First World War

and Army of Occupation

War Diary

France, Belgium and Germany

31 DIVISION
94 Infantry Brigade
York and Lancaster Regiment
12th (Service) (Sheffield) Battalion
1 March 1916 - 28 February 1918

WO95/2365/1

The Naval & Military Press Ltd
www.nmarchive.com
Published in association with The National Archives

Published by

The Naval & Military Press Ltd

Unit 10 Ridgewood Industrial Park,

Uckfield, East Sussex,

TN22 5QE England

Tel: +44 (0) 1825 749494

www.naval-military-press.com

www.nmarchive.com

Contents

Document type	Place/Title	Date From	Date To
Heading	WO95/2365/1		
Map	War Diary. 12th Bn., York & Lancaster Regt., (Sheffield.) Volume II Period, From March 28, 1916 To. April 30, 1916		
Heading	Confidential. War Diary Of 12th Service. Battn. York And Lancaster Regiment. (Sheffield) From 1-3-16 To 29-3-16. Volume I.		
War Diary	Kantara	01/03/1916	15/03/1916
War Diary	France.	16/03/1916	29/03/1916
War Diary	Boulogne	28/03/1916	28/03/1916
War Diary	Bertrancourt	02/04/1916	05/04/1916
War Diary	Colincamps	03/04/1916	03/04/1916
War Diary	Trenches	04/04/1916	12/04/1916
War Diary	Bertrancourt	13/04/1916	28/04/1916
War Diary	Colincamps	28/04/1916	30/04/1916
Heading	War Diary 12th (Service) Bn., York & Lancaster Regiment (Sheffield). Volume III. From 1st May 1916 To 31st May 1916		
War Diary	Colincamps	01/05/1916	01/05/1916
War Diary	Trenches	02/05/1916	06/05/1916
War Diary	Bois De Warnimont	07/05/1916	14/05/1916
War Diary	Trenches	15/05/1916	20/05/1916
War Diary	Courcelles Au Bois	21/05/1916	21/05/1916
War Diary	Trenches	22/05/1916	28/05/1916
War Diary	Colincamps	23/05/1916	23/05/1916
War Diary	Trenches	27/05/1916	27/05/1916
War Diary	Courcelles	30/05/1916	30/05/1916
War Diary	Bus Wood	31/05/1916	31/05/1916
War Diary	Bus	01/06/1916	05/06/1916
War Diary	Gezaincourt	06/06/1916	12/06/1916
War Diary	Bus	13/06/1916	14/06/1916
War Diary	Trenches	15/06/1916	19/06/1916
War Diary	Warnimont Wood.	20/06/1916	30/06/1916
Heading	94th Bde. 31st Div. War Diary 12th Battalion York & Lancaster Regiment 1st To 31st July 1916. Appendices Attached-Preliminary Operation Order. Sketches Showing Assembly Positions.		
Heading	War Diary. 12. S. Battalion, York And Lancaster Regiment. (Sheffield). Volume V. From 1st July. 1916. To 31st July. 1916. B.E.F., 1st June. 1916		
Heading	War Diary Of 12th (S) Bn. York & Lancaster Regt. For July 1916		
War Diary	Colincamps Sector.	01/07/1916	03/07/1916
War Diary	Colincamps Sector.	01/07/1916	04/07/1916
War Diary	Louvencourt	05/07/1916	06/07/1916
War Diary	Longuevillette	07/07/1916	08/07/1916
War Diary	Steenbecque	09/07/1916	09/07/1916
War Diary	Merville	10/07/1916	15/07/1916
War Diary	Vieille Chapelle Area.	16/07/1916	27/07/1916
War Diary	Lestrem.	28/07/1916	31/07/1916

Miscellaneous	Public Record Office		
Miscellaneous	12th (S) Battalion, York & Lancaster Regiment. (Preliminary) Operation Order. No 14	26/06/1916	26/06/1916
Miscellaneous			
Operation(al) Order(s)	12. S. Battalion. York & Lancaster Regiment. (Preliminary) Operation Order. No. 14	27/06/1916	27/06/1916
Diagram etc	1st Phase. Position Of Assembly 1.30 a.m. "A"		
Diagram etc	2nd Phase. Position Of Assembly At-10 "B"		
Diagram etc	3rd Phase Immediately Prior To Assault "Zero" "C"		
Diagram etc	4th Phase Occupation of 1st Bound O-20" D		
Diagram etc	5th Phase Commencement Of 2nd Bound "0-40" E		
Diagram etc	6th Phase 2nd Bound "0-50" F		
Diagram etc	7th Phase 1.40 G		
Heading	War Diary Of 12th (S) Bn York & Lanc Rgt. Aug 1916. Vol 6		
War Diary		01/08/1916	31/08/1916
War Diary	War Diary. 12th. (Service) Battalion York And Lancaster Regiment. Volume IX From 1st. September 1916 To 30th. September 1916. B.E.F. September 30th. (Midnight).		
War Diary	South of Neuve Chapelle	01/09/1916	10/09/1916
War Diary	South Of Neuve Chapelle	09/09/1916	10/09/1916
War Diary	La Fosse	11/09/1916	12/09/1916
War Diary		11/09/1916	14/09/1916
War Diary	La. Fosse.	15/09/1916	16/09/1916
War Diary	Festubert.	17/09/1916	23/09/1916
War Diary	Le Touret	24/09/1916	25/09/1916
Heading	War Diary. 12th. (Service) Battalion York And Lancaster Regiment. Volume X For 1st, October 1916, To 31st. October 1916		
War Diary	Le Touret.	26/09/1916	02/10/1916
War Diary	Festubert Sector.	03/10/1916	03/10/1916
War Diary	Map. Ref. X.17d. 1.4. Bethune Combined Sheet	03/10/1916	03/10/1916
War Diary	Le-Touret	04/10/1916	05/10/1916
War Diary	Vendin-Lez-Bethune	06/10/1916	06/10/1916
War Diary	Robecq	07/10/1916	08/10/1916
War Diary	Marieux.	09/10/1916	16/10/1916
War Diary	Marieux. Famechon.	17/10/1916	18/10/1916
War Diary	Warnimont Wood.	19/10/1916	30/10/1916
War Diary	Hebuterne	30/10/1916	31/10/1916
Miscellaneous	Scheme. Reference Map, France. Sheet 57 D., 1/40.000. General Idea.		
Miscellaneous	Instructions.	13/10/1916	13/10/1916
War Diary	Hebuterne	01/11/1916	02/11/1916
War Diary	Sailly-Au-Bois.	03/11/1916	03/11/1916
War Diary	Thievres	07/11/1916	07/11/1916
War Diary	Warnimont Wood.	12/11/1916	12/11/1916
War Diary	Hebuterne	14/11/1916	17/11/1916
War Diary	The Dell. Sailly-Au-Bois.	18/11/1916	18/11/1916
War Diary	Courcelles	21/11/1916	21/11/1916
War Diary	Hebuterne	22/11/1916	27/11/1916
War Diary	The Dell Sailly-Au-Bois.	29/11/1916	29/11/1916
Heading	War Diary. 12th. S. Battalion York And Lancaster Regiment. (Sheffield) Volume XI From 1st. November 1916. To 30th. November 1916 B.E.F. December 1st. 1916		

Heading	War Diary. 12th. (Service) Battalion York And Lancaster Regiment. (Sheffield). From 1st. December 1916. To 31st. December 1916. B.E.F. January 1st, 1917		
War Diary	The Dell, Sailly Au-Bois. J 17 634	01/12/1916	03/12/1916
War Diary	Hebuterne	05/12/1916	07/12/1916
War Diary	Rossignol Farm.	09/12/1916	16/12/1916
War Diary	Hebuterne	17/12/1916	20/12/1916
War Diary	Sailly-Au-Bois	21/12/1916	21/12/1916
War Diary	The "Dell" Sailly-Au-Bois.	25/12/1916	28/12/1916
Heading	War Diary. 12. S Battalion, York & Lancaster Regiment. Volume XI. From 1st January, 1917. To 31st January. 1917. B.E.F., Feby 1st. 1917		
War Diary	The Dell. Sailly Au Bois.	01/01/1917	03/01/1917
War Diary	The Line.	04/01/1917	08/01/1917
War Diary	Sailly Au Bois	10/01/1917	11/01/1917
War Diary	Beauval	12/01/1917	22/01/1917
War Diary	Candas	23/01/1917	31/01/1917
Heading	War Diary. 12th York Lanc. Regt 31st Division February 1917. Volume XIV.		
War Diary	Bonneville	01/02/1917	08/02/1917
War Diary	Terramesnil	09/02/1917	09/02/1917
War Diary	Courcelles Au-Bois	12/02/1917	28/02/1917
Heading	War Diary. 12 (Service) Battalion And Lancaster Regt Volume XV From 1st. March. 1917 To 31st. March. 1917. BEF. April 1st. 1917		
War Diary	Sailly Dell	01/03/1917	01/03/1917
War Diary	Hebuterne.	02/03/1917	03/03/1917
War Diary	German 1st Line About 500 N.W. of "Nameless Farm."	04/03/1917	04/03/1917
War Diary	German 1st Line About 500 N.W. of "Nameless Farm."	05/03/1917	05/03/1917
War Diary	Hebuterne.	06/03/1917	08/03/1917
War Diary	Puisieux.	09/02/1917	12/02/1917
War Diary	Puisieux.	10/02/1917	13/03/1917
War Diary	Bus.	14/03/1917	18/03/1917
War Diary	Beauval	19/03/1917	19/03/1917
War Diary	Bouret Sur Canche.	20/03/1917	20/03/1917
War Diary	Valhuon	21/03/1917	21/03/1917
War Diary	Aumerval	22/03/1917	23/03/1917
War Diary	Equedecques	24/03/1917	24/03/1917
War Diary	Merville	25/03/1917	31/03/1917
Heading	War Diary 12th Bn Yorks Lanc Regt. 31st Division April 1917. Volume XVI Vol 14		
War Diary	Merville	01/04/1917	13/04/1917
War Diary	Hermin	14/04/1917	30/04/1917
Heading	12th. Service. Battalion. York And Lancaster Regiment. War Diary. Vol. XVII From 1st. May 1917. To 31st. May 1917 BEF June 1/17		
War Diary	Mardeuil	01/05/1917	01/05/1917
War Diary	G.6. Control	02/05/1917	02/05/1917
War Diary	H.1.F.&.d	03/05/1917	03/05/1917
War Diary	R.C.2.	03/05/1917	04/05/1917
War Diary	B.30.a.7.9	05/05/1917	05/05/1917
War Diary	R.C.2	06/05/1917	07/05/1917
War Diary	B.25.a	08/05/1917	10/05/1917
War Diary	Right Subsector	11/05/1917	14/05/1917
War Diary	B.25.b.x.d.	15/05/1917	18/05/1917

War Diary	Right Subsector	19/05/1917	19/05/1917
War Diary	B.25.b.2.d.	18/05/1917	18/05/1917
War Diary	Right Subsector	19/05/1917	20/05/1917
War Diary	Maroeuil	21/05/1917	26/05/1917
War Diary	Mardeuil	22/05/1917	27/05/1917
War Diary	A.28.a.	28/05/1917	31/05/1917
Miscellaneous	The Battalion Provided The Following To Take Charge of Dumps As Shewn:-		
Miscellaneous	3rd May 1917 OC 12 Y & L		
Miscellaneous	A Form. Messages And Signals.		
Heading	12 (S) Bn. York Lancaster Regt. War Diary. Vol XVIII From 1st June 1917 To 30 June 1917. B.E.F. July 6/17		
War Diary	A28a (Nr Ecurie)	01/06/1917	10/06/1917
War Diary	B25A.	11/06/1917	13/06/1917
War Diary	Front Line Gavrelle.	14/06/1917	14/06/1917
War Diary	Roclincourt	19/06/1917	27/06/1917
War Diary	Front line.	28/06/1917	28/06/1917
War Diary	Cadorna (Near Front Line)	29/06/1917	30/06/1917
Operation(al) Order(s)	Operation Orders No. 58		
Operation(al) Order(s)	Amendments To Operation Order No 58	10/06/1917	10/06/1917
Operation(al) Order(s)	Stay Operation Order No. 59	14/06/1917	14/06/1917
Operation(al) Order(s)	Stay Operation Order No 61	18/06/1917	18/06/1917
Operation(al) Order(s)	12th S. Battalion York & Lancaster Regiment Operation Orders No. 62	25/06/1917	25/06/1917
Heading	War Diary		
Map			
Operation(al) Order(s)	Operation Order No. 63		
Miscellaneous	12th S. Battalion York And Lancaster Regiment. Part Taken By This Battalion In The Offensive Operations of 28th. June 1917	28/06/1917	28/06/1917
Miscellaneous	Observations.		
Operation(al) Order(s)	Operation Order No 64	30/06/1917	30/06/1917
Operation(al) Order(s)	Stay Operation Order No 65	01/07/1917	01/07/1917
Miscellaneous	12th (S) Battalion, York And Lancaster Regiment. Preliminary Instructions For Attack On German Trenches From Trench Junction C.19.C.4.9. (Exclusive) To Bend C.19.a.25.35	22/06/1917	22/06/1917
Miscellaneous	Administrative Supplement. to Preliminary Instructions For Attack on German Trenches.		
Miscellaneous	Reference Administrative Supplement, Para 4 (C)		
Miscellaneous	Supplement		
Miscellaneous	Administrative Supplement. Appendix "C" Signal Communication.		
Miscellaneous	Preliminary, Instructions & C Amendments And Addenda	25/06/1917	25/06/1917
Miscellaneous	Administrative Supplement. Appendix "E". Rations And Water.		
Miscellaneous	Administrative Supplement. Appendix "I". Arrangements For Holding The Line On "Z" Day.		
Miscellaneous	Administrative Supplement. Appendix "N" Carrying Parties	25/06/1917	25/06/1917
Miscellaneous	Administrative Supplement.-Appendices Referred To In Paragraph 5	26/06/1917	26/06/1917
Miscellaneous	Co		
Miscellaneous	Public Record Office Pro Document Reference WO95/2365	12/03/2003	12/03/2003

Heading	War Diary. 12th. S. Battalion York And Lancaster Regt. Period. July 1st 1917 To July 31st. 1917. Volume 19. Date 1.8.17. B.E.F.		
War Diary		02/07/1917	02/07/1917
War Diary	Bray	03/07/1917	11/07/1917
War Diary	Painsley Camp N St. Vaast	12/07/1917	25/07/1917
War Diary	N St Vaast	25/07/1917	31/07/1917
Operation(al) Order(s)	Stay Operation Order No 66	02/07/1917	02/07/1917
Operation(al) Order(s)	Stay Operation Order No. 67	12/07/1917	12/07/1917
Miscellaneous	Adjutant		
Operation(al) Order(s)	Operation Order No 68	17/07/1917	17/07/1917
Operation(al) Order(s)	Stay Operation Order. No 69	20/07/1917	20/07/1917
Miscellaneous			
Operation(al) Order(s)	12th. S. Battalion York And Lancaster Regt. Operation Orders No. 70	28/07/1917	28/07/1917
Miscellaneous	Special Order Of The Day By Brigadier-General G.T. Carter Campbell, D.S.O., Commanding 94th Infantry Brigade.	03/07/1917	03/07/1917
Miscellaneous	Congratulatory Messages.	01/07/1917	01/07/1917
Heading	War Diary. 12th S. Bn York & Lancaster Regt Period August 1st 1917 to August 31st 1917 Volume 20 Date 1.9.17 BEF.		
War Diary	Support Trenches Acheville Sector	01/08/1917	12/08/1917
War Diary	Vimy Ridge.	12/08/1917	16/08/1917
War Diary	Mont St Eloi	17/08/1917	24/08/1917
War Diary	Trenches. Front Line. Acheville. Sector	25/08/1917	29/08/1917
War Diary	Brigade Support.	30/08/1917	30/08/1917
War Diary	Beehive & Canada Tr.	31/08/1917	31/08/1917
Operation(al) Order(s)	Stay Operation Order No 72	08/08/1917	08/08/1917
Operation(al) Order(s)	Stay Operation Order No. 73	15/08/1917	15/08/1917
Operation(al) Order(s)	Administrative Instructions Issued With Operation Order No. 73		
Operation(al) Order(s)	Amendment To Operation Order No. 74	23/08/1917	23/08/1917
Operation(al) Order(s)	Ibex Operation Order No. 74	23/08/1917	23/08/1917
Operation(al) Order(s)	Administrative Instructions Issued With Operation Order No. 74, Dated 23.8.17	23/08/1917	23/08/1917
Operation(al) Order(s)	Bn York Lancaster Regt. Operation Order No 75.		
Heading	War Diary. 12th (S) Bn. York Lancaster Regt 31st Division September 1917. Volume XXI		
War Diary	Beehive & Canada Trench Area. T 27d.	01/09/1917	02/09/1917
War Diary	In Front of Railway Embarkment & Petit Vimy & Vimy	03/09/1917	05/09/1917
War Diary	Front Line Acheville	05/09/1917	07/09/1917
War Diary	Front Line	08/09/1917	11/09/1917
Miscellaneous	Acheville		
War Diary	Roclincourt.	11/09/1917	17/09/1917
War Diary	Brown Line. Vimy Ridge.	18/09/1917	25/09/1917
War Diary	Red Line Acheville.	26/09/1917	29/09/1917
War Diary	Front Line Acheville	30/09/1917	30/09/1917
Operation(al) Order(s)	Ibex Operation Order No. 76	04/09/1917	04/09/1917
Miscellaneous			
Operation(al) Order(s)	Operation Order No 77	06/09/1917	06/09/1917
Operation(al) Order(s)	Operation Order No 78	08/09/1917	08/09/1917
Operation(al) Order(s)	Ibex Operation Order No. 79	11/09/1917	11/09/1917
Operation(al) Order(s)	12th. S. Battalion York And Lancaster Regiment. Operation Order No. 80	17/09/1917	17/09/1917

Operation(al) Order(s)	Administrative Instructions Issued With Operation Order No. 80. Dated. 17.9.17	17/09/1917	17/09/1917
Operation(al) Order(s)	12th. S. Battalion York And Lancaster Regiment. Operation Order No. 81	23/09/1917	23/09/1917
Operation(al) Order(s)	Administrative Instructions Issued With Operation Order No 81		
Miscellaneous	Adjt		
Operation(al) Order(s)	12th (Service) Battn, York & Lancaster Regiment. Operation Order. No 82	29/09/1917	29/09/1917
Operation(al) Order(s)	Administrative Instructions Issued With Operation Order No. 82		
Miscellaneous	Reference Scheme For Tactical Exercise.		
Miscellaneous	12th S Battalion York And Lancaster Regiment. Operation Order For battalion Tactical Exercise 16.9.17	16/09/1917	16/09/1917
Miscellaneous	12th. S. Battalion York And Lancaster Regiment. Tactical Exercise.		
Heading	War Diary. 12th. S. Battalion York And Lancaster Regiment. Period-October 1st 1917 To October 31st 1917 Volume XXII Date of despatch. November 1st 1917 BEF.		
War Diary	Front Line. Acheville Sector.	01/10/1917	01/10/1917
War Diary	Front Line Acheville	01/10/1917	07/10/1917
War Diary	No Man's Land Acheville.	06/10/1917	07/10/1917
War Diary	Roclincourt Springvale Camp.	07/10/1917	11/10/1917
War Diary	Brown Line	12/10/1917	17/10/1917
War Diary	Red Line	18/10/1917	23/10/1917
War Diary	Front Line	24/10/1917	29/10/1917
War Diary	Roclincourt Springvale Camp.	30/10/1917	31/10/1917
Miscellaneous	Post Office Telegraphs.		
Operation(al) Order(s)	12th York & Lanc Rgt Operation Order No 84	05/10/1917	05/10/1917
Operation(al) Order(s)	Administrative Instructions Issued With 12th Operation Orders No 84		
Miscellaneous	Adjt		
Operation(al) Order(s)	12th. S. Battalion York And Lancaster Regt. Operation Order No 85	11/10/1917	11/10/1917
Operation(al) Order(s)	Administrative Instructions Issued With Operation Order No. 85 Dated 11.10.17	11/10/1917	11/10/1917
Operation(al) Order(s)	12th. S. Battalion York And Lancaster Regt. Operation Order No. 86	17/10/1917	17/10/1917
Operation(al) Order(s)	Administrative Instructions Issued With Operation Order No 86	17/10/1917	17/10/1917
Operation(al) Order(s)	12th. S. Battalion York And Lancaster Regt. Operation Order No. 87	19/10/1917	19/10/1917
Operation(al) Order(s)	12th. S. Battalion York And Lancaster Regt. Operation Order No. 88	23/10/1917	23/10/1917
Operation(al) Order(s)	Administrative Instructions Issued With Operation Order No 88		
Operation(al) Order(s)	Addition To Operation Orders No 89 Dated 30/10/17	30/10/1917	30/10/1917
Operation(al) Order(s)	12th. Bn. York & Lancaster Regt. Operation Order No 89	29/10/1917	29/10/1917
Operation(al) Order(s)	Administrative Instructions Issued With. 12th York & Lanc Regt Operation Order No 89, Dated 29/10/17	29/10/1917	29/10/1917
Operation(al) Order(s)	94th Infantry Brigade Order No. 183	01/10/1917	01/10/1917

Heading	War Diary 12th. S. Battalion York & Lancaster Regiment. Period:- November 1st 1917 To November 30th 1917. Volume XXIII Date of despatch. December 1st 1917 B.E.F.		
War Diary	Spring-Vale Camp. Roclincourt	01/11/1917	04/11/1917
War Diary	Brown Line.	05/11/1917	11/11/1917
War Diary	Red Line.	11/11/1917	16/11/1917
War Diary	Ecurie	17/11/1917	19/11/1917
War Diary	Red Line Oppy Sector.	20/11/1917	20/11/1917
War Diary	Front Line Oppy Wood	21/11/1917	22/11/1917
War Diary	Oppy Sector.	22/11/1917	26/11/1917
War Diary	Railway Cutting.	27/11/1917	28/11/1917
War Diary	Railway Cutting. Red Line.	29/11/1917	30/11/1917
Operation(al) Order(s)	12th. S. Battalion York & Lancaster Regiment. Operation Order No 89	04/11/1917	04/11/1917
Operation(al) Order(s)	Administrative Instructions Issued With Operation Order. No 89, Dated 4/11/17	04/11/1917	04/11/1917
Operation(al) Order(s)	12th S. Battalion York And Lancaster Regiment. Operation Order No. 90	10/11/1917	10/11/1917
Operation(al) Order(s)	Administrative Instructions Issued With Operation Order No. 90		
Operation(al) Order(s)	12th. S. Battalion York And Lancaster Regiment. Operation Order No. 91	16/11/1917	16/11/1917
Operation(al) Order(s)	Administrative Instructions Issued With Operation Order. No. 91, Dated 16/7/17	16/07/1917	16/07/1917
Operation(al) Order(s)	12th. S. Battalion York And Lancaster Regt. Operation Order No. 92	19/11/1917	19/11/1917
Operation(al) Order(s)	Administrative Instructions Issued With Operation Order. No. 92 Dated 19/11/17	19/11/1917	19/11/1917
Operation(al) Order(s)	12th S Bn. York & Lancaster Rgt. Operation Order 93	20/11/1917	20/11/1917
Miscellaneous	Administrative Instructions To Operation Order No.	20/11/1917	20/11/1917
Operation(al) Order(s)	12th S Bn York & Lancaster Rgt Operation Order No 94	24/11/1917	24/11/1917
Operation(al) Order(s)	12th S. Bn York Lancaster Regt Operation Order No 95	26/11/1917	26/11/1917
Operation(al) Order(s)	Administrative Instructions Issued With 12th York Lancaster Regt O.O. No 95	26/11/1917	26/11/1917
Heading	War Diary 12th S Battalion York & Lancaster Rgt. Period- December 1st 1917. To December 31st 1917 Volume XXIV Date of despatch. January 2nd 1918 B.E.F.		
War Diary	Red Line & Railway Cutting	01/12/1917	02/12/1917
War Diary	Oppy Wood. Front Line	03/12/1917	07/12/1917
War Diary	Mont St Eloy.	08/12/1917	21/12/1917
War Diary	A.22.C, 6.4, (Near Roclincourt)	22/12/1917	23/12/1917
War Diary	A22C6.4 (Sheet 51B)	24/12/1917	24/12/1917
War Diary	Acheville (Hudson Post)	25/12/1917	30/12/1917
War Diary	Neuville St Vaast.	31/12/1917	31/12/1917
Operation(al) Order(s)	Administrative Instructions To Accompany Operation Order No. 96		
Operation(al) Order(s)	12th. S. Battalion York & Lancaster Regiment. Operation Order. No 96	02/12/1917	02/12/1917
Operation(al) Order(s)	12th. S. Battalion York & Lancaster Regt. Operation Order No. 97	07/12/1917	07/12/1917
Operation(al) Order(s)	Administrative Instruction Issued With Operation Order No. 97 Dated 7.12.17	07/12/1917	07/12/1917

Operation(al) Order(s)	12th. S. Battalion York And Lancaster Regiment. Operation Order No. 98	21/12/1917	21/12/1917
Operation(al) Order(s)	12th. S. Battn York & Lancaster Regt. Operation Order No. 99	24/12/1917	24/12/1917
Operation(al) Order(s)	12th. S. Battn York And Lancaster Regt. Operation Order No. 100	30/12/1917	30/12/1917
Miscellaneous	12th. S. Battalion York & Lancaster Regiment. Tactical Exercise.		
Heading	War Diary. 12. S. Bn. York & Lancaster Rgt. Period. January 1, 1918 To January 31, 1918 Vol. XXV Date of Despatch. Feby 1/18		
War Diary	Cubitt Camp	01/01/1918	01/01/1918
War Diary	Neuville St Vaast.	01/01/1918	01/01/1918
War Diary	A9.a24	01/01/1918	06/01/1918
War Diary	Vancouver Road	07/01/1918	11/01/1918
War Diary	Spring-Vale Camp.	12/01/1918	13/01/1918
War Diary	Roclincourt	14/01/1918	18/01/1918
War Diary	Front Line.	19/01/1918	24/01/1918
War Diary	Cubitt Camp.	24/01/1918	25/01/1918
War Diary	Neuville St Vaast.	26/01/1918	29/01/1918
War Diary	Red Line.	30/01/1918	31/01/1918
Operation(al) Order(s)	12th. S. Battalion York And Lancaster Regiment. Operation Order No. 101	05/01/1918	05/01/1918
Operation(al) Order(s)	12th. S Bn York And Lancaster R. Operation Order No 102	11/01/1918	11/01/1918
Operation(al) Order(s)	12th. S. Bn. York & Lancaster Regiment. Operation Order No. 103	17/01/1918	17/01/1918
Operation(al) Order(s)	12th S. Bn York Lancaster Regt. Operation Order No 104	23/01/1918	23/01/1918
Operation(al) Order(s)	12th. S. Bn. York & Lancaster Regt. Operation Order No. 105	29/01/1918	29/01/1918
Miscellaneous	Administrative Instructions.	29/01/1918	29/01/1918
Heading	12 (S) Battn York & Lancaster Regiment Last Volume. Feb 1 To Feb 26 1918. Feby 28/18. Vol 24		
War Diary	Vancouver Road.	01/02/1918	01/02/1918
War Diary	Brigade Support.	02/02/1918	05/02/1918
War Diary	Cubitt Camp.	06/02/1918	11/02/1918
War Diary	Lancaster Camp	11/02/1918	11/02/1918
War Diary	York Camp.	12/02/1918	15/02/1918
War Diary	Pernes.	16/02/1918	16/02/1918
War Diary	Pernes & York Camp.	17/02/1918	28/02/1918
Operation(al) Order(s)	12th. S. Battalion York And Lancaster Regiment. Operation Order No. 110	10/02/1918	10/02/1918
Miscellaneous			
Miscellaneous	Special Order Of The Day By Brigadier-General G.T.C. Carter-Campbell D.S.O., Commanding 94th Infantry Brigade.	29/01/1918	29/01/1918
Miscellaneous	OC. C Coy		
Operation(al) Order(s)	12 Bn York Lancs R. Operation Order No 108	04/02/1918	04/02/1918
Miscellaneous	Administrative Instructions		
Miscellaneous	Re-Postings.	09/02/1918	09/02/1918
Operation(al) Order(s)	Operation Orders. No. 109	09/02/1918	09/02/1918

CONFIDENTIAL -- WAR DIARY.

12th S Bn., York & Lancaster Regt., (Sheffield.)

V O L U M E II

Period, from March 28, 1916

To .. April 30, 1916.

B E F., France. 30 4 16.

CONFIDENTIAL.

WAR DIARY

of

12th Service. Battn. York and Lancaster Regiment. (Sheffield)

from 1-3-16 to 29-3-16.

Volume 1.

Army Form C. 2118

Instructions regarding War Diaries and Intelligence Summaries are contained in F. S. Regs., Part II. and the Staff Manual respectively. Title Pages will be prepared in manuscript.

12 Y & L.

WAR DIARY
or
INTELLIGENCE SUMMARY
(Erase heading not required.)

Page 8.
Vol. 1.

Place	Date	Hour	Summary of Events and Information	Remarks and references to Appendices
Kantara	1.3.16	Noon.	"B" Company rejoined Battalion.	HWT
Do	7.3.16	6 pm	Battalion struck Camp.	HWT
Do	8.3.16	4 am.	Marched out of KANTARA & entrained for PORT SAID	HWT
Do	9.3.16	11 am.	Received instructions to embark next day with detachment of 18 West Yorks & 14 Y & L.	HWT
Do	10.3.16	10 am.	Embarked on H.M.T. "Briton", & sailed about five pm.	HWT
Do	15.3.16	Noon.	Arrived MARSEILLES.	HWT
France.	16.3.16	7 am.	Disembarked. Entrained 11 am.	HWT
	18.3.16	2 pm.	Detrained PONT REMY. & marched to billets at HUPPY.	HWT
	22.3.16 23.3.16	-	Musketry on temporary range at POULTIERES	HWT

1875 Wt. W593/826 1,000,000 4/15 J.B.C. & A. A.D.S.S./Forms/C. 2118.

Army Form C. 2118

Instructions regarding War Diaries and Intelligence Summaries are contained in F. S. Regs., Part II. and the Staff Manual respectively. Title Pages will be prepared in manuscript.

12 Y & L.

WAR DIARY
or
INTELLIGENCE SUMMARY
(Erase heading not required.)

Page 9.
Vol. 1.

Place	Date	Hour	Summary of Events and Information	Remarks and references to Appendices
France.	26.3.16	8 am.	Marched to LONGPRE. Billeted in town.	HWP
	27.3.16	8 am.	Marched to VIGNACOURT. Billeted in town. 10 Officers & 40 N.C.O.'s proceeded for 72 hours duty in trenches, with 8th Worcesters (TF)	HWP
	28.3.16	8 am.	Marched to BEAUQUESNE. Billeted in town.	HWP
	29.3.16	8 am.	Marched to BERTRANCOURT. & encamped in canvas huts.	HWP
			[illegible signature] Major Lieut. Colonel Comdg. 12th (S) Bn. York. & Lancs. Rgt. (Sheff[illegible])	
			End of Vol I	

1875 Wt. W593/826 1,000,000 4/15 J.B.C. & A. A.D.S.S./Forms/C. 2118.

Instructions regarding War Diaries and Intelligence Summaries are contained in F. S. Regs., Part II. and the Staff Manual respectively. Title Pages will be prepared in manuscript.

12 Y+L.

WAR DIARY
or
INTELLIGENCE SUMMARY
(Erase heading not required.)

Army Form C. 2118

P1

March – April 1916

Place	Date 1916	Hour	Summary of Events and Information	Remarks and references to Appendices
Boulogne	28 March	–	Lieut R.D. BERRY transferred to Hospital ship for England, & struck off strength	
BERTRANCOURT	April 2nd	1 pm	Battn commenced move to COLINCAMPS – Billets in village for the night.	H.W.T.
COLINCAMPS	3rd	12.30 pm	Commenced to move from COLINCAMPS to take up front-line trenches about 1300 yds long, 3/4 mile W. of Serre, extending from Q4.B55 to K35 A 44 (Ref. Trench map, 1-10,000, Sheet "BEAUMONT & HEBUTERNE.")	H
			Relieved 18th Durham Light Infantry from Q4 B55 to K34 B90, and 8th Bn WORCESTER Regt (T.F) from K34 B90 to K35 A 44.	
			"D" Coy plus 1 Platoon "C" Co occupied line held by 18th D L I, and remaining three platoons "C" Coy that held by Worcesters: with "A" Coy & one platoon of "B" supporting "D", & remaining 3 platoons of "B" supporting "C" Co.	
			On our right, Battn of K.O.S.B's (29th Divn) – on our left, 14th York & Lancs	H.W.T.
Trenches	4th	12 noon	Relief completed. No casualties. During the day there was slight activity by enemy with rifle grenades & canister bombs. Casualties – 1 man killed.	H.W.T.

124th · April 1916

Page 2

Army Form C. 2118

WAR DIARY
or
INTELLIGENCE SUMMARY
(Erase heading not required.)

Instructions regarding War Diaries and Intelligence Summaries are contained in F. S. Regs., Part II. and the Staff Manual respectively. Title Pages will be prepared in manuscript.

Place	Date	Hour	Summary of Events and Information	Remarks and references to Appendices
Trenches	April 1916 5th		Quiet day. Snipers active.	HWP
"	6th		Up to about 8 p.m. the day was quiet, but after this the enemy artillery was heard to be very active towards the South, the activity gradually extending in our direction.	
"		8.58 p.	Enemy commenced to bombard our line, fire being concentrated round the REDAN, rather more on the support lines than the front. Our own artillery replied on to enemy front & second lines. With the exception of some damage in one or two places to the trenches, the enemy's artillery had little effect & caused no casualties.	
"		10.32 p.	Bombardment practically ceased & enemy put up quantity of Very lights from their front line facing us.	
"		10.45 p.	Working parties set on & damage done to trenches was repaired during the night.	

1875 Wt. W593/826 1,000,000 4/15 J.B.C. & A. A.D.S.S./Forms/C. 2118.

124 Bn

Instructions regarding War Diaries and Intelligence Summaries are contained in F. S. Regs., Part II. and the Staff Manual respectively. Title Pages will be prepared in manuscript.

Page 3 – Apl 1916.

Army Form C. 2118

WAR DIARY
or
INTELLIGENCE SUMMARY
(Erase heading not required.)

Place	Date Apl '16	Hour	Summary of Events and Information	Remarks and references to Appendices
Trenches	6th		Remainder of night quiet except that a canister bomb was thrown into one of our trenches on the left, wounding one man.	H.W.T.
"	7th		Day quiet but towards evening another canister bomb was thrown into the same trench & two more men were wounded. Captain COUSIN joins 94th Inf. Bde Staff as Intelligence Officer. Coys in front line were relieved by those in support.	
"	"	10.30pm	– Relief completed – no casualties.	H.W.T.
"	8th		Situation normal. Rifle grenade activity at the Redan.	
"	"	8.30pm	Enemy threw minenwerfer bomb into No 10 post, killing two men, wounding [illegible]4, & causing much damage to parapet. It was decided after this to hold this Post with small parties at either end, leaving centre clear, as experience showed that the trench was very well registered by enemy.	
			Strength – 2nd Lieut F A BEAL & 12 o.r. struck off, on joining 94/1 Light Trench Mortar Battery.	H.W.T.

1875 Wt. W593/826 1,000,000 4/15 J.B.C. & A. A.D.S.S./Forms/C. 2118.

12 Y & L – Page 4. April 1916. Page 4

WAR DIARY
or
INTELLIGENCE SUMMARY
(Erase heading not required.)

Army Form C. 2118

Instructions regarding War Diaries and Intelligence Summaries are contained in F. S. Regs., Part II. and the Staff Manual respectively. Title Pages will be prepared in manuscript.

Place	Date April 16	Hour	Summary of Events and Information	Remarks and references to Appendices
Trenches	9th	–	Situation normal. – Lieut C.H. WOODHOUSE and one or wounded.	H.W.T.
"	10th	–	Wet day. Trenches bad.	H.W.T.
"	11th	–	Rain made trenches very muddy. Telephone wires were broken down from sides of trenches in many places.	H.W.T.
"	12th	1.30p	Commencement of relief by 13th East Yorks.	
"		10.30p	– Relief completed. No casualties. Battalion moved to hutments at BERTRANCOURT.	
			NOTES.– During the Battalions 9-days occupation of the trenches, a great deal of very necessary work was done, such as deepening communication trenches, making front line continuous & opening up communication trenches between front line & support line, which had been allowed to fall into disuse. Also in making dug-outs for accomodation of the men. No wiring was done owing to the imperative nature of trench improvements required. Telescopic rifles were received after the first four days, & from this time the enemy sniping became considerably less. Our snipers accounted for several of their men.	H.W.T.
BERTRANCOURT	13th to 24th	–	Battalion training resumed. Special attention to wiring, bombing & reconnoitring. Working parties on trench-cutting, dug-outs, &c in COLINCAMPS area.	H.W.T.

1875 Wt. W593/826 1,000,000 4/15 J.B.C. & A. A.D.S.S./Forms/C. 2118.

12 Y&L - April 1916

Page 5.

Army Form C. 2118

Instructions regarding War Diaries and Intelligence Summaries are contained in F. S. Regs., Part II. and the Staff Manual respectively. Title Pages will be prepared in manuscript.

WAR DIARY
or
INTELLIGENCE SUMMARY
(Erase heading not required.)

Place	Date April	Hour	Summary of Events and Information	Remarks and references to Appendices
BERTRANCOURT	28	8.30 am	Battalion less "B" Coy. marched to billets at COLINCAMPS, to act as Brigade Reserve.	H.W.F.
Do	Do	10.0 am	"B" Coy joined 11th S.B. East Lancs, – who had a company away on Corps duty, – & marched with them to section of trenches formerly held by 12th Y.&L. "B" became the supporting Coy of 11th East Lancs.	
Colincamps	Do	-	"D" Coy. having marched to COLINCAMPS with Battalion, later in the day sent on 2½ platoons into supporting points at FORT HOYSTED, ELLIS SQUARE, and HITTITE Trench.	
Do	Do	-	Working parties sent out. One man wounded, machine gun fire, while clearing new communication trench.	
Do	29-30		Working parties ordered to be in billets by 11-30 p.m. Promptly at the hour, our artillery opened up on the whole Divisional front. This lasted until 12.30 am, desultory fire continuing until 12.50 am.	H.W.F.

[signature] Lieut. Colonel Comdg.
12th (S) Bn. York & Lancs. Rgt. (Sheffield.)

1875 Wt. W593/826 1,000,000 4/15 J.B.C. & A. A.D.S.S./Forms/C. 2118.

WAR DIARY CONFIDENTIAL.

12th (Service) Bn., York & Lancaster Regiment (Sheffield).

VOLUME III.

From 1st May 1916

To 31st May 1916.

B E F., 1st June 1916.

12 York & Lancs — Page 1 — May 1916

Instructions regarding War Diaries and Intelligence Summaries are contained in F. S. Regs., Part II. and the Staff Manual respectively. Title Pages will be prepared in manuscript.

WAR DIARY
or
INTELLIGENCE SUMMARY
(Erase heading not required.)

Army Form C. 2118

Place	Date May	Hour	Summary of Events and Information	Remarks and references to Appendices
COLINCAMPS	1st		Working party under Lt Ingold & Lt Storry shelled at ELLIS SQUARE. Casualties. Other Ranks, 1 killed, 3 wounded.	[illegible]
TRENCHES	2		Battalion, less "D" Coy, took over trenches from K35A 4085 to K23 d 35 45 from 14 York & Lancs. One Coy 14 Y & L in support. 6th Gloucesters on R, 11 E Lancs on L.	
"	"	1.30pm	Relief completed – no casualties. – Rest of evening quiet, with one burst of artillery. Cas: 2 o.r. slightly wounded	[illegible]
"	"		"D" Co. at COLINCAMPS, as permanent Working Party.	
"	3		Enemy early active with tr. mortars & H.E. Shells. Our artillery replied. – In afternoon enemy constantly shelled & bombed JOHN COPSE. Three wounded were being attended to when a mine ("Minnie") was thrown into "C" Coy telephone dug-out, killing 6 men including C-S-M Ellis J.W. – Quiet evening. – Cas. – Other ranks, killed 6 (John Copse) died of wounds, 1 (John C.) Wounded, 5 (1 John C, 2 Rob Roy, 1 No 4 Post, 1 No 13 Post.)	[illegible]
			Officers who had been left at BERTRANCOURT (isolated for measles) rejoined Battn.	
"	4	–	Early morning enemy shelled LE CATEAU & TOUVENT Fm. Our art replied. Between 9 & 10.30am enemy threw Tr Mortar bombs in vicinity of MATTHEW COPSE without doing any damage. Later 'whizz bangs' & light tr. m. bombs were directed at MATTHEW COPSE & BLENEAU AV. Art. retaliated in each case. During afternoon our art was registering enemy's lines.	[illegible]
"	"	10.10pm	Shower of rifle grenades on right sub-sector & bombs on left sub-sector.	

1875 Wt. W593/826 1,000,000 4/15 J.B.C. & A. A.D.S.S./Forms/C. 2118.

12 York & Lancs. Page 2 - May 1916.

Instructions regarding War Diaries and Intelligence Summaries are contained in F. S. Regs., Part II. and the Staff Manual respectively. Title Pages will be prepared in manuscript.

WAR DIARY
or
INTELLIGENCE SUMMARY
(Erase heading not required.)

Army Form C. 2118

Place	Date	Hour	Summary of Events and Information	Remarks and references to Appendices
Trenches	4	(cont).	Our art. silenced enemy. Bombs on left believed to come from Bombing Party outside German lines. Cas. - o.r. killed 1 (by sniper, ~~[illegible]~~ in No 4 post), wounded 1 o.r. (rifle grenade, No 5 Post).	M.H.
"	5	5 a.m.	Intermittent shelling of JOHN C. & NAIRN Tr. lasting $\frac{3}{4}$ hr. Our aeroplanes very active, one flying very low & firing his machine gun into enemy trenches after flying behind their lines.	M.H.
		9-11 AM	MATTHEW C. JOHN C. shelled with h.e. & t.m.s. No damage. Our art. replied.	
		3.30 PM	Similar effort by enemy. No 4 Post blown in for 3rd time in 4 days. After 6 p.m. all quiet.	
"	6	4 p.m.	Relief commenced. Finished 4.30. No cas. All in billets BOIS DE WARNIMONT 10.30 p.m. - new Rest Camp. - "D" Coy remained at COLINCAMPS.	M.H.
BOIS DE WARNIMONT	4	2 p.m.	Draft of 20 o.r. arrived. Quarantined. - During stay at WARNIMONT WOOD, Battalion devoted a good deal of time to "refresher" training.	M.H.
"	10	Noon	- Visit of General Sir Douglas Haig, Commander-in-Chief.	M.H.
"	11	noon	- "D" Coy's Working Party shelled at ROB ROY. Cas. - o.r. - wounded 1.	M.H.
"	12	-	Major A. Plackett proceeded to 31 Divisional School as Chief Instructor.	M.H.
"	14	-	Batt. ordered to return to trenches, less 2 platoons of "D" Co. to be left at COLINCAMPS to carry on as permanent working party with 2 platoons 5 Lancs.	M.H.

1875 Wt. W593/826 1,000,000 4/15 J.B.C. & A. A.D.S.S./Forms/C. 2118.

12 York Hussars - Page 3 - May, 1916.

WAR DIARY
or
INTELLIGENCE SUMMARY
(Erase heading not required.)

Army Form C. 2118

Instructions regarding War Diaries and Intelligence Summaries are contained in F. S. Regs., Part II. and the Staff Manual respectively. Title Pages will be prepared in manuscript.

Place	Date	Hour	Summary of Events and Information	Remarks and references to Appendices
Trenches	15	–	Relieved 16 W. Yorks in sector (N) K23 d 4040 – (S) K29. C 80.84. – 4th Bn Royal Berks, 48th Div. on our left, 16 W. Yorks on our right.	
"	"	7-30 p.	Relief completed. No casualties.	[illegible]
"	16	12-20 a.	Up to this hour, enemy activity was normal. No immediate signal was observed, but intense fire was opened simultaneously from Batteries, direction L 8 D. east of SERRE; rear of PENDANT COPSE on JOHN COPSE & sector to North K23.d. Shells of exceptionally heavy calibre H.E., on front line & supports.	
			Following a red flare from direction of JOHN COPSE fire became more intense on support line. 12.50 from OBSERVATION WOOD on EXCEMA, LE CATEAU, NAIRN, and Communication trenches to north, while the heavy fire on front line of our sector from JOHN C to MATTEW C. continued.	
			Our artillery replied vigorously, & sharp rifle fire was kept up on German trenches.	[illegible]
			The bombardment commenced to abate in intensity at 2-10 a.m. and ended at 2-20 a.m. Chief damage – EXCEMA in vicinity of OBSERVATION WOOD LE CATEAU (badly) ROB ROY at Junction with NAIRN. NAIRN. Front line damaged especially at LUKE COPSE, some of the trenches being levelled.	
			This bombardment was employed to cover a raid on 4th Berkshires on our right, who reported sixteen killed, 43 wounded, 24 missing.	
			(Our casualties were 15 killed, 1 missing (afterwards traced to hospital, wounded) & 45 wounded. – all "other ranks". Most occurred in front line, K29 B18 LUKE C to MARK C. with 16 in ROB ROY.	

(875 Wt. W593/826 1,000,000 4/15 J.B.C. & A. A.D.S.S./Forms/C. 2118.

12 York Lancs - Page 4 - May 1916

Instructions regarding War Diaries and Intelligence Summaries are contained in F. S. Regs., Part II. and the Staff Manual respectively. Title Pages will be prepared in manuscript.

WAR DIARY
or
INTELLIGENCE SUMMARY
(Erase heading not required.)

Army Form C. 2118

Place	Date	Hour	Summary of Events and Information	Remarks and references to Appendices
Trenches	16	–	Our men were very steady during the bombardment. The disposition was – "B" Coy (under Lieut J. L. MIDDLETON) and "C" Coy (under 2/Lt TE A GRANT) in the Front Line, with "A" Coy (under Lieut F.C. EARL) in support. A number of Senior officers were absent on this date for various causes. Valuable assistance was given by sappers + miners of 257 Coy R.E and 14th Bn, York Lancs Regt, in digging out men buried by shell bursts. During the morning, one man was killed by a sniper in JORDAN. At night Capt Allen, Capt + adjt Tunbridge, Lieut Woodhouse + Lt Moxey rejoined from hospital.	MH
"	17	–	Hostile art. fairly active all day. During afternoon our heavy art. bombarded German front lines + supports. Cas – OR. killed 1, wounded 3. (Shell).	MH
"	18	–	Normal. Our men still very busy repairing damage done in bombardment of night 15-16th. "A" Coy snipers reported having hit two men on left of Sector, one man being hit through his steel helmet. Quiet night. Cas – OR. 4 wounded (shell).	MH
"	19	–	Shortly after midnight a burst of 10 H.E. shells on S. of Sector toward REDAN was followed by a succession of peculiar star-lights in sky each light lasting about a second. – Sector N. of JOHN COPSE was briskly shelled with HE	MH

1875 Wt. W593/826 1,000,000 4/15 J.B.C. & A. A.D.S.S./Forms/C. 2118.

12 Y&L – Page 5 – May 1916

Instructions regarding War Diaries and Intelligence Summaries are contained in F. S. Regs., Part II. and the Staff Manual respectively. Title Pages will be prepared in manuscript.

WAR DIARY
or
INTELLIGENCE SUMMARY
(Erase heading not required.)

Army Form C. 2118

Place	Date	Hour	Summary of Events and Information	Remarks and references to Appendices
Trenches	19 (cont'd)		& shrapnel about 2 a.m., our guns replying heavily. Considerable machine gun activity by both sides for next 2 hrs. A special patrol was sent out during night to search for German believed to have been killed or wounded in No Man's Land but nothing was found. Patrol reports enemy wiring party busy. – Enemy sent over a number of rifle grenades & canister bombs, but we had no casualties. Enemy anti aircraft guns particularly busy. 200 shells were fired at one British machine over the German lines, without doing any damage as far as could be seen. Lieut J.L. Ward appointed 94 Inf Bde Orderly Officer.	M.W.
"	20	–	Battalion was relieved by 11 E. Lancs. Relief completed 4.15 p.m. No cas. Batt marched into billets at COURCELLES, leaving 2 platoons of D Coy at COLINCAMPS to continue work in trenches in sector. This work includes improvement of old trenches, reopening disused trenches & cutting new ones. – The work done by 'D' Coy has previously been very favourably commented upon by the R.E. Officer in charge. – 2/Lt Grant appointed Pioneer Officer, 94 Inf Bde.	M.W.
COURCELLES AU BOIS	21	–	Took over duties in COURCELLES & provided working parties for trenches, mostly at night.	M.W.

1875 Wt. W593/826 1,000,000 4/15 J.B.C. & A. A.D.S.S./Forms/C. 2118.

1244 – Page 6 – May 1916

Instructions regarding War Diaries and Intelligence Summaries are contained in F. S. Regs., Part II. and the Staff Manual respectively. Title Pages will be prepared in manuscript.

WAR DIARY
or
INTELLIGENCE SUMMARY
(Erase heading not required.)

Army Form C. 2118

Place	Date	Hour	Summary of Events and Information	Remarks and references to Appendices
Trenches	22/28	–	Reopening Northern part of HITTITE Trench, & converting it into a fire trench as far as PALESTINE, about 200 yds of trench were completed; old wire repaired & strengthened.	[initials]
				[initials]
COLINCAMPS	23	–	1 o.r. wounded during shelling of COLINCAMPS	[initials]
Trenches	24	–	"D" Coy's working party, wiring, came under machine-gun fire. Cas. o.r. 1 killed 2 wounded.	[initials]
COURCELLES	30	9.30a	~~Moved to Rest Camp~~ in BUS WOOD, with COLINCAMPS party included.	[initials]
BUS WOOD	31	–	Resumed "refresher" & specialist training.	

[signature] Lieut. Colonel Comdg.
12th (S) Bn. York & Lancs. Rgt. (Sheffield.)

1875 Wt. W593/826 1,000,000 4/15 J.B.C. & A. A.D.S.S./Forms/C. 2118.

Instructions regarding War Diaries and Intelligence Summaries are contained in F. S. Regs., Part II. and the Staff Manual respectively. Title Pages will be prepared in manuscript.

WAR DIARY
~~or~~
~~INTELLIGENCE SUMMARY~~
(Erase heading not required.)

XXXI

Army Form C. 2118

9 Jun

12 York & Lancs

Vol 4

Place	Date	Hour	Summary of Events and Information	Remarks and references to Appendices
BUS	1/6/16	9.30 a.m.	C.O., Adj., Coy. Commanders, & M.G. officer & Signalling Sergt. went up to the trenches, which according to instructions received, the Batt. was to take over from 10th E. Yorks. on the following day. Sector (N) K.29.C. [illegible]	
		[illegible] a.m.	Wire received, postponing relief till following Sunday 4th inst.;	
		5 op.m.	Inspection of Batt. by Major-General O'Gowan, who complimented officers and men on their behaviour during the bombardment when the Batt. was last in trenches. i.e. night 15/16 5.16.	
		6.30 p.m.	Word received of further alteration in programme. Forthcoming tour of duty in trenches still further postponed.	C.E.
"	2.6.16.	9.0 a.m.	Usual programme of training was carried out during the day.	C.E.
"	3.6.16.	9.30 a.m.	Batt. carried out Aeroplane Contact Patrol practice on ground J.25 d & C — I 30. b & C. Ref. France 57D. 1/40,000.	C.E.
"	4.6.16.	9.30 am – 1.00 pm	Batt. provided working parties for work behind the lines.	C.E.
"	5.6.16.	9.30 a.m.	Batt. marched from BUS to GEZAINCOURT, arriving 2.15 p.m. Position of Batt. H.Q. (Map Ref. France 57D 1/40,000) A.21 C.5.3. "D" Coy. billeted apart at BRETEL, i.e. A.15 C. and D.	C.E.
GEZAINCOURT	6.6.16	9.0 a.m. – 4.30 p.m.	Training Continued.	C.E.
	7.6.16.		The following two officers arrived for duty from the base, and were posted as under:— Lieut. H. OXLEY appointed Batt. Signalling Officer vice Sec. Lt. J.C.G. BARDSLEY, evacuated to England. 2/Lt. C.H. WARDILL, to "C" Coy.	C.E.

1875 Wt. W593/826 1,000,000 4/15 J.B.C. & A. A.D.S.S./Forms/C. 2118.

Army Form C. 2118

Instructions regarding War Diaries and Intelligence Summaries are contained in F. S. Regs., Part II. and the Staff Manual respectively. Title Pages will be prepared in manuscript.

WAR DIARY

~~or~~

~~INTELLIGENCE SUMMARY~~

(Erase heading not required.)

Place	Date	Hour	Summary of Events and Information	Remarks and references to Appendices
GEZAINCOURT	8.6.16	8.0 a.m.	Draft of forty four (44) O.R. arrived for duty from the base.	
		9.0 a.m.	Bde. Route march; Chief points to be noticed :- March Discipline. Route :- A.21.C.5.3. — A.15.C.3.7. — Crossroads N.E. of CITADELLE — Road junction N. of LE BON AIR — BAGNEUX — GEZAINCOURT.	C.E.
"	9.6.16	2.15 p.m.	Bde. practice of assembly in assembly trenches preparatory to the assault. Carried out on training ground in E. 7. and 8.	C.E.
"	10.6.16	9.30 a.m. 2.45 p.m.	Repetition of Bde. practice in assembly and assault.	C.E.
"	11.6.16	~~[illegible]~~ C.E. 2.0 p.m.	" " " " ~~[illegible]~~ " " in conjunction with Aeroplane Contact patrol.	C.E.
"	12.6.16	9 a.m. 2.0 p.m.	Repetition of Bde. practice in assembly and assault.	C.E.
BUS	13.6.16	8.7 a.m.	Commenced march back to BUS from GEZAINCOURT via same route as outward journey i.e. via DOULLENS, SARTON, and AUTHIE. Arrived in BUS 1.30 p.m. 1½ Coys. and all officers in huments in BUS WOOD; remainder billeted in village. Position of H.Q. :- J.20.c.8.2. (map ref. France, 57 D. N.E., Edition 2.A. 1/20,000.).	C.E.
"	14.6.16	8.30 a.m.	Adv. party, (usual composition) moved off to trenches to take over stores etc. from 10th (S.) Bn. E. YORKS. REGT., in Sector K.23.d.35.40. — K.29.c.80.90. Batts. on our right and left respectively :- 11th (S.) Batt. E. YORKS. REGT. & 8th Batt. OXFORD & BUCKS. LIGHT INFANTRY. Batt. left BUS at 1.0 p.m. Relief reported complete 6.10 p.m., no Casualties. Distribution of Coys.:- Left Coy. = A Coy.; Right Coy. = D Coy.; Left Reserve Coy. = C Coy.; Right Reserve Coy. = B Coy. Quiet night. Position of Batt HQ = K.28.b.7.5.	C.E.

Army Form C. 2118

Instructions regarding War Diaries and Intelligence Summaries are contained in F. S. Regs., Part II. and the Staff Manual respectively. Title Pages will be prepared in manuscript.

WAR DIARY

~~or~~

~~INTELLIGENCE SUMMARY~~

(Erase heading not required.)

Place	Date	Hour	Map Ref.:- France 57D 1/40,000. Summary of Events and Information	Remarks and references to Appendices
TRENCHES	15.6.16.	3.0.a.m. 9.15.p.m	Work commenced on deepening parts of front line to 7' where necessary. Quiet day on the whole. Enemy knocked in LE CATEAU trench between FRONT LINE and ROB ROY with 6 trench mortar shells. Dug out by Right Coy.	
		10.30.p.m.	A few shrapnel put over on to ration party at 10.30. p.m. Casualties during the day:- 1 O.R. killed (C. Coy.), 1 O.R. shell-shock (D. Coy), 3 O.R. wounded (2 C. Coy. + 1 A. Coy.).	C.E.
"	16.6.16	8.0.a.m.	Enemy artillery and trench mortars quiet during the morning, enabling working parties to carry on undisturbed.	
		4.0.p.m	Batt. on our right relieved by 12th (S). Batt. E. YORKS. REGT.	
		9.30.p.m	LE CATEAU knocked in again, and dug out by Right Coy. Trenches becoming drier owing to fine weather	C.E.
"	17.6.16	8-30a.m. to 5.30p.m.	Slow consistent shelling by heavy battery (H.E.) of our front line from K. 23. d. 25.30, to approx. 100x South. Some bays were knocked in, and all the traffic trench for that distance levelled up. Casualties during the day:- 3 O.R. killed (including 12/s C.S.M. Marsden — buried in dug-out — + 12/1388 Sgt. Clay), all of A. Coy. 7 O.R. shell shock, all A. Coy. Immediately after cessation of bombardment work was commenced on attempting to dig C.S.M. Marsden out. This was stopped by the enemy firing a few 77mm. shells + rifle grenades.	
		10.30.p.m to 2.0.a.m	At night work was recommenced on this and digging out the traffic trench. The whole of the available men of Right reserve Coy. being called on to dig. Traffic trench cleared by daylight, but dug out not. Quiet night from the shelling point of view.	C.E.
"	17.6.16	1.40 a.m	Enemy blew land mine on JOHN TUNNEL, killing 3 O.R. (not of this batt.)	

1875 Wt. W593/826 1,000,000 4/15 J.B.C. & A. A.D.S.S./Forms/C. 2118.

Instructions regarding War Diaries and Intelligence Summaries are contained in F. S. Regs., Part II. and the Staff Manual respectively. Title Pages will be prepared in manuscript.

Army Form C. 2118

WAR DIARY
~~or~~
~~INTELLIGENCE SUMMARY~~
(Erase heading not required.)

Place	Date	Hour	Map Ref:- France 57D. NE 1/20,000 Summary of Events and Information	Remarks and references to Appendices
TRENCHES	18.6.16.	8.0 a.m.	Work continued on C.S.M. Marsden's dug-out. Quiet day. Work carried on of deepening and consolidating front line bays and traffic trench.	
		10.0 p.m.	Working party of 14th Y. & L. at work making our ammunition, water and ration dumps at junction of JONES and JORDAN.	
		11.0 p.m.	Work on C.S.M. Marsden's dug-out given up as hopeless by left coy.	
		1.0 a.m.	Order received from G.O.C. to convert JOHN TUNNEL into sap-head, and post sentries at night. Order transmitted to left Coy. Casualties:- 2 O.R. wounded (A & C [acc.]); 3 O.R. shell shock (2C + 1A).	C.E.
"	19.6.16.	9.0 a.m. to 3.0 p.m.	Slow heavy shelling commenced again on practically same front as before, only continuing about 50x further South. Total estimated at 160 15 c.m. H.E. Retaliation by our artillery succeeded in stopping it about 3.0 p.m. Bde. Chaplain, who had come up to read burial service over C.S.M. Marsden's dug-out was unable to do so, as enemy were continually shelling this spot.	
		3.0 p.m.	Commenced to be relieved by 11th (S) Batt. E. Lancs. Regt.. Owing to misty weather it became possible to relieve the left coy (whose line had been blocked and coy split up) by daylight, instead of at night, as at first arranged. Casualties previous to relief:- 1 Off. i.e. 2/Lt. H.S. LUMB (A. Coy.), shell shock, 1 O.R. wounded (A. Coy.). Relief reported complete 7.0 p.m. no casualties. Batt marched to hutments in WARNIMONT WOOD. Last Coy. arrived 12.30 a.m. 20/6/16. Position of Batt H.Q.:- I.24.d.5.7.	C.E.
WARNIMONT WOOD	20.6.16.	9.0 a.m.	Quiet day. Men allowed to rest and clean themselves up.	C.E.
	21.6.16.	9.0 a.m.	Batt provided carrying parties from COLINCAMPS to trenches for ammunition etc.	
	22.6.16.	9.0 p.m.	EUSTON DUMP to front line for gas cylinders. Also digging parties in JONES and JORDAN. Working all night 22/23.6.16.	C.E.

1875 Wt. W593/826 1,000,000 4/15 J.B.C. & A. A.D.S.S./Forms/C. 2118.

Instructions regarding War Diaries and Intelligence Summaries are contained in F. S. Regs., Part II. and the Staff Manual respectively. Title Pages will be prepared in manuscript.

WAR DIARY

~~or~~

~~INTELLIGENCE SUMMARY~~

(Erase heading not required.)

Army Form C. 2118

Place	Date	Hour	Summary of Events and Information	Remarks and references to Appendices
WARNIMONT WOOD	23.6.16	12 noon	Working parties supplied to trenches. 1 O.R. killed (B Coy.)	C.E.
	24.6.16		Quiet day. Nothing to report.	C.E.
	25.6.16		Divine services during the day, both in the Y.M.C.A tent and the wood.	C.E.
	26.6.16	8.30 a.m.	Batt. move off to training ground to re-practice assembly and assault.	
		5.15 p.m.	Major-General O'Gowan, the Div. Commander, spoke a few words of encouragement to the Batt. prior to its going into action.	C.E.
	27.6.16	11 a.m.	~~Lieut Gen Sir Aymler Hunter Weston VIII Corps commander visited the battalion & addressed the men with regard to forthcoming operations~~ AHH	AHH
	~~28.6.16~~	11.55 p.m.	Two patrols left our front line trenches under Lieut F.W.S. STORRY and Sgt F. DONOGHUE "B" Coy - carrying Bangalore torpedoes - The patrols examined the enemy wire and reported it to be considerably damaged by our shell fire - the Bangalore torpedoes were not fired owing to casualties in men trained in their use - two gaps were reported on right of our front wire thin & damaged on the left - Sgt Henderson, Pte Storey & Pte Gambles severely wounded. Patrols returned to front line about 1-10 a.m.	AHH
	28.6.16		Quiet day - very heavy rain - commencement of operations postponed 48 hrs	AHH
	29.6.16		Busy day issuing stores for assaulting troops.	AHH
	30.6.16	10 a.m.	Lieut. Col. Crosthwaite taken ill and evacuated. Major Plackett recalled from Div. School & assumed command of battalion.	AHH
		11 a.m.	Lieut General Sir Aymler Hunter Weston VIII Corps Commander visited battalion & addressed the men with regard to forthcoming operations.	
		9 p.m.	Battalion moved out of WARNIMONT WOOD to march to assembly trenches behind JOHN COPSE & MARK COPSE. Battalion halted just W of COURCELLES till 9.40 pm - hot tea & rum being issued -	AHH
		9.40 pm	March continued via NORTHERN AVENUE, PYLON, NAIRNE - to assembly trenches. Battalion took up position as follows: Front line MARK COPSE to JOHN COPSE - 1st wave "C" & "A" Coy (A on right). 2nd wave in bombardment slits dug between front line & traffic trench and COPSE TRENCH.	

1875 Wt. W593/826 1,000,000 4/15 J.B.C. & A. A.D.S.S./Forms/C. 2118.

Army Form C. 2118

Instructions regarding War Diaries and Intelligence Summaries are contained in F. S. Regs., Part II. and the Staff Manual respectively. Title Pages will be prepared in manuscript.

WAR DIARY

~~or~~

~~INTELLIGENCE SUMMARY~~

(Erase heading not required.)

Place	Date	Hour	Summary of Events and Information	Remarks and references to Appendices
	30.6.16		3rd Wave of attack (B & D) Coys were disposed as follows – 'B' Coy on right in CAMPION 'D' on left also CAMPION. 4th Wave 'B & D' Coys in MONK TRENCH. Battalion H.Q. in the ~~[illegible]~~ tunnel in JOHN COPSE. 11th East Lancs on our right – 14th York & Lancs in support behind this battalion. Enemy artillery very quiet during assembly.	[illegible]

A.L. Gumbridge Capt & Adjt
12th York & Lancs Regt
for O/C

94th Bde.
31st Div.

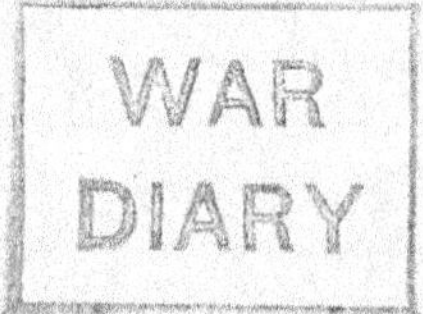

12th BATTALION

YORK & LANCASTER REGIMENT

1st to 31st JULY 1916.

Appendices attached=
Preliminary Operation Order.
Sketches showing assembly positions.

CONFIDENTIAL.

WAR DIARY.

12.S.Battalion,York and Lancaster Regiment. (Sheffield).

VOLUME V.

From 1st July.1916.

To 31st July. 1916.

B.E.F., 1st June.1916.

94
31.

War Diary

of

12th (S) Bn. York & Lancaster Regt.

for

July 1916

Army Form C. 2118.

Instructions regarding War Diaries and Intelligence Summaries are contained in F. S. Regs., Part II. and the Staff Manual respectively. Title Pages will be prepared in manuscript.

WAR DIARY
or
~~INTELLIGENCE SUMMARY~~
(Erase heading not required.)

Place	Date	Hour	Summary of Events and Information	Remarks and references to Appendices
COLINCAMPS SECTOR	1.7.16	1.40 am	Battalion Headquarters consisting of Major A.Plackett ,Commanding;Major A R Hoette,second-in-Command;Captain & Adjutant N.L.Tunbridge,Lieutenant H. Oxley,Signalling Officer,and other Headquarters' Details arrived at JOHN Copse. All quiet.Nothing seen of "A" & "C" Companies.	
Do	Do	1.55 am	Captain Clarke reported our own wire cut on our front and tapes laid out in front of our line,vide Battalion Operation Order,No.15,para.2 (a,b,c,d.) Laying of tape completed about 12-30.am.Report sent to Brigade Hdqtrs in DUNMOW.	
Do	Do	2.40 am	The first and second waves of "A" Coy reported in position in the Assembly trenches.Company Hdqtrs established in the front line near its junction with JORDAN.	
Do	Do	3.45 am	Lieut.ELAM reported Battalion in position in the Assembly trenches.Reports not yet received from "B","C",& "D" Coys,however.	
Do	Do	3.50 am	"D" Coy reported in position.	
Do	Do	4.5 am	Enemy started shelling JOHN COPSE and front line.	
Do	Do	4.25 am	Report sent to 94th Infantry Brigade.Battalion in position in Assembly trenches.	
Do	Do	6.0 am	"C" Company report our own guns firing short on the front line between JOHN & LUKE COPSES causing casualties. Reported to Brigade by runner telephonic communication being cut.	
Do	Do	6.30 am	"C" Coy reported Bays 31 to 38 heavily shelled.8 killed & 6 wounded--principally No 12 platoon. Reply sent "Report again at 7-0 am.Nothing can be done at present."	
Do	Do	7.0 am	"C" Coy reported no further casualties ,but that our guns had been firing short, and had been hitting our own parapet in the front line.This was reported to Brigade.	
			NOTES: The Communication trenches i.e.,NORTHERN AVENUE,PYLON,& NAIRNE were in an exceedingly bad condition owing to the heavy rain;in places the water	

2449 Wt. W14957/M90 750,000 1/16 J.B.C. & A. Forms/C.2118/12.

Instructions regarding War Diaries and Intelligence Summaries are contained in F. S. Regs., Part II. and the Staff Manual respectively. Title Pages will be prepared in manuscript.

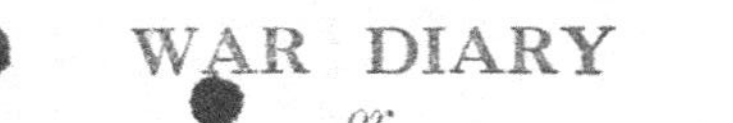

PAGE 2.

WAR DIARY
or
INTELLIGENCE SUMMARY
(Erase heading not required.)

Army Form C. 2118.

Place	Date	Hour	Summary of Events and Information	Remarks and references to Appendices
COLINCAMPS. SECTOR.			was well above the knees. This caused great fatigue to the men and consequently delayed assembly of Battalion in the trenches at least $2\frac{1}{2}$ hours. The Eastern end of NAIRNE was found to be considerably blown in, but was passable. The front line was badly smashed up throughout its length; also the Traffic trench. COPSE trench was also badly smashed up. MONK & CAMPION were in a bad state, but this was due to the weather rather than to the enemy shelling. From the outset telephonic communication with the Brigade was cut, and the only means of communication throughout the day was by runner. The enemy artillery continued shelling heavily from 4.5 am, until the attack commenced. In view of the fact that the enemy artillery became active as soon as it was daylight, it would appear likely that the enemy was warned of the attack by observing gaps cut in our own wire and tapes laid out in No Man's Land, thus obtaining at least three and a half hours warning of the attack. "A" Coy reported no sign of the tape which was laid during the night; it had, apparently, been removed. It served no purpose at all except to give the enemy warning. The wire in front of our lines had been cut away too much and as the gaps were not staggered, our intention to attack must have been quite obvious to the enemy.	
	1.7.16	7.20 AM	The first wave of "A" and "C" proceeded into No Man's Land and laid down about 100 yards in front of our trenches under cover of intense bombardment by Stokes Mortars and Artillery. Casualties were not heavy up to this point.	
	1.7.16	7.29 AM	Second wave moved forward and took up a position about 30 yards in rear of the first wave. The third and fourth waves left CAMPION & MONK and advanced in section columns. The enemy started an artillery barrage commencing at MONK and gradually rolling forward to the front line, where it finally settled .	

2449 Wt. W14957/M90 750,000 1/16 J.B.C. & A. Forms/C.2118/12.

Army Form C. 2118.

Instructions regarding War Diaries and Intelligence Summaries are contained in F. S. Regs., Part II. and the Staff Manual respectively. Title Pages will be prepared in manuscript.

WAR DIARY
or
INTELLIGENCE SUMMARY

(Erase heading not required.)

PAGE 3.

Place	Date	Hour	Summary of Events and Information	Remarks and references to Appendices
COLIN CAMPS SECTOR	1.7.16	7.30.am	Barrage lifted from the German front line and first and second waves moved forward to the assault. They were immediately met with very heavy machine gun and rifle xxx fire and artillery barrage. The left half of "C" Coy was wiped out before getting near the German wire, and on the right the few men who reached the wire were unable to get through. As soon as our barrage lifted from their front line, the Germans, who had been sheltering in Dug-outs immediately came out and opened rapid fire with their machine guns. Some were seen to retire to the second and third lines. The enemy fought very well throwing Hand grenades into his own wire. NOTES: A great many casualties were caused by the enemy's machine guns; infact the third and fourth waves suffered so heavily that by the time they had reached No Man's Land they had lost at least half their strength. Whole sections were wiped out. The German front line wire was found to be almost intact, particularly on the left. A few men of both "A" and "C" Coys managed to enter the German trenches on the right of the attack, but in all other parts of the line men were held up, being shot down by the Germans in front of them. The few survivors took shelter in shell holes in front of the German wire and remained there until they could get back under cover of darkness. The failure of the attack was undoubtedly due to the wire not being sufficiently cut. Had this been cut the enemy's machine guns could have been dealt with by the men who managed to reach the front line. As it was, they could not be reached and there was no means of stopping their fire. Bombers attempted to silence them with grenades but could not reach them - consequently succeeding waves were wiped out and did not arrive at the German wire in any strength. --------------	

2449 Wt. W14957/M90 750,000 1/16 J.B.C. & A. Forms/C.2118/12.

Instructions regarding War Diaries and Intelligence Summaries are contained in F. S. Regs., Part II. and the Staff Manual respectively. Title Pages will be prepared in manuscript.

Army Form C. 2118.

WAR DIARY
or
INTELLIGENCE SUMMARY

(*Erase heading not required.*)

PAGE 4.

Place	Date	Hour	Summary of Events and Information	Remarks and references to Appendices
COLINCAMPS SECTOR	1.7.16.	10.30 am.	Major Hoette wounded in JOHN COPSE. No reports from Coys yet to hand. Reported to Brigade.	
	"	1. pm	Battalion Hdqtrs moved to MARK COPSE, as JOHN COPSE was full of wounded. Still out of touch with Coys; reported to Brigade.	
	"	8.21 pm	Reply sent to BM 41, enquiring as to strength, ammunition, bombs, Lewis guns, &c., in front line: "Strength of Battalion-10 men unwounded. These are runners and Signallers. Have no Lewis Guns. 3000 S.A.A. 350 Bombs. Lewis pans--nil."	
	"	10 pm	Message received from Brigade that we should be relieved by the 13th and 14th S. Battalions, York & Lancaster Regiment, in the front line; The Battalion to withdraw to ROLLAND trench. Hdqtrs withdrew from MARK COPSE at 10-15 am, and was established in a deep sap in ROLLAND. During the night message received from Brigade to say that information had been received that about 150 of our men had penetrated the German front line opposite MARK COPSE, and were still maintaining their position in the German front line. Every endeavour was to be made to get into touch with them and withdraw them	
	July 2	1.30 am to 3.15 am.	Two Officer patrols were sent out from MARK COPSE with men borrowed from the 14 Battn, York & Lancaster Regiment. These went out into No Man's Land and approached the German wire. No Signs of any fighting were apparent, and wounded men, who were met and brought in, stated that any men left in the trenches, had become casualties and unable to offer further resistance. Patrols consequently withdrew. German machine guns were very active, sweeping No Man's Land and a large number of Very Lights were sent up. Lieut. H. Oxley was slightly wounded.	
			Captain E.G.G. Woolhouse and 2nd Lieut. W.H. Rowlands arrived with 80 1st reinforcements. These joined up in ROLLAND trench with the remainder of the Battalion. The Officers now with the Battalion were: Capt. E.G.G. Woolhouse, Captain & Adjutant. N.L. Tunbridge, Lieutenant E.L. Moxey. (M G Officer) 2nd Lieut. C C Cloud, 2nd Lieut. W.H. Rowlands, also Major A Plackett & Lieut H Oxley.	

2449 Wt. W14957/M90 750,000 1/16 J.B.C. & A. Forms/C.2118/12.

Army Form C. 2118.

WAR DIARY
or
INTELLIGENCE SUMMARY
(Erase heading not required.)

Instructions regarding War Diaries and Intelligence Summaries are contained in F. S. Regs., Part II. and the Staff Manual respectively. Title Pages will be prepared in manuscript.

PAGE 5.

Place	Date	Hour	Summary of Events and Information	Remarks and references to Appendices
COLINCAMPS SECTOR.	2.7.16	12 Noon	Casualty Return: Killed in Action: Captain W.A.Colley. Captain.W.S.Clark. 2nd Lieut.C.H.Wardill. 2nd Lieutenant.E.M.Carr. Wounded: Major A.R.Hoette. Captain.R.E.J.Moore. Lieut.C.H.Woodhouse. Lieut.G.H.J.Ingold. Lieut.F.C.Earl. Lieut.F.W.S.Storry. Lieut.H.W.Pearson. Missing, Believed wounded: Lieut.C.Elam. 2nd Lieut.P.K.Perkin. 2nd Lieut.A.J.Beal. 2nd Lieut.F.Dinsdale. Killed, Wounded & Missing: Other Ranks: 468. LATER: Major A.Plackett and Lieut.H.Oxley, evacuated wounded. Headquarters removed from ROLLAND to TROSSACHS, owing to there being better dug-out accommodation. SPECIAL ORDER OF THE DAY: In a Special Order of the Day, Brigadier-General H.C.Rees.D.S.O., prior to handing over the Command of the 94th Infantry Brigade, to Brig: General T.Carter-Campbell.D.S.O., said: "In giving up the Command of the 94th Brigade to Brigadier-General T. Carter-Campbell, whose place I have temporarily taken during this great battle, I wish to express to all ranks my admiration of their behaviour. I havebeen through many battles in this war and nothing more magnificent has come under my notice. The waves went forward as if on a drill parade and I saw no man turn back or falter. I bid good-bye to the remnants of as fine a Brigade as has ever gone into action."	
	3.7.16	12 Noon	Casualties: Officers as reported yesterday. Other ranks: 468 previously reptd "Killed, wounded & Missing", now 21 Missing rejoined Unwounded. 67 wounded, 6 killed. Casualty since 1 o r., --373 Missing."	
	1.7.16		NOTES ON THE GERMAN TRENCHES. ETC., (1). The German front line trench was 12 ft deep and 3 ft wide at the bottom sloping upward. There was no parapet at all, but a very high parados-	

2449 Wt. W14957/M90 750,000 1/16 J.B.C. & A. Forms/C.2118/12.

Instructions regarding War Diaries and Intelligence Summaries are contained in F. S. Regs., Part II. and the Staff Manual respectively. Title Pages will be prepared in manuscript.

PAGE 6.

WAR DIARY
or
INTELLIGENCE SUMMARY
(Erase heading not required.)

Army Form C. 2118.

Place	Date	Hour	Summary of Events and Information	Remarks and references to Appendices
COLINCAMPS SECTOR			3 or 4 ft in height, immediately behind the fire trench. There were no fire steps at all. The wire in front of the German trench is very thick, from 2 to 3 ft high, thinner at the bottom than at the top, and comes to within three feet of the edge of the trench.	
			Trenches revetted with basket work and floor-boarded. The traverses were very wide. No information is available regarding the second line, reserve and communication trenches.	
			(2). <u>DUG-OUTS</u>. One Dug-out was noted. This was deep and of a type similar to those in MONK trench. It had about 18 steps and would accommodate eight men. The Dug-out was run out under the parapet and was just at the corner and close to a traverse. The man who saw this states that there was a notice up with the following in English characters: "M G No. 1. POST."	
			He was quite positive about this. The Dug-out was not damaged by our fire.	
			(3). <u>MACHINE GUNS</u>. Machine guns were fired both from emplacements and from behind parados. One emplacement in particular was noted to be situated in a parados. The parados was hollowed out and a mound raised behind it, so as to conceal the emplacement. This gun caused a great number of casualties and was situated in the German front line just to the South of MARK COPSE.	
			(4). <u>UNDERGROUND TUNNELS</u>. Although no underground tunnels were actually seen leading to the front line, it is suspected that these exist, owing to large numbers of the enemy apparently appearing from nowhere, in the front line.	

	1.7.16		<u>SUGGESTIONS & CRITICISMS</u>: (A) The wait in the Assembly trenches was too long.	

2449 Wt. W14957/M90 750,000 1/16 J.B.C. & A. Forms/C.2118/12.

Instructions regarding War Diaries and Intelligence Summaries are contained in F. S. Regs., Part II. and the Staff Manual respectively. Title Pages will be prepared in manuscript.

Army Form C. 2118.

WAR DIARY
or
INTELLIGENCE SUMMARY

(Erase heading not required.)

PAGE 7.

Place	Date	Hour	Summary of Events and Information	Remarks and references to Appendices
COLINCAMPS SECTOR.			(B) The first wave should not have occupied the front line. Owing to the Trench Mortars being in position in the front line, it became a death trap when the enemy retaliated against them. (C) More bombardment slits should have been dug. It was found that men occupying these suffered very slightly compared with those in Assembly trenches; those that were dug should have been deeper. (D) More men should have been trained in the use of the Bangalore torpedo. It was found that all trained men had become casualties by the time the torpedoes were actually required. (E) Smoke bombs would have been useful to conceal our efforts to cut the enemy's wire, As it was, anyone attempting to cut the wire was immediately sniped. TACTICS. (i) The assault should have been made at dawn or soon after. As it was the enemy had 4½ hours to prepare for an attack, as our intention was undoubtedly given away by the gaps cut in our wire and the tapes laid out in front. Men who reached the German wire state that on looking towards our own lines, they could see almost every movement. This being so any attack by day was scarcely likely to succeed. (ii) The attack should have been in double time. (iii) The waves were too far apart, the distance between them allowing the enemy to pay attention to each wave before the next came up. MISCELLANEOUS. Assaulting bombers state that they think they could have carried their bombs better in jackets than in the buckets. The general opinionwas that Officers, N.C.O's and Machine gunners were marked men. ---------	

2449 Wt. W14957/M90 750,000 1/16 J.B.C. & A. Forms/C.2118/12.

Army Form C. 2118.

Instructions regarding War Diaries and Intelligence Summaries are contained in F. S. Regs., Part II. and the Staff Manual respectively. Title Pages will be prepared in manuscript.

WAR DIARY
or
INTELLIGENCE SUMMARY

(Erase heading not required.)

PAGE 8.

Place	Date	Hour	Summary of Events and Information	Remarks and references to Appendices
COLINCAMPS SECTOR.	3.7.16		The Battalion continued to be in support in Trossachs trench. Little activity on either side, though at 4 am there was a Gas Alarm. Night and day saw many dead carried out and placed in Red Cottage and dis-used trenches. Odd survivors crawled in from No Man's Land under cover of darkness. Draft of 56 other ranks arrived at the Base in Warnimont Wood. <u>Evacuated to England:</u> Lieut-Colonel J.A.Crosthwaite, Major A.R.Hoette, Captain R.E.J.Moore, Lieut.F.W.S.Storry.	
	4.7.16	8 pm	Relief by Oxon and Bucks.Battn, 48th Division, commenced. Relief completed by 10 pm, without any further casualties. Battn marched to billets at LOUVENCOURT. Captain D.C.Allen rejoined Battn from 4th Army School of Instruction & took over the command of Battn., from Captain E.G.G.Woolhouse. Of the 22 Officers, who went into the trenches on June 30, the following only marched out with the Battn: Capt. & Adjutant N.L.Tunbridge, Lieut.E.L.Moxey, 2nd Lieut. C.C.Cloud, and the Medical Officer; Lieut.E.C.Cunnington. In addition, of course, were Capt.Woolhouse & 2nd Lieut Rowlands-reinforcements. The marching out strength of the rank and file was 202, which included 82 reinforcements. Lieut.C.H.Woodhouse and Lieut.H.W.Pearson evacuated to England.	
LOUVENCOURT.	5.7.16.		Quiet day. Preparations made for move to GEZAINCOURT. At 5-0 pm. Lieut-Gen. Sir Aylmer Hunter-Weston made laudatory speech to the troops of the 94th Infty Brigade, who took part in the assault. Major Plackett evacuated to England.	
do.	6.7.16	10. am	Battalion fell in for march to GEZAINCOURT. Owing to artillery and transport congestion start was delayed. Route: via SARTON, MARIEUX, & DOULLENS. Further delays at DOULLENS and GEZAINCOURT owing to movement of troops and lack of billeting accommodation. Proceeded to LONGUEVILLETTE, N of GEZAINCOURT. Arrived 5-30 pm.	
LONGUEVILLETTE	7.7.16	10. am	Battalion Roll Call. Strength proved to be 18 Officers, 541 other ranks., out of totals of 36 Officers and 1036 (including draft) other ranks. Casualties	

2449 Wt. W14957/M90 750,000 1/16 J.B.C. & A. Forms/C.2118/12.

Army Form C. 2118.

Instructions regarding War Diaries and Intelligence Summaries are contained in F. S. Regs., Part II. and the Staff Manual respectively. Title Pages will be prepared in manuscript.

WAR DIARY
or
INTELLIGENCE SUMMARY

(Erase heading not required.)

PAGE 9.

Place	Date	Hour	Summary of Events and Information	Remarks and references to Appendices
Longuevillette	7.7.16		proved to be as follows:	

	"A" Coy.	"B" Coy.	"C" Coy.	"D" Coy.	Battn Total.
Killed:	6.	15.	8.	16.	45.
Died of Wounds.	1.	2.	2.	7.	12.
Wounded:	76.	62.	43.	56.	237.
Missing:	44.	44.	71.	42.	201.
TOTALS.	127.	123.	124.	121.	495.

Place	Date	Hour	Summary of Events and Information	Remarks and references to Appendices
			Re-organising and refitting commenced. Draft of 56 allotted to Coys. Lieut. G.H.J. Ingold evacuated to England.	
	8.7.16	1.30am	Received orders to move to STEENBECQUE, in rear of line between YPRES & ARMENTIERES. Moved off 12 noon., entraining at 9-30 pm at FREVENT. ROUTE:-- DOULLENS & BOUQUE MAISON.	
Steenbecque	9.7.16	2 am	Detrained at STEENBECQUE. Now in area of 1st Army and under jurisdiction of X1 Army Corps. Marched via ST FLORIS, CALONNE-SUR-LA-LYS to MERVILLE, arriving there at 2 pm.	
Merville	10.7.16		Quiet day. Following messages received: From Lieut-Gen. Sir Aylmer Hunter-Weston, K.C.B., D.S.O., Commander V111th Army Corps:--"G O C. Anzac Corps has sent the following message to me which I desire to pass on at once to the Officers, N.C.O's and men, V111th Army Corps, to show them the opinion held of them by the rest of the British troops-- 'Just a line to say how sorry we are to hear of the losses which your magnificent Corps has recently suffered in its gallant fighting in German trenches. They are, indeed, heroes and their name will live for ever'" The Vice-Chancellor, Sheffield University wrote "Congratulate Battalion on its superb courage, while deeply deploring severe losses."	
	11.7.16		Battalion training commenced.	
	12.7.16 13.7.16		Quiet days. Nothing to report.	
	14.7.16		Moving order: Warning of.	

2449 Wt. W14957/M90 750,000 1/16 J.B.C. & A. Forms/C.2118/12.

Instructions regarding War Diaries and Intelligence Summaries are contained in F. S. Regs., Part II. and the Staff Manual respectively. Title Pages will be prepared in manuscript.

PAGE 10.

WAR DIARY
or
INTELLIGENCE SUMMARY
(Erase heading not required.)

Army Form C. 2118.

Place	Date	Hour	Summary of Events and Information	Remarks and references to Appendices
MERVILLE	15.7.16	1.0 am	Operation Orders received. 31st Division ordered to take over part of the line held by 61st Division.	
"		7.0 am	1 Officer (2 Lt W.H. Rowlands) 8 N.C.Os and 60 men-"A" Coy. 8 " " 20 " "D" " moved to PONT DU HEM, ROUGE CROIX, E & W., CROIX BARBEE, RUE DU PUITS, ETON, CHARTERHOUSE, HARROW, WELLINGTON, EUSTON, LORETTO, LA VENTE FARM--defensive posts in NEUVE CHAPELLE sector.	
"		12 Noon	Battalion, less personnel detailed above moved off. Destination-RUE DU PUITS (M 26 & M 27). Route: L'EPINETTE, LESTREM, BOUT DEVILLE. Arrived 5-0 pm.	
VIEILLE CHAPELLE AREA	16.7.16	3.0 pm	Battn Hdqtrs removed to R 29 d 57. Ref. Map: FRANCE 36 a. 1/40,000.	
	17.7.16		Quiet day. Regtl classes for the training of Machine gunners and bombers commenced.	
"	18.7.16		Quiet. Nothing to report.	
"	19.7.16	8. pm.	Enemy aircraft active. Bomb dropped in rear of transport line. Congratulatory message from VIII Corps Commander received. The following is an extract: "The 31st Division (New Army) and the 48th Territorial Division, by the heroism and discipline of the units engaged in this their first big battle (July 1), have proved themselves worthy to fight by the side of such magnificent regular Divisions as the 4th and 29th. There can be no higher praise." Brigade bombing school of instruction opened. 2nd Lieut. J.C. Cowen appointed instructor. Four day courses.	
"	20.7.16		Men confined to billeting area owing to attack on enemy trenches by neighbouring Divisions--Anzacs and 61st Divn.	
"	21.7.16	10. am	PONT DU HEM & CHARTERHOUSE Posts handed over to 10th Battn. East Yorks Regt.,	
"	22.7.16	2. pm	Relief of "A" and "D" Coys in Posts by "B" and "C" Coys.	
"	24.7.16	5.15 pm.	Fighting strengths of "A", "B" and "C" Coys formed into composite Coy, and attached to 14.S. Battn. York & Lancaster Regiment, for duty in front line from CHURCH ROAD to OXFORD STREET. Captain E.G.G. Woolhouse in charge of Coy, 160 strong. "D" Coy furnished garrisons for the following posts: EDWARD, HENS, and LANSDOWNE.	

2449 Wt. W14957/M90 750,000 1/16 J.B.C. & A. Forms/C.2118/12.

Army Form C. 2118.

WAR DIARY
or
INTELLIGENCE SUMMARY
(Erase heading not required.)

Instructions regarding War Diaries and Intelligence Summaries are contained in F. S. Regs., Part II. and the Staff Manual respectively. Title Pages will be prepared in manuscript.

PAGE 11.

Place	Date	Hour	Summary of Events and Information	Remarks and references to Appendices
			The night of 24/25 passed very quietly.	
VIELLE CHAPELLE AREA.	25.7.16		Hostile srtillery and trench mortars were active the greater part of the day on the sector occupied by the Coy on our left and on the sector on the right, but the sector occupied by our detachment was left alone. The night was quiet.	
	26.7.16		During the morning Detachment Coy reported the enemy artillery registering two points behind the front line: some buildings at S 5 a 77 and S 5 c 37. From 2 pm to 4-30 pm the enemy shelled these points without ceasing with heavy shells, the greater proportion of these being "blind".	
	"	5-15 pm	Our sector subjected to three separate Trench Mortar Bombardments, each bombardment of 30 to 45 minutes duration. The enemy traversed the line from left to right from 5-15 pm to 6 pm: from 6-30 pm to 7-0 pm and from 7-45 pm to 8-15 pm causing many casualties and doing a great deal of damage to our defences. The night 26/27 was comparatively quiet. Hostile machine guns, however, were fairly active. Our casualties were 3 other ranks killed; 18 wounded, two so seriously as to die at Medical stations the next day.	
	27.7.16	11.30 am	Detachment sector taken over by "A" Coy, Durham Light Infty, 18th Battn. Posts also relieved by 16th and 15 Battns, West Yorks. Regt. No casualties occurred during the relief.	
	"	4. pm	Moved to L'EPINETTE and LESTREM. Battn H Qs being R 9 a 0.50. Reference map: FRANCE 36 a. 1/40,000. Arrived 6-0 pm. 2nd Lieut. G.C.M.L. PIRKIS joined the Battn for duty from the Base.	
LESTREM.	28.7.16		Quiet day. Nothing to report.	
	29.7.16		Quiet day. ~~xxxxxxxxxx~~. Draft of 12 other ranks arrived 7-30 pm.	
	30.7.16		Quiet. Lieut. H. Oxley rejoined Battalion from base.	
	31.7.16	11.30 am	Captain C.H. Gurney, 13th S. Battn, York & Lancaster Regiment, on appointment to 12 Y & L, assumed command of the Battn.	
		9.0 am	Field Work school commenced by Brigade: Subjects taught- Wiring, Sandbagging, Revetting. Demolition. Coys instructed also by 223rd Field Coy. R.E., in the erection of various forms of wire entanglements. Six-day programme arranged.	

C H Gurney Captain T O/C,
12th (S) Bn. York & Lancaster Regt.

2449 Wt. W14957/M90 750,000 1/16 J.B.C. & A. Forms/C.2118/12.

PRO document reference: WO 95/2365 ⟨1⟩

The item(s) described below have been extracted from this document for reasons of preservation.

Tracing of a printed map of area around Serre, France, showing trenches, copses, wires

Please order as: MF 1/53

Date: 12 March 2003

Signed: G. L. Beech

Name: G. L. BEECH

SECRET.

COPY NO...9...

12th(S) BATTALION, YORK & LANCASTER REGIMENT.
(PRELIMINARY)OPERATION ORDER, NO 14.

Reference HEBUTERNE Trench Map. 1/10,000.

26.6.16.

1. GENERAL.

1. Outline. The troops of the 4th Army are about to attack the German first line system.

The duty of the 31st Division will be to form a defensive flank for the remainder of the Army.

In order to be in a position to form this flank, they must first capture the village of SERRE. The taking of the village is essential to the success of the general operations.

It will be the duty of the 94th Infantry Brigade to carry this operation to a successful conclusion.

2. DISTRIBUTION of Troops. The attack of the 94th Infantry Brigade will be carried out by two Battalions, 11th EAST LANCS. REGT., on the right and the 12th YORK & LANCS. REGT., on the left. The 13th YORK & LANCS. REGT., will be in reserve on the right, 14th YORK & LANCS REGT., on the left.

3. Division of Line. The dividing line between the 11th East Lancs. Regt., and the 12th York & Lancs. Regt., will be as follows:

For purposes of Attack: The line North corner of MARK COPSE at Point K 29 a 98 65, Point K 30 a 21 20, Point K 30 c 66 91, North-Western boundary SERRE, to Point K 30 b 50 68. Point (68) as shown on sketch map already issued to Companies.

4. Conduct of Attack. THE ATTACK WILL BE MADE ACROSS THE OPEN.

TROOPS WILL NOT ENTER TRENCHES UNTIL THEY HAVE REACHED THEIR OBJECTIVE.

ALL MOVEMENTS OF TROOPS IN REAR OF THE TWO LEADING WAVES WILL BE IN LINES OF SECTION COLUMNS.

The attack will be carried out in three "bounds", 11th East Lancs. Regt., completing its task in three and the 12th York & Lancs. Regt., in two.

As soon as troops have reached the objective of any "bound", immediate steps will be taken to consolidate prior to further advance. Special parties have been detailed for the construction and garrison of 9 Strong Points, positions of which have been indicated on map previously issued.

3. Objectives. The objectives of the two "bounds" of the 12th York and Lancs. Regt., are shown on the map already issued. It will be seen that its final objective is the [illegible] portion of a defensive line facing North, formed by [illegible] Brigade. This line will be held against any counter-[illegible]

[illegible]

II. DISPOSITIONS AND FORMATIONS FOR THE ATTACK.

4. [illegible] The Battalion will attack on a frontage of [illegible] yards, starting from the North corner of MARK COPSE Post No. 21, to the most Easterly corner of JOHN COPSE, both inclusive, two Companies to be in the front line, two Companies in support, each Company on a frontage of approximately [illegible] yards.

Right Assaulting Coy: "A" Coy. — From North corner of MARK COPSE to Post 37 inclusive.

Left Assaulting Coy: "C" Coy. — From Post 37 inclusive to corner of JOHN COPSE inclusive.

Right Support Coy: "B" Coy.
Left Support Coy: "D" Coy.

Objectives.

First "bound" — Fourth German line between Points K 30 a 6x 61 and K 30 a 21 20. Dividing point between Companies is K 30 a 37 41. True bearing of centre of the attack 113 degrees from junction of Points 30 & 61.

Second "bound" — (a) The German trenches running in an East and Westerly direction joining Points K 30 a 44 85 to Point (82) (85). This line is divided as follows: K 30 a 44 85 to Point 29, "D" Coy; Point 29 to 6[illegible], "B" Coy.

(b) "A" Company will follow in rear of "B" and establish a defensive flank facing South-East in the trench running round North Westerly boundary of SERRE village up to Point [illegible].

Company [illegible] trenches [illegible] will block [illegible]

[illegible] the Battalion in the trenches [illegible] the night prior to the attack, in accordance with Diagram [illegible] attached; they will move into the position from which the attack will be delivered, at times which are notified below. Absolute silence will be maintained from the time of entering the communication trenches.

No SMOKING will be permitted, and great care MUST be taken that bayonets are not shewn above the parapet prior to the advance.

3. Movements. At 1-30 am the following movements will take place:
Two Companies, 10th East Yorks. Regt., 92nd Brigade, will withdraw from the Front Line trenches via JORDAN and LE CATEAU.

The second wave of "A" and "C" Coys, 12th York & Lancs. Regt., in COPSE will move overland into the Front Line; this movement will be made as quietly as possible, a few men being sent forward at a time. On the completion of these movements, the Battalion will occupy positions as shown on Diagram "B".

4. Assault. First Bound. The Assault will take place at zero hour; times shown below prior to zero hour will be indicated by the minus sign. Body of the order shows movement of troops that take place at the times indicated.

TIME.

- 10. "A" and "C" Coys will each have two platoons in front fire trench, each Coy occupying frontage, approximately 175 yards, disposed as follows: On the fire step one platoon to form the first wave. On the floor of trench - one platoon to form second wave.

DIAGRAM C.

At this hour platoons forming the first wave will advance from the fire step into "No man's Land", as far towards the German wire as our bombardment will permit and lie down.

The Trench Mortar Section at the head of Sap E, will commence a hurricane bombardment of the hostile trenches, firing at the rate of ten rounds per gun per minute.

- 5. The second wave moves out into "No man's Land" and lies down 50 yards in rear of the first wave.

ZERO. The leading Companies "A" and "C" will advance to the assault in two waves, and will proceed in quick time to their first objective.

DIAGRAM D.

The artillery will sweep in front of them, lifting slowly, until at 0.20 it will lift from the fourth German line to enable the attacking troops to enter.

On arrival at the first objective the leading Companies will push out bombing parties along all trenches leading to their flanks or to their front and will block these with bombing stops.

Two clearing parties, each of one platoon of the 14th York and Lancs. Regt., will advance out of COPSE and follow the first and second waves respectively. These will clear the German lines as the waves pass over them.

The following further movement will commence at zero hour. Two guns of a section of 94th T M B, emerging from sap-head E will follow the leading Companies working up to a position in fourth German line, with "A" Cey.

3\. Movements. At 1-30 am the following movements will take place: Two Companies,10th East Yorks.Regt.,92nd Brigade,will withdraw from the Front Line trenches via JORDAN and LE CATEAU.

The second wave of "A" and "C" Coys,12th York & Lancs.Regt., in COPSE will move overland into the Front Line; this movement will be made as quietly as possible,a few men being sent forward at a time. On the completion of these movements,the Battalion will occupy positions as shown on Diagram "B".

4\. Assault. First Bound. The Assault will take place at zero hour; times shown below prior to zero hour will be indicated by the minus sign. Body of the order shows movement of troops that take place at the times indicated.

TIME.

\- 10. DIAGRAM C. "A" and "C" Coys will each have two platoons in front fire trench,each Coy occupying frontage,approximately 175 yards,disposed as follows: On the fire step one platoon to form the first wave.On the floor of trench - one platoon to form second wave.

At this hour platoons forming the first wave will advance from the fire step into "No man's Land",as far towards the German wire as our bombardment will permit and lie down.

The Trench Mortar Section at the head of Sap E, will commence a hurricane bombardment of the hostile trenches,firing at the rate of ten rounds per gun per minute.

\- 5. The second wave moves out into "No man's Land" and lies down 50 yards in rear of the first wave.

ZERO. The leading Companies "A" and "C" will advance to the assault in two waves,and will proceed in quick time to their first objective.

DIAGRAM D. The artillery will sweep in front of them, lifting slowly,until at 0.20 it will lift from the fourth German line to enable the attacking troops to enter.

On arrival at the first objective the leading Companies will push out bombing parties along all trenches leading to their flanks or to their front and will block these with bombing stops.

Two clearing parties,each of one platoon of the 14th York and Lancs.Regt.,will advance out of COPSE and follow the first and second waves respectively. These will clear the German lines as the waves pass over them.

The following further movement will commence at zero hour. Two guns of a section of 94th T M B, emerging from sap-head E will follow the leading Companies working up to a position in fourth German line,with "A" Coy.

0.5. CAPTAU. Third and fourth waves, "B" and "D" Coys, will leave their trenches in ROB ROY and CAMPION, and advance to the third and second German lines, where they will [illegible].

0.20. Artillery fire lifts from the objective of First "bound" to Western edge of SERRE village. Diagram "B".

4. Assault. First Bound.

0.20. Third and Fourth waves again advance, and pass through [illegible] below [illegible] as possible to our barrage. [illegible] the first two waves be held up, third and fourth waves will carry them on to the first objective and immediately re-organise for a further advance.

DIAGRAMS B. 0.40. C.

Second "bound". The artillery barrage lifts from Western edge of SERRE village, and the third and fourth waves advance to secure the second objective. "A" Company, after pushing forward bombing parties up communication trenches running to North West corner of the orchard and round the orchard, as far as the barrage permits, will move forward behind "B" Coy, occupying the trench running round North-westerly boundary of SERRE village up to Point (68), thus forming defensive flank facing South East. This Coy will leave two sections in the trench on the North-Western edge of the orchard.

DIAGRAM C.

No. 3 platoon, K.O.Y.L.I. will follow "A" Coy, and occupy the latter trench, in addition to the two sections of "A" Coy, and will remain there until it is practicable to construct a new trench running through Point (74) to K 30 b 24.50.

DIAGRAM D.

The barrage will move slowly up the village at a rate of 4 minutes for the first 200 yards, afterwards lifting at the rate of 4 minutes for each 100 yards. This barrage finally lifts from the North-East edge of SERRE at 1.20.; two 18pounder batteries and two 4.5 howitzers continue firing on the orchard near L 23 a 16, and neighbouring trenches, until 1.40.

DIAGRAM D.

Companies "B", "D" and "A" Coys will occupy, and consolidate trenches [illegible] of the trench selected as a defensive [illegible] front and will block them [illegible].

1.20. The consolidation of the North-West corner of SERRE village immediately it has been seized, at 1.20, is of vital importance.

A strong bombing party from "B" Coy will immediately proceed along the communication trench running towards the orchard near L 23 a 16, blocking all trenches running off to the North-East.

1.40. Artillery barrage lifts from the orchard near L 25 a 16. "B" Coy will detail one platoon in addition to the Bombing party mentioned in preceding para., to push on and support the attack of the 11th East Lancs. Regt. at L 25 a 16. This party will get up as close to our artillery barrage as safety will permit and will make every effort to capture the orchard by 1.40, or immediately after.

Final Positions. On completion of the third "bound" the position will be as follows:-- The Battalion will be holding defensive flank facing North connecting with 11th East Lancs., on the right at Point (68) (The platoon of "B" Coy, mentioned in previous para., having rejoined remainder of the Coy-if circumstances permit- after East Lancs., have established themselves in the orchard, near L 25 a 16) and with 14th York & Lancs Regt., at the road and trench junction at Point X 30 a 44 85, Coys occupying positions as stated in para. (1) 1, 2, a & b.

Strong Points. Each strong point will be constructed by a party of one N.C.O and 12 men, assisted by 5 Pioneers and by a detachment of one Machine Gun, Brigade Machine Gun Coy, as follows:--

Strong Pt.	Bound.	Inft. Pty found by.	Assembling with, & accompanying.	On completion of work, Pioneers rejoin
C.	2nd.	[illegible] Coy.	4th wave. "D"	) Battn H.Q.
H.	2nd.	"A" Coy.	4th wave. "B"	)

)(- This party will join "A" Coy at the fourth German line.

Above Pioneers will report to their respective Coys at 5 pm on X day.

Responsibility for the exact siting of Strong Points will rest with the nearest Officer at the time work is commenced.

The garrison of each post will consist of construction party, less pioneers.

Bombing Stops. When the troops reach their objective at any stage of the attack, strong bombing parties will be sent forward along all communication trenches leading towards the next objective, and when the final objective has been reached Bombing stops will be constructed between 80 and 100 yds in front of the line to be held.

Co-operation. All troops will push forward to their objective regardless of movements or checks of other troops to their right and left. On reaching their objective every effort will be made to assist by fire or by flank attacks, any portions of our own troops in their neighbourhood who may be held up.

In the event of the leading troops being held up at any [illegible] the succeeding waves will carry the attack forward, and capture the objective, immediately re-organising in order to be ready to continue the attack on the next objective at the right time.

20. Troops which have captured a hostile trench, or any portion of it, will hold it at all costs. The word "Retire" will not be used. All men will be informed that should they hear the word "Retire" they may be quite certain it has been shouted by the enemy.

As a general principle, re-inforcements should not be sent to the assistance of troops who have been held up, but rather to the assistance of troops who are making progress.

Messages describing briefly the situation, will be sent to Battalion Hdqrs at 20 minutes intervals throughout the operations. Two runners should be sent with each important message. Every Officer and N.C.O going into action will have a notebook prepared with addresses etc., The time of despatch must be clearly stated. A untimed message is useless.

All attacking parties will follow up our barrage as close as safety permits.

MISCELLANEOUS.

14. (a) Screens. If any screens are found in the captured trenches they should not be pulled down, as they are a sign to the German Artillery not to fire on the trenches where they are placed.

(b) Mis-Use of White Flag. All men should be warned against the probable mis-use of white flags, and signs of surrender by the enemy. They have also been known to sham death, and then shoot into the back of our assault.

(c) The construction of a second line to the defensive flank will be undertaken along the line of trenches Point 74 — K 30 b 24.55 – Strong Point H. Strong Point J. For this purpose the 12 K O Y L I have been specially allotted.

(d) (1) There are two Outward and two Homeward communication trenches in the 94th Brigade area., viz.—

	JORDAN (Homeward)
NICEMA (Outward)	NAIRNA (Outward).
LE CATEAU (Homeward).	

(2) West of SACKVILLE STREET the communication trenches are as follows:

Outward: NORTHERN . NAGRAM . SOUTHERN.

Homeward: CENTRAL . RAILWAY.

The German communication trenches marked blue on map previously ~~map~~ issued will be cleared by two Coys of the 12th K O Y L I Pioneer Battalion.

(e) After the fourth wave has passed over the third German line, the Battalion Forward Report Centre, will be established near K 29 b 95.66, junction of communication trench marked blue on sketch of the third line German trench.

(f) Battalion Battle Hd'qrs. in the first instance will be JOHN COPSE and will move forward along the line of communication trenches marked Blue on map already issued up to Point K 29 b 95,66, [illegible] point 52.

(g) Brigade Battle Hdqrs will be in DUNMOW, NORTH of junction with [illegible] Advance Report Centre [illegible] (MARK COPSE).

A. L. Lumbridge Capt. & Adjt.,
12.S.Battalion, York & Lancaster Regt.,

[illegible] 2 p.m

Copy No. 1. C.O.
2. 2nd in Command.
3. 12 K O Y L I.
4. Adjutant.
5. "A" Coy.
6. "B" "
7. "C" "
8. "D" "
9. L G Officer.
10. Bombing Offr.
11. Signalling Offr.
12. Intelligence Offr.
13. M.O.
14. Q M.
15. Transport Offr.
16. Brigade. (4 [illegible])
17. Files.

SECRET.

12.S.Battalion,York & Lancaster Regiment.
(Preliminary) Operation Order. No 14.

Reference Section II. Paragraph C."Strong Points".For line:

7½ N. 2nd. "A" Coy. 4th wave. "B". read

N. 2nd. "A" Coy. 2nd wave. "A".

Delete line: "This party will join "A" Coy at the fourth German line."

Administrative.

Reference Supplement Orders. III/

In para., 5.Rations. For line:"A" Coy.(a) One platoon 12 K O Y L I."

read

"B" Coy.(A) One platoon 12.K.O.Y.L.I."

June 27.1916.

Capt & Adjt.
12.S.Battalion,York & Lancs.Regt.,

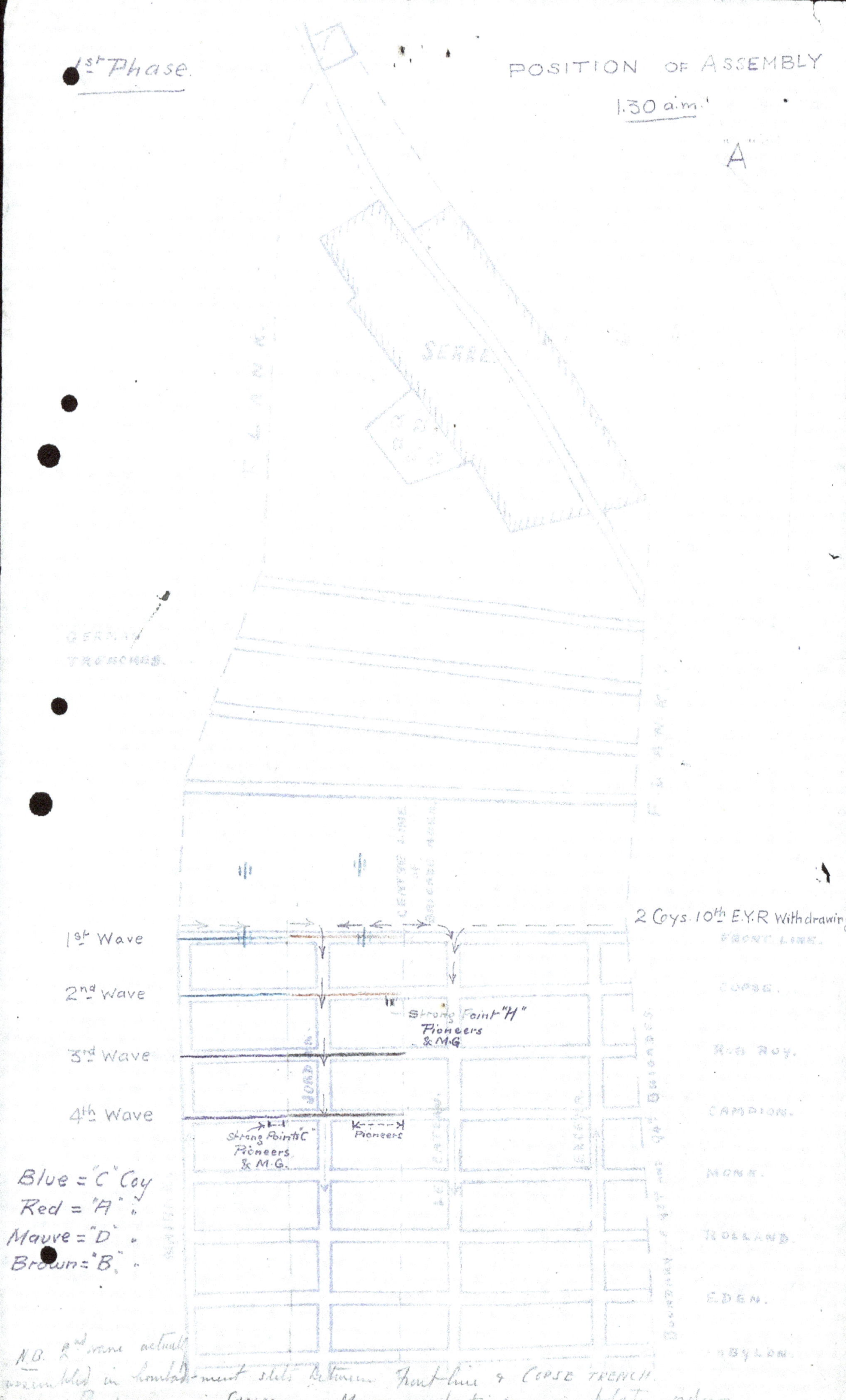
1st Phase.
POSITION OF ASSEMBLY
1.30 a.m.
"A"
SERRE
GERMAN TRENCHES.
2 Coys. 10th E.Y.R Withdrawing.
1st Wave
2nd Wave
3rd Wave
4th Wave
FRONT LINE.
COPSE.
ROB ROY.
CAMPION.
MONK.
ROLLAND.
EDEN.
Strong Point "H"
Pioneers
& M.G
Strong Point "C"
Pioneers
& M.G.
Pioneers
Blue = "C" Coy
Red = "A" "
Mauve = "D" "
Brown = "B" "
N.B.
Front line & COPSE TRENCH.
CAMPION & MONK

2nd PHASE

POSITION OF ASSEMBLY

AT −10

B

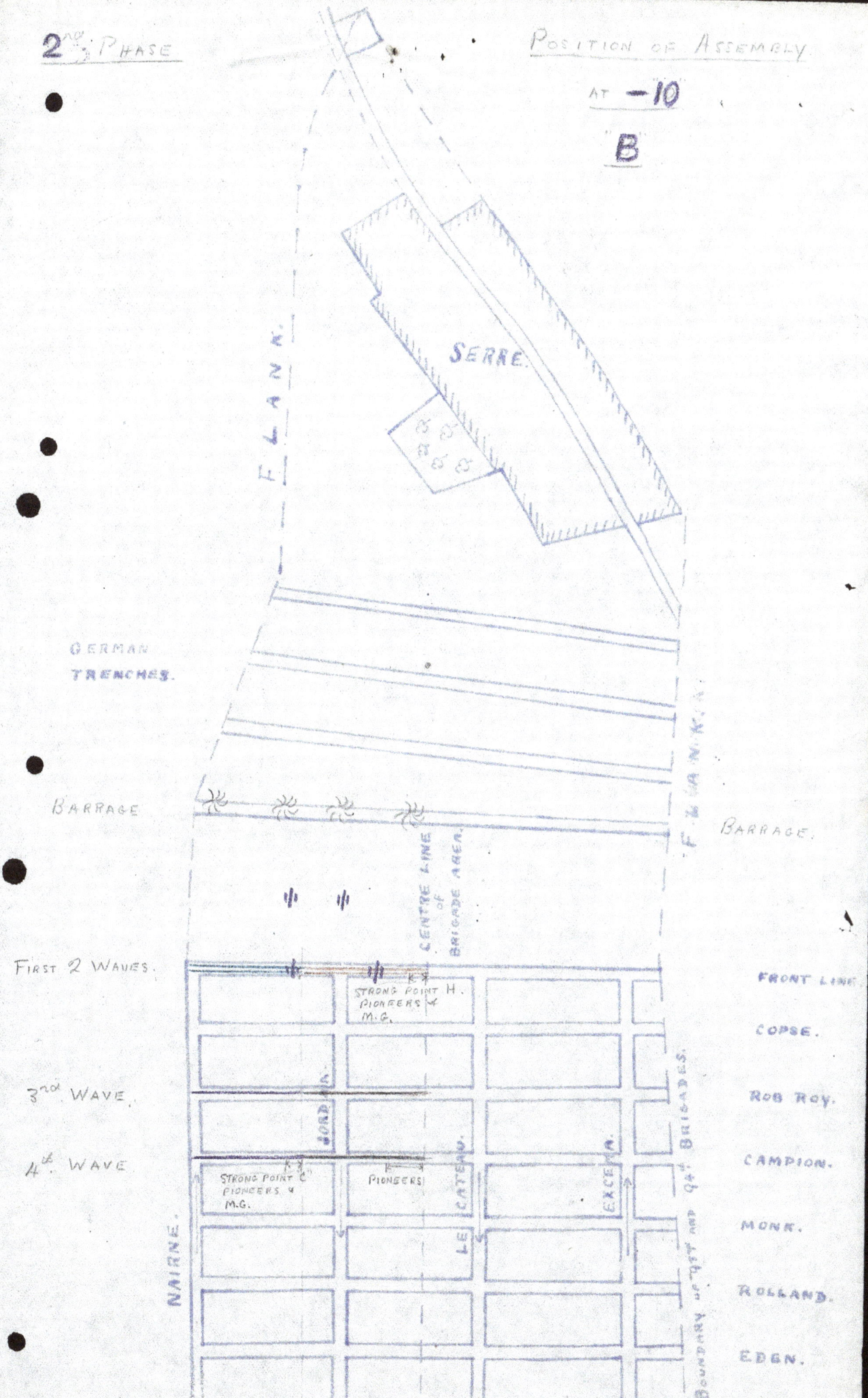

See notes sheet "A"

IMMEDIATELY PRIOR TO ASSAULT

"ZERO"

"C"

3RD PHASE

BARRAGE

BARRAGE

1st Wave

2nd Wave

Strong Point H
Pioneers of M.G

3rd Wave

4th Wave

Strong Point C
Pioneers & M.G.

Pioneers

See note diagram "A"

4th PHASE

OCCUPATION OF 1st BOUND

0-20" D

SERRE

FLANK

Barrage

First 2 Waves

Barrage

Strong Pt "H"
Pioneers
M.G.

GERMAN
TRENCHES.

3rd Wave

4th Wave

Pioneers

Strong Point
Pioneers
M.G.

CENTRE LINE of BRIGADE AREA

FLANK

FRONT LINE.

COPSE.

ROB ROY.

CAMPION.

MONK.

HOLLAND.

EDEN.

BABYLON.

NAIRNE.

JORDAN.

LE CATEAU.

EXCEMA.

BOUNDARY OF 93rd AND 94th BRIGADES.

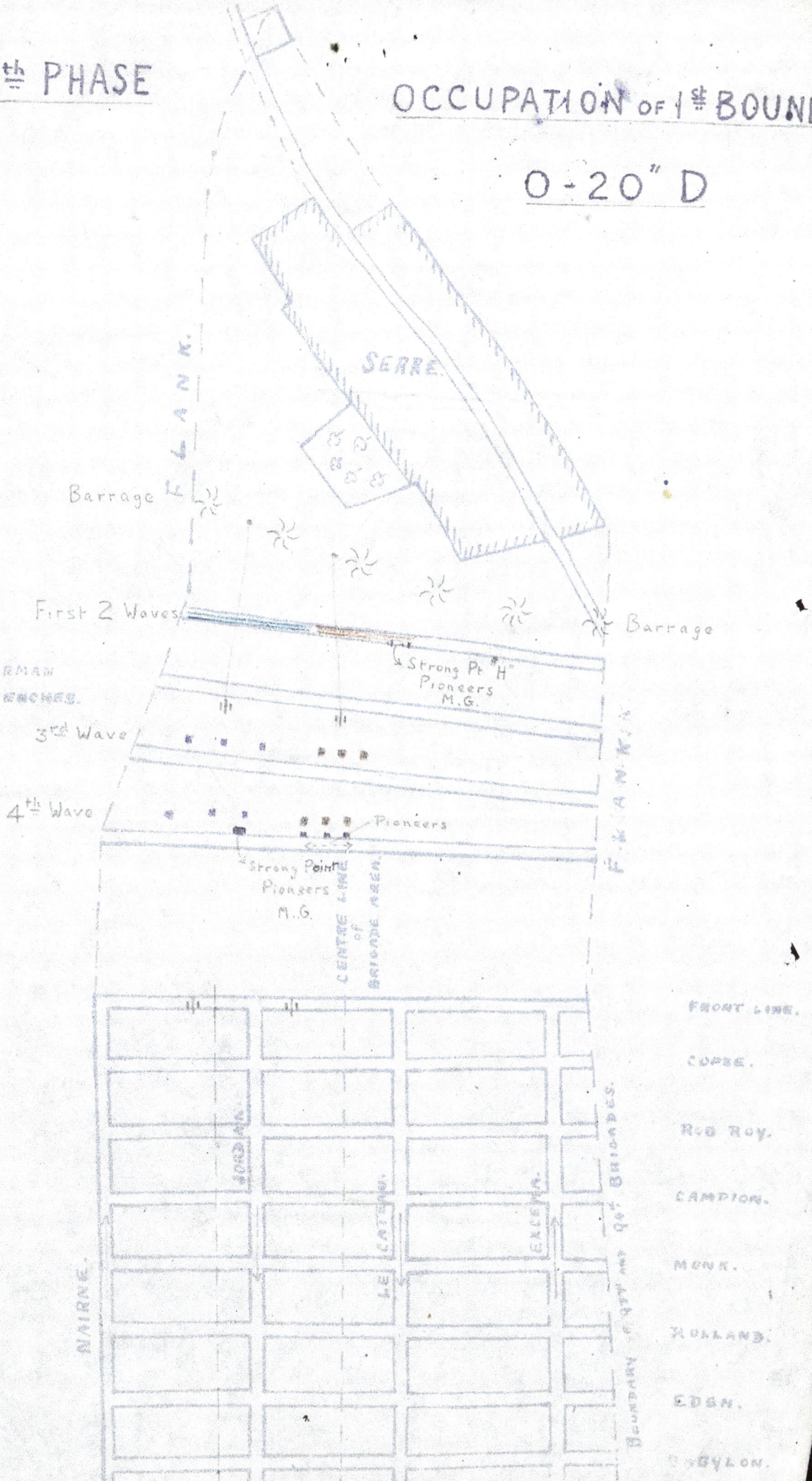

5th PHASE

COMMENCEMENT OF 2nd BOUND—

"0-40" E

Barrage

Barrage

3rd Wave

4th Wave

1st 2 Waves

Strong Point "C" Pioneers & M-G

Strong Point "H" Pioneers & M.G.

Pioneers

GERMAN TRENCHES.

CENTRE LINE OF BRIGADE AREA

FRONT LINE.

COPSE.

ROB ROY.

CAMPION.

MUNN.

HOLLAND.

EDEN.

6th PHASE — 2nd BOUND

"O-50" F

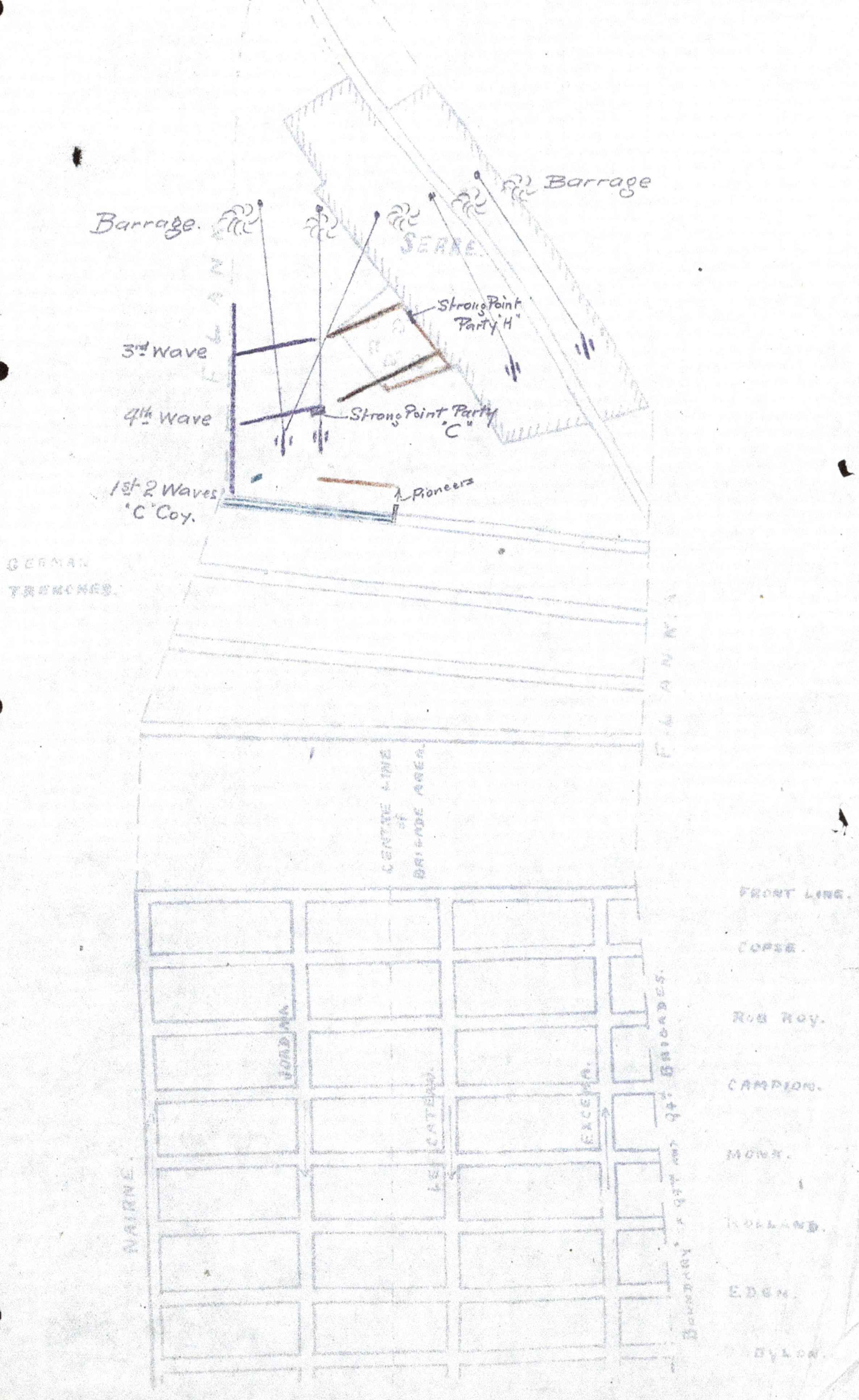

Barrage.

Barrage

SERRE

FLANK

Strong Point Party 'H'

3rd Wave

4th Wave

Strong Point Party 'C'

1st 2 Waves 'C' Coy.

Pioneers

GERMAN TRENCHES.

FLANK

CENTRE LINE OF BRIGADE AREA.

FRONT LINE.

COPSE.

ROB ROY.

CAMPION.

MONK.

ROLLAND.

EDEN.

DYLON.

JORDAN.

LE CATEAU.

EXCEMA.

NAIRNE.

BOUNDARY of 93rd and 94th BRIGADES.

2nd Phase

7th PHASE

1.40

G

STRONG POINT PARTY

STRONG POINT PARTY

SERRE

GERMAN TRENCHES

1 wave FRONT LINE

2 wave COPSE.

Clearing up party

ROB ROY.

3rd wave

4th wave

3rd wave CAMPION.

4th wave MONK

ROLAND

EDEN.

TAYLOR.

Confidential Vol ~~vii~~ 6

War Diary

12th (S) Bn York + Lanc. Rgt.

Aug 1916.

Instructions regarding War Diaries and Intelligence Summaries are contained in F. S. Regs., Part II. and the Staff Manual respectively. Title Pages will be prepared in manuscript.

WAR DIARY
or
INTELLIGENCE SUMMARY
(Erase heading not required.)

12th York & Lancs. Regt

Army Form C. 2118

Place	Date	Hour	Summary of Events and Information	Remarks and references to Appendices
	Aug 1.	3pm	Battalion inspected whilst on parade (Musketry) by the Commander of the First Army, Gen. Sir Charles Monro GCMG, KCB.	
	" 2		2nd Lieutenant R.B. Wayland was attached to this Battalion from 11th E. Lancs	
	" 3		Quiet day. 2nd Lieut V.S. Simpson joined the Battalion for duty from Base. Captain D.C. Allen went as Instructor at Divisional School of Instruction.	
	" 4		Battalion took over trenches forming a Composite Battalion with the 11th E. Lancs. Our portion Vine Street (inclusive) to Oxford Street (exclusive). Major Rees of the 11th East Lancs in command. Relief completed at 5.30 pm	
	" 5		Draft of 19 men came from Base & joined the Battalion in the trenches.	
	" 6		Heavy trench mortar fire in the morning & afternoon on Plum St. Very little activity during the day	
	" 7		Our trench mortar & artillery active on German front line.	
	" 8		Draft of 28 men arrived. Very little activity.	
	" 9		Heavy trench mortar & rifle grenade fire between Plum Street & Vine Street in the morning. Our artillery replied effectively. The 13th Y&L took over the line held by this battalion. Relief completed at 6pm. The battalion took over the following posts :- CURZON, HILLS, PORT ARTHUR, COPSE, LANSDOWNE, HENS, EDWARD, GROTTO, ANGLE, ST VAAST, LORETTO, EUSTON, RUE DU PUITS, CROIX BARBÉE. Battalion Headquarters was established at M 31 D 68 (Total casualties 1 private killed)	
	" 10		Quiet day.	
	" 11		B and D companies supplied men for fatigue work with the RE's. Telegram from Brigade Headquarters stating that No. 12/338 Pte. C. CORTHORN (B Coy) and 12/275 Pte G.C. WRIGHT (A Coy) were awarded Distinguished Conduct Medal for services rendered during the attack on Serre, July 1st 1916	

1875 Wt. W593/826 1,000,000 4/15 J.B.C. & A. A.D.S.S./Forms/C. 2118.

Instructions regarding War Diaries and Intelligence Summaries are contained in F. S. Regs., Part II. and the Staff Manual respectively. Title Pages will be prepared in manuscript.

WAR DIARY
or
INTELLIGENCE SUMMARY
(Erase heading not required.)

Army Form C. 2118

Place	Date	Hour	Summary of Events and Information	Remarks and references to Appendices
	Aug 12		Quiet day. Nothing to report.	
	13		Fatigue parties at work removing ammunition, rations etc from keeps & posts in the Brigade Area & refitting keeps & posts according to Establishment	
	14		Fatigue parties as yesterday.	
	15		ditto; Second Lt. J. E. Davies & Second Lt. J. B. Wilson joined the Battalion for duty from the Base Depot	
	16		Divisional Bombing School opened at PACAUT. Second Lt. Westby & Second Lt. Wilson with 18 other ranks proceeded to PACAUT for six days' course.	
	17		Second Lt. C. A. Jackson rejoined Battalion for duty from 4th Army School of Mortars; Captain & Adjutant N. R. Tunbridge attached for duty to 11th Bn E. LANCS REGT. as Second in Command (actg) Lt. J. L. Ward assumes duties of adjutant	
	17		Quiet day.	
		8pm	Operation Orders received from Brigade for relief of Brigade in the line by 183rd Inf. Bde. (30th Division) on August 18th	
	18		Battalion relieved in posts by 2/8 WORCESTER REGT and 2/4 GLOUCESTERSHIRE Regt. Relief completed at 6 pm. Battalion marched to LESTREM	
			Major H. B. Fisher joined Battalion as C.O. from 92nd Infantry Brigade (Brigade Major)	
	19		Quiet day. Second Lt. T. E. A. GRANT rejoined Battalion from 94th Inf. Bde. HQs.	
		10pm	50 men under Capt. Woolhouse (C & D Companies) detailed to proceed to RICHEBOURG ST. VAAST, where they ~~[illegible]~~	

1875 Wt. W593/826 1,000,000 4/15 J.B.C. & A. A.D.S.S./Forms/C. 2118.

Instructions regarding War Diaries and Intelligence Summaries are contained in F. S. Regs., Part II. and the Staff Manual respectively. Title Pages will be prepared in manuscript.

WAR DIARY
or
INTELLIGENCE SUMMARY
(Erase heading not required.)

Army Form C. 2118

Place	Date	Hour	Summary of Events and Information	Remarks and references to Appendices
	Aug 19		billeted + from where they went into trenches as working party in B lines	
	20		Captain A.N. Cousin rejoined Battalion from 94th Inf Bde	
			Second Lt. J.H. Thompson rejoined Battalion from the [illegible]	
			Ordinary parades.	
	21		Quiet day. Company parades	
	22		Major H.B. Fisher appointed Lt. Colonel	
	23		Second Lt. Wilson and 18 Other Ranks proceeded to join Capt. Woolhouse at RICHEBOURG ST VAAST.	
	24, 25		Quiet days. Nothing to report.	
	26		Battalion came in Trenches. relieved 2/4th Glosters (T.F) Relief complete 3/30 pm. Battn Hqrs CURZON POST. Sector taken over :- PIONEER TRENCH inclusive to CHURCH ROAD exclusive. Quiet day.	
	27		Enemy trench mortars active on right sector. Our artillery and Stokes guns bombarded enemy front line trench at 10.50 am. Enemy shelled PORT ARTHUR with shrapnel. Heavy trench mortars active against PIONEER TRENCH Machine guns active during the night. Our artillery bombarded DISTILLERY S.17.b 505, and caused a fire. Also bombarded enemy front line opposite LIVERPOOL STREET and OXFORD STREET.	
	28		Enemy shelled PORT ARTHUR and vicinity with shrapnel between 7.40 & 8.20 am; also OXFORD STREET and front line between 9.45 + 9.56. Heavy trench	

1875 Wt. W593/826 1,000,000 4/15 J.B.C. & A. A.D.S.S./Forms/C. 2118.

Instructions regarding War Diaries and Intelligence Summaries are contained in F. S. Regs., Part II. and the Staff Manual respectively. Title Pages will be prepared in manuscript.

WAR DIARY
or
INTELLIGENCE SUMMARY
(Erase heading not required.)

Army Form C. 2118

Place	Date	Hour	Summary of Events and Information	Remarks and references to Appendices
	Cont. 28		mortars against front line and North South of PIONEER TRENCH all morning. Our artillery bombarded enemy front line opposite PIONEER TRENCH between 10.20 & 11.30. am. Stokes guns bombarded enemy front line south of PIONEER TRENCH at 8.10pm.	
	29		Enemy shelled PIONEER TRENCH and along front line with H.E. and shrapnel between 5.45 & 6.30pm. Enemy trench mortars very active along our front line. Our artillery bombarded enemy front line opposite our right half, and our right sector with H.E. and shrapnel between 5.45 & 6.30pm. Stokes guns very active against enemy front line opposite PIONEER TRENCH. Machine guns active during night	
	30.		Quiet day. Weather very bad.	
	31.		Quiet day.	

H B Fisher [signature]
Lieut. Col.
Commanding
12. S. Batt. York & Lancaster Regt.

1875 Wt. W593/826 1,000,000 4/15 J.B.C. & A. A.D.S.S./Forms/C. 2118.

C O N F I D E N T I A L.

W A R D I A R Y.

12th.(Service) Battalion York and Lancaster Regiment.

VOLUME ~~VIII~~ IX

From 1st.September 1916.

To 30th. September 1916.

B.E.F.
September 30th.(Midnight).

Army Form C. 2118

WAR DIARY
or
INTELLIGENCE SUMMARY
(Erase heading not required.)

Instructions regarding War Diaries and Intelligence Summaries are contained in F. S. Regs., Part II. and the Staff Manual respectively. Title Pages will be prepared in manuscript.

Place	Date	Hour	Summary of Events and Information	Remarks and references to Appendices
South of NEUVE CHAPELLE	Sept 1	7.30–7.45am	Our artillery bombarded enemy front line opposite NEUVE CHAPELLE. Fairly quite day.	
	" 2		Enemy artillery active against our batteries in the morning, also T.M. fire on our front line.	
		7.10am	Our artillery retaliated opposite NEUVE CHAPELLE on first & second lines, also in rear of enemy lines.	
		4.20pm	Enemy artillery very active against LANSDOWNE POST and CURZON POST also front line.	
	" 3	12.10pm	Enemy T.M. fire on our front line and CHURCH STREET. Both our artillery and enemy artillery quite	
	" 4	4.15 & 5.15pm	Enemy shelled heavily RICHEBOURG L'AVOUE and RUE DU BOIS with 25c. H.E. shells, also enemy artillery shelled front line near PIONEER TRENCH. Enemy T.M's also active against this part. Our artillery and Stokes guns retaliated on enemy front line opposite PIONEER and LANSDOWNE TRENCHES.	
	" 5	12.45pm	Enemy shelled our trenches to the N.W. of NEUVE CHAPELLE.	
		12.55pm	Our artillery bombarded enemy front line opposite NEUVE CHAPELLE in retaliation.	
	" 6	1.12pm	Enemy artillery shelled our front line ~~between~~ at junction of OXFORD STREET.	

1875 Wt. W593/826 1,000,000 4/15 J.B.C. & A. A.D.S.S./Forms/C. 2118.

2

Army Form C. 2118

Instructions regarding War Diaries and Intelligence Summaries are contained in F. S. Regs., Part II. and the Staff Manual respectively. Title Pages will be prepared in manuscript.

WAR DIARY
or
INTELLIGENCE SUMMARY
(Erase heading not required.)

Place	Date	Hour	Summary of Events and Information	Remarks and references to Appendices
South of NEUVE CHAPELLE	Sept 6	3.25 to 6.10 pm	Enemy Trench Mortars very active on front line between CHURCH ROAD and PIONEER TRENCH.	
		3.25 to 6.15 pm	Our artillery retaliated on first & second lines enemy trenches between CHURCH ROAD and PIONEER TRENCH. Stokes' guns also bombarded the above points.	[illegible] //
	Sept 7	8.0 am & 2.30 pm	Enemy shelled our front line and supports continually.	
		11.35 am	Also enemy T. M's active against our front line opposite CHURCH ROAD at 11.35 am.	
		5.30 & 6.15 pm	Enemy T. M's active against our front line between CHURCH ROAD and LANSDOWNE TRENCH	
		6.55 & 12.20 pm	Our artillery bombarded enemy first and second lines opposite CHURCH ROAD and OXFORD STREET.	
	Sept 8	8.25 to 9.15 am	Enemy shelled NEUVE CHAPELLE.	
		11.20 & 11.25 am	" " front line between PIONEER and CRESCENT TRENCHES	
		1.10 p.m	" " second line near LANSDOWNE TRENCH.	
		12.20 pm & 12.20 pm	" T. M's also active on above points.	

1875 Wt. W593/826 1,000,000 4/15 J.B.C. & A. A.D.S.S./Forms/C. 2118.

3

Army Form C. 2118

WAR DIARY
or
INTELLIGENCE SUMMARY
(Erase heading not required.)

Instructions regarding War Diaries and Intelligence Summaries are contained in F. S. Regs., Part II. and the Staff Manual respectively. Title Pages will be prepared in manuscript.

Place	Date	Hour	Summary of Events and Information	Remarks and references to Appendices
SOUTH OF NEUVE CHAPELLE	Sept 8	8.25 & 8.50am	Our artillery shelled enemy front line, opposite LANSDOWNE TRENCH and PLUM STREET.	
		11.45am & 12.10pm	Our artillery shelled enemy front line opposite PIONEER TRENCH and NEUVE CHAPELLE.	
			Enemy also shelled above points in the afternoon	
		5.8 & 5.27pm	Our artillery shelled enemy from line opposite FIFTHTEENTH STREET to HUN STREET.	CW
		6.0 & 7.0pm	also first and second lines during general bombardment of sector. Enemy replied very weakly to our bombardment.	
	Sept 9	10.16am	Enemy shelled our front line on La Bassee Road also front line between OXFORD and PIONEER TRENCHES,	
		10.28 & 10.36 a.m.	also second line between PIONEER and CRESCENT TRENCHES.	
		10.am & 10.30am.	Enemy T. M's active on above points.	
			Our artillery shelled enemy first and second lines opposite PIONEER and CRESCENT TRENCHES.	
		12.30 to 12.50pm	Our medium T. M's cutting wire at S.11 A.30.22. also S.11 A.36.28	
			Our artillery bombarded enemy first and second lines opposite PIONEER TRENCH and LIVERPOOL STREET throughout the afternoon and evening intermittently.	

1875 Wt. W593/826 1,000,000 4/15 J.B.C. & A. A.D.S.S./Forms/C. 2118.

Instructions regarding War Diaries and Intelligence Summaries are contained in F. S. Regs., Part II. and the Staff Manual respectively. Title Pages will be prepared in manuscript.

WAR DIARY
or
INTELLIGENCE SUMMARY
(Erase heading not required.)

Army Form C. 2118.

Place	Date	Hour	Summary of Events and Information	Remarks and references to Appendices
South of Neuve-Chapelle	1916 Sept 9th		Day spent quietly.	
	" 10th		During the night the Battalion carried out a raid on the enemy trenches at S11a, South of Neuve Chapelle. To a certain extent the success of the operation was marred by the fact that German front line was in rear of what had hitherto been assumed to be its position. The real front line trench was practically undamaged by the preliminary bombardment; in addition it was blocked, and the party entering it were at a great disadvantage. A Gas Alarm on the left, caused by one of the men complaining of choking and saying he was gassed, led to some confusion, which, together with the Machine Gun and Rifle fire prevented a satisfactory re-organisation on the Left section. Our casualties were: 4 killed, 1 Died of Wounds, 20 Wounded and 4 missing. About thirty Germans are known to have been killed: no prisoners were taken.	CW
		8 p.m.	Patrol Parties sent out.	
		9.5 pm	German Working Party dispersed by our Machine Gun Fire.	
		10.0 pm – 11.10 pm	Patrols withdrawn. Casualties: One ~~ordinary~~ other rank killed.	
			Captain T. E. A. Grant arranged the details of the raid, and supervised from our front line trench, with great energy and determination.	

2449 Wt. W14957/M90 750,000 1/16 J.B.C. & A. Forms/C.2118/12.

Army Form C. 2118.

Instructions regarding War Diaries and Intelligence Summaries are contained in F. S. Regs., Part II. and the Staff Manual respectively. Title Pages will be prepared in manuscript.

WAR DIARY
or
INTELLIGENCE SUMMARY

(Erase heading not required.)

Place	Date	Hour	Summary of Events and Information	Remarks and references to Appendices
South of NEUVE CHAPELLE	Sep 9 / " 10		2nd Lts. V. S. Simpson and J. H. Thompson were in charge of the two parties.	
		11.45 pm	Both parties filed out into No-man's-land.	
		12.7 am	All parties out.	
		1.30 am	Both Officers took their parties forward. One of the men of 2nd Lt Thompson's party complained of choking and said he was gassed. This alarm spread and twenty men which occupied a position further back in No Mans Land ~~[illegible]~~. On going forward 2nd Lt. Thompson found that though the German wire had been badly knocked about, there were a good many strands still intact. After straggling about he found himself in a shell hole, about three yards from the German trench. One man was with him, and between them both they had 10 bombs. These they threw into the enemy's trench. At this point, the man, Pte. Wilson H. A. was shot through the head. ~~2nd Lieut. Thompson brought away all identification information from the man's body.~~	
			Within a minute of Zero, 2nd Lt. Simpson's party were in the German trench. They found that the enemy had blocked this trench on the right and left, also the communications behind. The trenches were found to be revetted with timber and very few sandbags used.	

2449 Wt. W14957/M90 750,000 1/16 J.B.C. & A. Forms/C.2118/12.

Army Form C. 2118.

WAR DIARY
or
INTELLIGENCE SUMMARY

(Erase heading not required.)

Instructions regarding War Diaries and Intelligence Summaries are contained in F. S. Regs., Part II. and the Staff Manual respectively. Title Pages will be prepared in manuscript.

Place	Date	Hour	Summary of Events and Information	Remarks and references to Appendices
South of NEUVE CHAPELLE	Sep 9 Sep 10		The real trench was 15 yards behind the dummy trench on which our Artillery had been playing. All men, except one, say the enemy trenches were practically undamaged and splendidly made. No Germans were found in the pocket of trench which had evidently been formed to make a trap. Enemy bombers attacked the party, but their bombs were not very destructive. 2nd Lt Simpson's party threw bombs all round until the supply ran out, and after examining shelters for papers etc, returned. The Germans were very brave. 2nd. Lieut Simpson intended to reform his party, but he was unable to do so. This party remained in the trench for about 15 mins, no men were wounded whilst in the pocket. About 15 men of 2nd Lieut Thompson's party were in the dummy trench, but the Machine Gun near La Bassée Rd was playing over the area between. These men threw their bombs whenever they saw flashes and then crept back. The parties returned at 2.10 am. Stretcher parties were immediately organised and good work done. Several N.C.O's & men rendered services ~~which~~ distinguished them. The Enemy's shelling of our front line was at no time very heavy. Medium Trench Mortar Batteries in rear proved valuable support. Much valuable information was gained. In connection with the above the following message was received.	RW

2449 Wt. W14957/M90 750,000 1/16 J.B.C. & A. Forms/C.2118/12.

Army Form C. 2118.

Instructions regarding War Diaries and Intelligence Summaries are contained in F. S. Regs., Part II. and the Staff Manual respectively. Title Pages will be prepared in manuscript.

WAR DIARY
or
INTELLIGENCE SUMMARY
(Erase heading not required.)

Place	Date	Hour	Summary of Events and Information	Remarks and references to Appendices
South of NEUVE CHAPELLE			"The Army Commander desires, that his congratulations may be conveyed to the 12th (S) Bn. York & Lancaster Regt, for their successful raid on the night of 9/10 September."	
LA FOSSE	Sept 11th.		The Battalion was relieved by the 18th. (Bn) Durham Light Infantry & 15 West York Regt moving back to Billets at LA-FOSSE	CW
	Sept 12th.		Working parties supplied for the trenches.	
	Sept 11 " 12		A special patrol went out into No-man's land to obtain a package which had been noticed the previous evening; it was found about half way across & on examination was seen to contain a large number of letters belonging to late members of the Royal Sussex Regiment and dated for June of this year. The parcel had been sent back, apparently from the German interior, after information had been extracted, & then placed in no-man's land by a German Patrol. Inside was written "Letters of Dead English Soldiers".	
	Sept 12th 13th 14th.		Working Parties provided for the trenches. On the 13th. the temporary appointment of 2nd Lieut. J. E. A. Grant to Captain was in Battn Orders. On the 14th. the temporary appointment of Capt. C. H. Gurney to be Major was published in Battalion Orders.	

2449 Wt. W14957/M90 750,000 1/16 J.B.C. & A. Forms/C.2118/12.

Instructions regarding War Diaries and Intelligence Summaries are contained in F. S. Regs., Part II. and the Staff Manual respectively. Title Pages will be prepared in manuscript.

8

Army Form C. 2118

WAR DIARY
or
INTELLIGENCE SUMMARY
(Erase heading not required.)

Place	Date	Hour	Summary of Events and Information	Remarks and references to Appendices
LA-FOSSE.	1916 Sept 15th		Battalion receives orders to proceed to FESTHUBERT section of the line to hold from LOTHIAN TRENCH inclusive and QUINQUE RUE exclusive, & relieve therefrom the 18th. Bn. Manchester Regiment.	
	Sept 16th		In the afternoon, the Battalion was conveyed in Motor Buses & Lorries to its new Sector. Battn Headquarters now S21a12. Military Medals were presented by the 11th. Army Corps Commander at Merville, to Cpl Kirkby, L/Cpl Garbutt, Ptes Arridge, Downing, Marsden & Vickers. During the relief there was one casualty, a machine gunner being sniped.	RW
FESTHUBERT.	Sept. 17th.		Quiet Day generally, but the Enemy Artillery was active against our front line between QUINQUE CROSSING and CANADIAN ORCHARD. between 9.50 and 10.30 a.m. Our Artillery replied opposite ORKNEY ROAD at 10.45 and 11.5 a.m.	
	Sept. 18th Sept 19th		Little activity shewn by either side.	

1875 Wt. W593/826 1,000,000 4/15 J.B.C. & A. A.D.S.S./Forms/C. 2118.

9

Army Form C. 2118.

Instructions regarding War Diaries and Intelligence Summaries are contained in F. S. Regs., Part II. and the Staff Manual respectively. Title Pages will be prepared in manuscript.

WAR DIARY
or
INTELLIGENCE SUMMARY

(Erase heading not required.)

Place	Date	Hour	Summary of Events and Information	Remarks and references to Appendices
FESTUBERT	1916 Sept. 20th.		Enemy Artillery active against our Aircraft.	
	Sept. 21st.		There was a good deal of Shelling on both sides about point S22C in which our Stokes Guns and enemy Trench Mortars took a prominent part.	
	Sept. 22nd.		Quiet Day.	WM
	Sept 23rd.		Under authority of H.M. The King, the Commander in Chief of the British Army in the field awarded to No 12/727 PTE. S. MATTHEWS a member of this Battalion, the Distinguished Conduct Medal. This soldier, a stretcher bearer, remained in a sap in JOHN COPSE, dressing wounded men for three days and nights from July 1st, of the remainder of his squad one was killed and two were wounded.	
LE TOURET	Sept. 24th.		Battalion were relieved by the 14th York & Lancaster Regt, they proceeded to Billets in the village line of Defence at LE TOURET. Before the relief was completed CAPTAIN T.E.A. GRANT was shot through the left arm by a sniper. Battalion Headquarters were at X17. c.19.	
	Sept. 25th.		Quiet Day.	

2449 Wt. W14957/M90 750,000 1/16 J.B.C. & A. Forms/C.2118/12.

CONFIDENTIAL.

WAR DIARY.

12th.(Service) Battalion York and Lancaster Regiment.

VOLUME X

From 1st.October 1916,

To 31st.October 1916.

B.E.F. November 1st. 1916.

Instructions regarding War Diaries and Intelligence Summaries are contained in F. S. Regs., Part II. and the Staff Manual respectively. Title Pages will be prepared in manuscript.

WAR DIARY
or
INTELLIGENCE SUMMARY

(Erase heading not required.)

Army Form C. 2118.

Place	Date	Hour	Summary of Events and Information	Remarks and references to Appendices
LE TOURET	Sept. 26th. 27th & 28th		Working Party 200 strong was provided in the evenings of these days, for work in the front line, improving trenches and sandbagging.	
	Sept 29th.		All available Officers and 100 other ranks attended Flammenwerfer Demonstration at PACAUT in the afternoon. No working parties were supplied in the evening.	CW.
	Sept. 30th.		Short Route Marches were carried out independently by Companies.	

[signature] Major, for Lt. Col. Commanding
12th S. Bn. York & Lancaster Regt.

2449 Wt. W14957/M90 750,000 1/16 J.B.C. & A. Forms/C.2118/12.

Instructions regarding War Diaries and Intelligence Summaries are contained in F. S. Regs., Part II. and the Staff Manual respectively. Title Pages will be prepared in manuscript.

WAR DIARY
or
~~INTELLIGENCE SUMMARY~~
(Erase heading not required.)

Army Form C. 2118.

Place	Date	Hour	Summary of Events and Information	Remarks and references to Appendices
LE-TOURET.	1916 Oct 1st.	1a.m. 10a.m.	Old time re-established. Battalion commenced to relieve the 14th.S.Battalion York and Lancaster Regt. in the line, FESTUBERT Sector. - Notice received of the impending move of the 31st.Division to a new area. The plans of the Battalion for a general advance or move were overhauled, and preparations made for leaving the area at short notice. The more important points attended to were :- 1. Condition of Boots. 2. Transport and Harness. 3. Prepartion for all the detached ranks to be re-called. 4. Orders relating to dumps for stores etc.	
LE-TOURET	Oct. 2nd.		LIEUT.-COLONEL.H.B.FISHER rejoined the Battalion from the Commanding Officers' Conference at 1st.Army School. Draft of 97 Other Ranks, transferred from the 1ST.NORTHANTS REGT., arrived and proceeded to the trenches.	
FESTUBERT SECTOR.	Oct. 3rd.	4·45 a.m.	LIEUT.-COLONEL.H.B.FISHER, whilst visiting the Island Posts was killed by a chance shot, presumably from an enemy fixed rifle. (Other casualty - 1 Other rank)	
MAP. REF. X.17a.2.4. BETHUNE Combined Sheet		2-30 p.m.	At a quiet burial, Divisional and Brigade Staffs were represented.	
LE-TOURET	Oct 4th.		The Battalion were relieved in the trenches by the 1ST.BN.ROYAL WEST KENT REGT., of the 5th.Division, who had very recently been fighting in the SOMME BATTLE. The night was spent in billets at LE TOURET.	
DITTO.	Oct. 5th.	2p.m.	Battalion moved off to billets at VENDIN - LEZ - BETHUNE, arriving there at 5 p.m. and staying there for one night.	
VENDIN-LEZ-BETHUNE	Oct 6th	2-30 p.m.	Battalion marched to ROBECQ, a distance of six miles, arriving there just before dusk.	
ROBECQ	Oct 7th.		In view of forthcoming events prominence was given in Company Training Programmes.	

2449 Wt. W14957/M90 750,000 1/16 J.B.C. & A. Forms/C.2118/12.

Army Form C. 2118.

Instructions regarding War Diaries and Intelligence Summaries are contained in F. S. Regs., Part II. and the Staff Manual respectively. Title Pages will be prepared in manuscript.

WAR DIARY
or
~~INTELLIGENCE SUMMARY~~

(Erase heading not required.)

Place	Date	Hour	Summary of Events and Information	Remarks and references to Appendices
ROBECQ	OCT. 7th.		to Musketry and Rapid Loading. The training of specialists was resumed.	
DO.		3.45pm 7.0pm	Operation Orders issued. 2/LIEUT. D. R. HINCKLEY joined the Battalion for duty, from the Base.	
DO.	OCT. 8TH.	8.30a.m.	On transfer of the 31st. Division to the 13TH. CORPS RESERVE ARMY, the Battn. moved by rail to the new Area. The Battalion proceeded to BERGUETTE, a march of six miles, entraining at 12.15 p.m. After a train journey lasting just over four hours, the Battalion detrained at DOULLENS, and marched to billets at MARIEUX.	
MARIEUX.	OCT. 9th.		Plans for Progressive training drawn up.	
DO.	OCT 10th	2.30pm.	Short Battalion parade.	
DO	OCT. 11th.		In view of the importance of maintaining communication between Infantry and Aircraft, during operations, a practice was arranged between the Battalion and the 5th. Squadron, R.F.C., which was successful and beneficial.	
DO.	OCT. 12th		Battalion practised the Attack. – MAJOR. C. H. GURNEY proceeded to England for Senior Officers' Course at ALDERSHOT, and MAJOR. C. P. B. RIALL assumed temporary Command of the Battalion.	
DO.	OCT. 13th	9.a.m.	Company Commanders' Parades and Training of Specialists. Company Commanders' Parades included the following:- Physical Exercises, (Running, Jumping, Football, etc.), Bayonet Fighting, Musketry, (including Training in Rapid Loading and Firing), Close and Extended Order drill, Advancing over rough ground in Artillery Formation.	
		2pm.	Commanding Officer's Parade. Route March via RAINCHEVAL – ARQUEVES – VAUCHELLES. 2ND. V. S. SIMPSON took over the Command of "A" Company, CAPT. N. L. TUNBRIDGE having	

2449 Wt. W14957/M90 750,000 1/16 J.B.C. & A. Forms/C.2118/12.

Army Form C. 2118.

WAR DIARY
or
~~INTELLIGENCE~~ SUMMARY

(Erase heading not required.)

Instructions regarding War Diaries and Intelligence Summaries are contained in F. S. Regs., Part II. and the Staff Manual respectively. Title Pages will be prepared in manuscript.

Place	Date	Hour	Summary of Events and Information	Remarks and references to Appendices
MARIEUX	OCT. 13th.		proceeded to 92nd. Infantry Brigade for Instruction in "G" Branch duties.	
			A number of Officers and N.C.O's. toured the Divisional Trench Area.	
DO.	OCT. 14th.	Morning	Commanding Officer's Inspection of the Battalion.- Battalion Drill and practice in Attack Formation.	
		afternoon.	Company Commanders' Parades. - Commanding Officer inspected the Transport.	
		5pm.	All available attendedthe lecture for Officers on "Tanks" at SARTON.	
DO.	OCT. 15th	Morning	Church Parade.	
		afternoon.	Kit Inspection. - Party of Officers and N.C.O's. proceeded to the tranches for purpose of touring the Divisional Area.	
		11-55 p.m.	Draft of 93 Other Ranks arrived.	
DO.	OCT. 16th	Morning	Brigade practice in Attack. (Copy of scheme attached).	
		afternoon	Company Commanders' Parades and Training of Specialists.	
DO. FAMECHON.	OCT. 17th	2p.m.	Battalion proceeded to billets at FAMECHON, arriving there at 3.45 p.m.	
		5pm.	A draft of 48 Other Ranks joined the Battalion.	
		11-5pm	Notice received of probable move at very short notice.	
DO.	OCT. 18th	Morning.	Companies at the disposal of their Commanders. - Training Ground being in the neighbourhood of HURTEBISE FARM.	
		1·25pm	Operation Orders received.	
		2·15pm	Battalion marched off to WARNIMONT WOOD near AUTHIE.	
WARNIMONT WOOD.	OCT. 19th		Company Commanders' Parades and Training of Specialists.	
DO.	OCT. 20th.		Weather fine, but cold, the men in canvas huts feeling very severely in the night, the keenness of the air.	

2449 Wt. W14957/M90 750,000 1/16 J.B.C. & A. Forms/C.2118/12.

Army Form C. 2118.

Instructions regarding War Diaries and Intelligence Summaries are contained in F. S. Regs., Part II. and the Staff Manual respectively. Title Pages will be prepared in manuscript.

WAR DIARY
or
INTELLIGENCE SUMMARY

(Erase heading not required.)

Place	Date	Hour	Summary of Events and Information	Remarks and references to Appendices
WARNIMONT WOOD	1916 Oct. 21st.		"C" & "D" Companies, under the Command of CAPTAIN.D.C.ALLEN,(acting Second in Command) proceeded to COURCELLES for duty as VIII Corps Working Parties, with 93rd.Infantry Brigade, who relieved the 92nd.Infantry Brigade in the line this day. Officers in command of the two Companies,were:- "C" Company. LIEUT.R.W.LEAMON. "D" Company. CAPTAIN.E.G.G.WOOLHOUSE. Remainder of Battalion trained as usual. - Weather as yesterday.	HWD
WARNIMONT WOOD	Oct 22nd.		Quiet Day.	HWD
DO	Oct 23rd.		Company Route Marches. In the evening a working party of 3 Officers and 250 other ranks, was provided from "A" and "B" Companies, for "Carrying" work. A draft of 48 other ranks, transferred from the NORTHUMBERLAND FUSILIERS, joined the Battalion. - Coy.Sergt.Major Instr.F.W.FREESTONE, of the Army Gymnastic Staff, was attached to the Battalion for the purpose of instructing the Brigade Class in Bayonet Fighting.	HWD
DO.	Oct 24th.		Companies were at the disposal of their Commanders. - In the morning a working party of 1 Officer and 50 Other Ranks, was provided for "Carrying" work. LIEUT.S.W.MAUNDER,Quartermaster, was admitted to hospital.	HWD
DO.	Oct 25th.		Companies were at the disposal of their Commanders.	HWD
DO.	Oct 26th.		Two working parties, each 1 Officer and 100 Other Ranks strong, were provided for carrying T.M.Ammunition.	HWD
DO.	Oct 27th.		In the morning,"A" and "B" Companies proceeded to relieve"C" and "D" Companies at COURCELLES. "C" and "D" Companies returned to WARNIMONT WOOD. CAPTAIN D.C.ALLEN remained at COURCELLES in charge of detachment. O.C.Coys were:- "A"Company, 2ND.LIEUT.V.S.SIMPSON. "B" " CAPT.E.L.MOXEY.	HWD

2449 Wt. W14957/M90 750,000 1/16 J.B.C. & A. Forms/C.2118/12.

Army Form C. 2118.

WAR DIARY
or
~~INTELLIGENCE SUMMARY~~

(Erase heading not required.)

Instructions regarding War Diaries and Intelligence Summaries are contained in F. S. Regs., Part II. and the Staff Manual respectively. Title Pages will be prepared in manuscript.

Place	Date	Hour	Summary of Events and Information	Remarks and references to Appendices
WARNIMONT WOOD.	1916 Oct.29.		**In the morning Companies were** at the disposal **of their Commanders.**	
			Notice having been received from **Brigade Headquarters** that a working party would have to be provided in the evening, afternoon parades were suspended. **At night** a working party of **2** officers and **100** other ranks was provided for work in the trenches. **A H.E.** shell bursting near the cross roads, **HEBUTERNE, caused** 8 casualties in this party - **1** o.r. killed, 5 wounded and **2** shell-shock.	
DO.	Oct30.	12.10 a.m	Operation Orders received; **the Battalion** to take over the left section of the **HEBUTERNE** Sector, relieving the **18th.** Battalion Durham Light Infantry.	
		8.a.m	The Companies at **WARNIMONT WOOD** proceeded across country to the trenches.	
		10.30 a.m	The two Companies at **COURCELLES** met by guides of the **Durham Light Infantry** at **SAILLY-AU-BOIS.**	
		11 a.m	Transport and **Q.M.Stores** transferred to **COUIN.**	
HEBUTERNE	do.		**Owing** to the heavy rain the going was very hard. The main tracks to the trenches at parts were almost **2** feet in mud. The trenches also were in a bad state, and in the **front line** men had to stand in water, which in places was **Knee-deep**. **"A"** and **"B" Companies took** over the **front line**, and **"C"** and **"D"** were in support. The relief was completed without **any** casualties. Battalion Headquarters were in **HEBUTERNE, a shell-wrecked village.**	
DO	Oct. 31st.		**There was a good deal of activity in all arms.** Such activity had not been experienced **by the Battalion** since **July 1st.** Still no casualties.	
			Recently there has been a considerable amount of sickness amongst Officers and men and since October 20th. 3 Officers and **35** men have been admitted into hospital. **This ,of course,** does not include many of the sick cases treated by the **Medical Officer in camp.** The Officers evacuated were **:- CAPTAIN.A.N.COUSIN,**Intelligence Officer to the **94th.Infantry** Brigade, **LIEUT.S.W.MAUNDER,**Quartermaster, and **LIEUT.S.J.ATKINSON,**Transport Officer. On October 6th.,**2ND.LIEUT.F.A.DAVIES** was admitted to hospital, and **2ND.LIEUT.W.H.ROWLANDS,Lewis Gun Officer,** was evacuated to **ENGLAND** on the 13th.October.	

2449 Wt. W14957/M90 750,000 1/16 J.B.C. & A. Forms/C.2118/12.

Lieut. Col.
12 S.B. York Lancs Regiment

S C H E M E.

Reference Map,)
FRANCE.)
Sheet 57 D., 1/40,000.)

G E N E R A L I D E A.

The Enemy is strongly entrenched on the line REBEMPRE - BEAUQUESNE - SARTON - THIEVRES.

The G.O.C. intends to attack him on the front between BEAUQUESNE and SARTON, and to occupy the high ground immediately N. of the BEAUQUESNE - SARTON Road.

****

S P E C I A L I D E A.

1. The 31st Division will be in Corps Reserve, and after the high ground in ~~W~~ H.22.b. and c. has been captured, will pass through the original attacking Division, and continue the attack, having as its objectives, 1st, a marked position on the high ground in H.22.a. and H.21.d., 2nd, the eastern edge of the re-entrant from H.16.a. to forked roads H.21.b.
2. The 94th Infantry Brigade will form the centre of the 31st Divisional attack, with the 92nd Brigade on the right, and the 93rd Brigade on the left. The 94th Infantry Brigade will assemble at H.28., its right resting on the N.W. corner of the wood, and occupying a frontage of 600 yds.

INSTRUCTIONS.

1. The Brigade will form up in two lines of Battalions :

1st Line - Right, 13th Bn. York & Lancaster R.
Left, 14th Bn. York & Lancaster R.

2nd Line - Right, 11th Bn., East Lancashire R.
Left, 12th Bn., York & Lancaster R.

94 M.G. Company)
94 T.M.Battery) in Rear, in mass.

Battalions will be in four waves of shallow columns of half-platoons in file, each Battalion occupying a frontage of 300 yds, with 100 yds distance between waves.
Two hundred yds distance to be maintained between the rear wave of the leading Battalions, and the first wave of the rear Battns.

2. Immediately before the two leading waves of the first Battalions pass through the recently-captured front line trenches, they will deploy into waves in lines, and will attack and consolidate the line H.22.a.9.3. to H. 21.b. 5.1.

The two remaining waves of the leading Battalions will immediately before passing through the trenches taken by their leading waves, deploy into waves in line, as soon as the barrage flags are raised, press on within fifty yards of the barrage, and will seize and consolidate the second objective.

The two rear Battalions, etc., will maintain the same relative positions throughout the exercise, and whilst the first and second objectives are being taken, will lie down.

3. BARRAGE. An Artillery barrage will be represented by 12 men carrying blue signalling flags. This barrage will commence moving forward slowly, as soon as the leading waves of the Brigade pass through the marked position denoting the line held by the original attacking Division.
The first waves of the 13th and 14th Bns. York & Lanc R. will move forward fifty yards behind the Barrage.

4. The original attacking Division's line, and the first and second objectives, will each be marked by four white signalling flags.

[signature]
Captain,
Brigade Major,
94th Infantry Bde.

B.H.Q.
13.10.16.

Army Form C. 2118.

WAR DIARY

or

~~INTELLIGENCE SUMMARY~~.

(*Erase heading not required.*)

Instructions regarding War Diaries and Intelligence Summaries are contained in F. S. Regs., Part II. and the Staff Manual respectively. Title pages will be prepared in manuscript.

Place	Date	Hour	Summary of Events and Information	Remarks and references to Appendices
HEBUTERNE	1916 Nov 1st & 2nd		Battalion still holding Left Section of the HEBUTERNE SECTOR of the line.	RW.
SAILLY-AU-BOIS.	Nov 3rd		Battalion were relieved by the 14th. York and Lancaster Regt., and withdrew to billets at SAILLY-AU-BOIS, as Brigade Reserve.	RW.
THIÈVRES	Nov 7th.		Conveyed in Motor Buses , from SAILLY to billets at THIEVRES.	RW.
WARNIMONT WOOD.	Nov 12th		Battalion marched to hutments in WARNIMONT WOOD.	RW.
HEBUTERNE	Nov 14th		Took over again the same section of the line, relieving the 18th. WEST YORKS REGIMENT. 2nd. LIEUT. M. B. WALLACE joined the Battalion in the trenches.	RW.
"	Nov 16th/17th		A Patrol under Sergt. Boot of "B" Coy left our lines at 11.15.p.m., opposite K.17.b.02.18 and met a hostile party a short distance in front of our trench. The hostile party threw bombs and one of our patrol was killed. The enemy were estimated about 25 to 30 strong. Our patrol was considrably outnumbered and was forced to retire. A party was at once organised to bring in the body of the man killed, but this was impossible on account of hostile fire. Later a strong offensive patrol was sent out from the SUNKEN ROAD to sweep No-mans' -land, but could find no trace of either the enemy or the casualty. It is believed that this was a raiding party, as the volume of bombs thrown, was large.	RW.
"THE DELL." SAILLY-AU-BOIS.	Nov 18th		Battalion relieved by 14th. YORK & LANCASTER REGT., and moved back to the DELL (J 17.b.34.) The men were housed in dug-outs and temporary hutments.	RW.
COURCELLES	Nov 21st.		Headquarters, "A" & "C" Companies moved to bivouacs at COURCELLES, "B" & "D" remained at the DELL, under the command of MAJOR D.C. ALLEN.	RW.
HEBUTERNE	Nov 22nd.		The Battalion again took over the Left Section of the HEBUTERNE SECTOR, reliev -ing the 14th. YORK & LANCASTER REGT. A draft of 52 other ranks joined the Battn.	RW.

A5834 Wt. W4973/M687 750,000 8/16 D. D. & L. Ltd. Forms/C.2118/13.

Instructions regarding War Diaries and Intelligence Summaries are contained in F. S. Regs., Part II. and the Staff Manual respectively. Title pages will be prepared in manuscript.

WAR DIARY
or
INTELLIGENCE SUMMARY.

(Erase heading not required.)

Army Form C. 2118.

Place	Date	Hour	Summary of Events and Information	Remarks and references to Appendices
	1916			
HEBUTERNE	Nov 25		Lieut. E.G. HALPIN joined the Battalion for duty as Transport Officer. 2nd. Lieut. S. CRAWFORD joined this day.	
"	Nov 26		2ND. LIEUT. A.R. STEVEN joined Battalion.	
"	Nov 27		Prisoner, of the 8TH. BAVARIAN INFANTRY REGT, captured just outside our wire.	
"THE DELL" SAILLY-AU-BOIS	Nov 29		The Battalion was relieved by the 14th. YORK & LANCASTER REGT, and returned to the DELL. (J.17.b.34). A thick fog enabled a daylight relief to take place, but while this was in process, a temporary lifting of the fog disclosed a party of "A" Coy to the enemy, with the result that this party was fired on by an enemy machine gun. The range was badly judged. 1 other rank was killed.	
"	Nov 30th		Inspections of Rifles, Clothes and Feet.	

Lieut. Colonel Comdg.
12th (S) Bn. York & Lancs. Rgt. (Sheffield.)

C O N F I D E N T I A L.

WAR DIARY.

12th. S. BATTALION YORK AND LANCASTER REGIMENT. (SHEFFIELD)

VOLUME XI

From 1st. November 1916.

To. 30th. November 1916.

B.E.F. December 1st. 1916.

C O N F I D E N T I A L.

WAR DIARY.

12TH.(SERVICE) BATTALION YORK AND LANCASTER REGIMENT.(SHEFFIELD).

VOLUME XII

From 1st.December 1916.

To 31st.December 1916.

B E F. January 1st.1917.

Army Form C. 2118.

Instructions regarding War Diaries and Intelligence Summaries are contained in F. S. Regs., Part II. and the Staff Manual respectively. Title Pages will be prepared in manuscript.

WAR DIARY
or
~~INTELLIGENCE SUMMARY~~

(Erase heading not required.)

Place	Date	Hour	Summary of Events and Information	Remarks and references to Appendices
THE DELL, SAILLY AU-BOIS. J.14 b 3.4	1916 Dec. 1		The Battalion occupying the dug-outs etc at this place. Major D.C.ALLEN admitted to Hospital.	
do.	Dec 3rd		Lieut.Col.C.P.B.RIALL proceeded on Leave to U.K., Major F.J.COURTENAY HOOD assumed temporary command for the period of Lt.Col.Riall's absence.	
HEBUTERNE	Dec. 5th		Battalion again took over the Left Section of the HEBUTERNE SECTOR, relieving the 14th.Bn.York and Lancaster Regt.	
"	Dec 7th		Draft of 5 other ranks joined the Battalion.	
ROSSIGNOL FARM.	Dec. 9th		The Battalion were relieved in the line by the 14th.York and Lancaster Regt, plus two Companies of the 11th.East Lanc Regt, and proceeded to billets at ROSSIGNOL FARM. Major D.C.ALLEN rejoined the Battalion from Hospital.	
do	Dec. 10th		3 other ranks joined the Battalion.	
do	Dec 15th		2ND.LIEUT.F.G.MORRIS joined the Battalion for duty from the Base.	
do	Dec 16th		On the evening of this day a portion o f "B" & "D" Companies, took over the advanced posts in the Left Section of the HEBUTERNE SECTOR, relieving 11th.East Lanc Regt. garrisons.	
HEBUTERNE	Dec. 17th		The remainder of the Battalion completed the relief of the 11th.East Lanc Regt.	
do	Dec. 20th		"C" Company, 12th. Y & L.Rgt. relieved in the line by "C" Company 13th.Y & L Rgt., and went to billets at SAILLY-AU-BOIS. 100 other rank s joined the Battalion.	
SAILLY-AU-BOIS	Dec. 21st		"A" Company 12th Y & L Rgt., relieved by "A" Company 13th.Y & L Rgt., and marched to billets at SAILLY-AU-BOIS.	
THE "DELL" SAILLY-AU-BOIS.	Dec 25th		"B" & "D" Companies 12th Y & L Rgt., relieved by "B" & "D" Companies 14th.Y & L Regt., and moved to the DELL. "A"Company ~~Companies~~ left SAILLY and joined "B" & "D" Companies at the DELL. "C" Company remained at SAILLY.	
do	Dec 26th		Owing to the move yesterday the observation of Christmas was kept today, there were no parades or working parties.	
do	Dec 28th		Draft of 3 other ranks joined the Battalion.	
			During the time the Battalion has been at the DELL, large working parties have been provided daily.	

2449 Wt. W14957/M90 750,000 1/16 J.B.C. & A. Forms/C.2118/12.

L. Hawlt Maj Major ~~Lieut. Colonel~~ Comdg.
12th (S) Bn. York & Lancs. Rgt. (Sheffield.)

SECRET.

C O N F I D E N T I A L.

WAR DIARY .

12.S.Battalion,York & Lancaster Regiment.

---oo---

VOLUME XIII

From 1st January,1917.

To 31st January. 1917.

B.E.F., Feby 1st.1917.

Instructions regarding War Diaries and Intelligence Summaries are contained in F. S. Regs., Part II. and the Staff Manual respectively. Title pages will be prepared in manuscript.

WAR DIARY

or

~~INTELLIGENCE SUMMARY.~~

(Erase heading not required.)

Army Form C. 2118.

Place	Date 1917	Hour	Summary of Events and Information	Remarks and references to Appendices
THE DELL SAILLY AU BOIS.	Jany 1	–	"A" & "B" Companies proceeded to take over advanced posts in the LEFT Section of the HEBUTERNE Sector from 11th. S. Battn. EAST LANCS. REGT.	
"	2		Relief of the 11th S. Battn. EAST LANCS. Regt. completed.	
"	3		Nothing to report.	
The Line.	4		Captain R. W. LEAMON admitted to hospital, sick.	
"	5		On return of Lieut-Col. C. P. B. RIALL from leave, Major F. J. COURTENAY-HOOD ceased to hold temporary command of Battn.	
			"D" Coy relieved in the line by company of 13th S. Battn. YORK & LANCASTER REGT. Returned to billets at SAILLY-AU-BOIS.	
"	6		"B" Coy & H.Q. relieved by 13. S. Battn. YORK & LANCASTER REGT. Draft of 99 O.R. arrived	
"	8		Reinforcement of Officers (6). 2nd Lieut. E. M. BETHELL, 2nd Lieut. A. E. COLE, 2nd Lieut. J. M. SINCLAIR, 2nd Lieut. G. H. JARVIS, 2nd Lieut. A. L. TAYLOR, 2nd Lieut. A. W. LAIDLAW.	
SAILLY AU BOIS	10		Major C. H. GURNEY rejoined Battn. from Senior Officers Course, Aldershot. Assumed duties of Second-in-Command.	
"	11		In accordance with Divisional movement to back area the Battn. relieved by 9th Battn. ROYAL WELCH FUSILIERS, moved to BEAUVAL, arriving	

2353 Wt. W2544/1454 700,000 5/15 D. D. & L. A.D.S.S./Forms/C. 2118.

Instructions regarding War Diaries and Intelligence Summaries are contained in F. S. Regs., Part II. and the Staff Manual respectively. Title pages will be prepared in manuscript.

WAR DIARY

or

~~INTELLIGENCE SUMMARY.~~

(Erase heading not required.)

Page 2.

Army Form C. 2118.

Place	Date	Hour	Summary of Events and Information	Remarks and references to Appendices
	1917 Jany		there 5-0 AM. Battn "embussed" at J 10 c.	
BEAUVAL	12			
"	13			
"	14		Training by sections, platoons & Companies	
"	15			
"	16			
"	17			
"	18	5.15 pm	G.O.C, 31st Division lectured to all Officers of the Battn at THE MAIRIE.	
"	19	10am	General Sir H. de la P. GOUGH. K.C.B, Commanding FIFTH ARMY inspected the Battn whilst training was in progress.	
"	20	5.15 pm	G.O.C. 31st Division lectured to all N.C.Os of the Battalion.	
"	22	9.30am	Battn moved to CANDAS. G.O.C, 31st Division & G.O.C. 94 Infantry Brigade inspected Battn on line of march.	
CANDAS	23		Training.	

2353 Wt. W2544/1454 700,000 5/15 D. D. & L. A.D.S.S./Forms/C. 2118.

Instructions regarding War Diaries and Intelligence Summaries are contained in F. S. Regs., Part II. and the Staff Manual respectively. Title pages will be prepared in manuscript.

WAR DIARY
or
~~INTELLIGENCE SUMMARY.~~
(Erase heading not required.)

Army Form C. 2118.

Place	Date	Hour	Summary of Events and Information	Remarks and references to Appendices
	Jany			
CANDAS	24		Training.	
"	25		Do	
"	26		Battn in the morning practised Company attacks under the supervision of the XIII Corps Commander.	
"	27		Address to Officers of the Battn at GEZAINCOURT by XIII Corps Commander.	
"	28		Training.	
"	29	1 pm.	Battn moved to BONNEVILLE.	
"	30		Training	
"	31		Do	

C.A. Hill

Lieut. Colonel Comdg.
12th (S) Bn. York & Lancs. Rgt. (Sheffield.)

2353 Wt. W2514/1454 700,000 5/15 D. D. & L. A.D.S.S./Forms/C. 2118.

Confidential | Volume XIV.

Vol 12

War Diary.

12th York & Lanc. Regt. | 31st Division

February 1917.

Instructions regarding War Diaries and Intelligence Summaries are contained in F. S. Regs., Part II. and the Staff Manual respectively. Title pages will be prepared in manuscript.

WAR DIARY
or
~~INTELLIGENCE SUMMARY.~~
(Erase heading not required.)

Vol. XIV

Army Form C. 2118.

Place	Date	Hour	Summary of Events and Information	Remarks and references to Appendices
	1917			
BONNEVILLE	Feb 1st.		Battalion at BONNEVILLE carrying out training.	
Do.	" 4th.		Draft of 13 other ranks joined Battalion.	
Do	" 8th.		In the morning the Battalion left BONNEVILLE and marched via VALHEUREUX and BEAUVAL to TERRAMESNIL, arriving there soon after 1pm and staying for the night.	
TERRAMESNIL	" 9th		Battalion left TERRAMESNIL and marched to COURCELLES-AU-BOIS, arriving there at 2.30pm, and were billeted in the village. Battalion Headquarters at J.29 d.19. 2nd. Lieut. J. Buckland joined the Battalion for duty.	
COURCELLES AU-BOIS	" 12th		Working parties provided to the 2nd. Canadian Railway Troops, for railway construction work. These parties continued to be provided daily until the end of the month. 2nd Lieut. E.H. Taylor and 2nd Lieut. J.H. Wood joined the Battalion for duty from the Base	
DO.	" 16th		2nd. Lieut. J. Tonge joined for duty. German shell struck one of the billets occupied by men of "A" Company, causing seven casualties (2 killed & 5 wounded).	
DO	" 21st.	-	10. other ranks joined as a draft. 2nd. Lieut. H Booth joined Battalion	

2353 Wt. W2514/1454 700,000 5/15 D. D. & L. A.D.S.S./Forms/C. 2118.

Instructions regarding War Diaries and Intelligence Summaries are contained in F. S. Regs., Part II. and the Staff Manual respectively. Title pages will be prepared in manuscript.

Army Form C. 2118.

WAR DIARY
or
INTELLIGENCE SUMMARY.
(Erase heading not required.)

Place	Date	Hour	Summary of Events and Information	Remarks and references to Appendices
	1917			
COURCELLES-AU-BOIS.	Feb. 26		60 other ranks joined as a draft also 2nd Lieut. N. H. Malkin.	
DO	" 28		Wire received from Brigade informing us of a probable move to SAILLY DELL. Draft of 8 other ranks joined Battalion.	

C. Riall [illegible]
Cmdg 12 York & Lanc R.

2353 Wt. W2514/1454 700,000 5/15 D. D. & L. A.D.S.S./Forms/C. 2118.

S E C R E T.

CONFIDENTIAL.

W A R   D I A R Y.

12(SERVICE) BATTALION YORK AND LANCASTER REGT.

V O L U M E XV.

FROM 1st. March. 1917.
TO 31st. March. 1917.

x---------oooOooo---------x

BEF½ April 1st. 1917.

Vol

C. [illegible]
Cmdg 12 York & Lanc R.

12 York & Lanc R.

Army Form C. 2118.

VOL XV

page 1

Instructions regarding War Diaries and Intelligence Summaries are contained in F. S. Regs., Part II. and the Staff Manual respectively. Title pages will be prepared in manuscript.

WAR DIARY
or
INTELLIGENCE SUMMARY.
(Erase heading not required.)

Place	Date	Hour	Summary of Events and Information	Remarks and references to Appendices
SAILLY DELL	1.3.17		The Battalion marched from COURCELLES to SAILLY DELL, in column of fours, Companies maintaining 200x interval. They were comfortably billeted here in NISSEN huts. Owing to the bad condition of the roads, we were forced to march part of the way in the fields adjacent to the road.	CA
HEBUTERNE.	2.3.17		During the morning we marched, again in fours with 200x Coy. interval, to HEBUTERNE, and here relieved the 15th Bn. West Yorkshires, taking over their quarters. Although nominally holding the HEBUTERNE left sub-sector, the Regiment did not garrison this line, owing to the enemy's withdrawal, and the occupation of the German front line facing our front being occupied by the whole of the 18th Durham Light Infy. Sentry posts were, however, placed in the support trenches of our now disused front line, & kept us in connexion with the 18th Durhams, and No MANS LAND under observation.	CA

2353 Wt. W2544/1454 700,000 5/15 D. D. & L. A.D.S.S./Forms/C. 2118.

Page 2

Army Form C. 2118.

Instructions regarding War Diaries and Intelligence Summaries are contained in F. S. Regs., Part II. and the Staff Manual respectively. Title pages will be prepared in manuscript.

WAR DIARY
or
INTELLIGENCE SUMMARY.
(*Erase heading not required.*)

page 2

Place	Date	Hour	Summary of Events and Information	Remarks and references to Appendices
HEBUTERNE	3.3.17		The Colonel, Company Commanders & I.O. went in the morning to the German trenches held by the Fusiliers, to reconnoitre with a view to taking that line over. Route followed, SUNKEN ROAD, K.10. Central (Map 57.D N.E.). They returned about 4 pm. over NO MANS LAND N. of the road, owing to the enemy putting a barrage along that road. We were relieved by the 14th Gordons about 7 pm.	CR
GERMAN 1st LINE. ABOUT 500x N.W. of "NAMELESS FARM"	4.3.17		At 3 am the Bn. commenced its march across NO MANS LAND to the line held by the 18th Fusiliers, who provided each platoon with a guide, & reconnoitred a route for us during the afternoon of the 3rd. We arrived at our new line without incident, and relieved the Fusiliers by 6 am.	CR
SAME PLACE AS ABOVE.	5.3.17		Our posts are holding the 1st & 2nd GARDE STELLUNG from junction of SCHWEIKERT GARBEN and GARDE S. to Eastern edge of Rossignol WOOD, and the day has been spent in consolidating	CR

2353 Wt. W2544/1454 700,000 5/15 D. D. & L. A.D.S.S./Forms/C. 2118.

Page 3

Instructions regarding War Diaries and Intelligence Summaries are contained in F. S. Regs., Part II. and the Staff Manual respectively. Title pages will be prepared in manuscript.

WAR DIARY
or
~~INTELLIGENCE SUMMARY.~~
(*Erase heading not required.*)

Army Form C. 2118.

Page 3

Place	Date	Hour	Summary of Events and Information	Remarks and references to Appendices
	5.3.17		this line, and exploring enemy dugouts for information. Three dead Germans & two wounded, belonging to the 15th R.I.R. were found.	CA
HEBUTERNE.	6.3.17		Owing to the shortening of the British line incidental to our advance, we were withdrawn, and our front taken over by the 46th Div. who were on our left. We returned to HEBUTERNE during the afternoon in daylight. During the above operations our casualties only amounted to one O.R. wounded.	CA
HEBUTERNE	7.3.17		Nothing of interest to record. Bn. occupied in salvage work in old British line.	CA
	8.3.17		Ditto. Second in Command, Company officers & I.O., also S.O., reconnoitred line at PUISIEUX during the morning, the C.O. viewing it in the afternoon.	CA
PUISIEUX.	9.3.17		The Bn. relieved the 14th Gloucs at Puisieux: Route 16 POPLARS ROAD, LA LOUVIERE FARM, BOX WOOD, during the afternoon, their advanced posts being taken over after dark.	CA

2353 Wt. W2544/1454 700,000 5/15 D. D. & L. A.D.S.S./Forms/C. 2118.

Page 4

Instructions regarding War Diaries and Intelligence Summaries are contained in F. S. Regs., Part II. and the Staff Manual respectively. Title pages will be prepared in manuscript.

WAR DIARY
or
INTELLIGENCE SUMMARY.
(Erase heading not required.)

Army Form C. 2118.

Page 4

Place	Date	Hour	Summary of Events and Information	Remarks and references to Appendices
POISIEUX	10.3.17 to 12.3.17		Line now held by line of advanced posts, situated in consolidated shell holes. Dispositions as under: Front line comprised eight posts, co-ordinates; L9a 80. L9d 65. L9d 47. L9d 18. L9c 99. L9c 58. L9c 29 – L8d 9595. and three support posts:– L9d 41 – L9d 1065 – L9c 58. The average garrison of these posts was 1 NCO. & 12 men, the advanced posts all having a Lewis gun each, and these men were provided by two Companies, the balance of those Companies formed a Local Reserve & held a line from L8d 88 to L15c 29. (Map 57 D. NE.). The remaining two Companies formed the Supports & Bn. Reserves; the Support Coy. holding from L14a 7520 to L14a 28, and from L14d 4578 to L15c 08, whilst the Res. Coy. held from L14c 11 to L14c 39. this latter line being good trenches for giving cover. During the period under review the deep parsed unevent-	CA

2353 Wt. W2544/1454 700,000 5/15 D. D. & L. A.D.S.S./Forms/C. 2118.

Page 5

Instructions regarding War Diaries and Intelligence Summaries are contained in F. S. Regs., Part II. and the Staff Manual respectively. Title pages will be prepared in manuscript.

WAR DIARY
or
INTELLIGENCE SUMMARY.

(*Erase heading not required.*)

Army Form C. 2118.

Page 5

Place	Date	Hour	Summary of Events and Information	Remarks and references to Appendices
PUISIEUX 10.3.17 to 12.3.17			eventually for us, apart from the vigorous shelling the enemy gave PUISIEUX, & the wire cutting fire of our own Artillery. The nights were spent in wiring & generally strengthening the posts. A feature of this period was the abnormal number of officers from other Regiments who reconnoitred our line. We sent out many patrols.	CR
" 13.3.17.			Late in the afternoon the 2nd Queens arrived to relieve us, and we then marched to the "WHITE CITY", arriving there about 3 A.m. The Bn. then rested until next morning in dugouts & shelters. Although much fatigued the morale of the men was very good. Casualties: 11 O.R. wounded & 4 O.R. missing.	CR
BUS.	14.3.17		Marched to BUS, & occupied rest billets there.	CR
"	15.3.17		Day spent in cleaning up after the trenches & training.	CR
"	16.3.17		Training continued.	CR

2353 Wt. W2544/1454 700,000 5/15 D. D. & L. A.D.S.S./Forms/C. 2118.

Instructions regarding War Diaries and Intelligence Summaries are contained in F. S. Regs., Part II. and the Staff Manual respectively. Title pages will be prepared in manuscript.

WAR DIARY
or
~~INTELLIGENCE SUMMARY.~~
(Erase heading not required.)

Army Form C. 2118.

page 6

Place	Date	Hour	Summary of Events and Information	Remarks and references to Appendices
BOS.	17.3.17		Day spent in training. Draft of seven O.R. arrived.	CA
"	18.3.17		" " "	CA
BEAUVAL	19.3.17		Bn. marched to BEAUVAL, and billeted here.	CA
BOURET SUR CANCHE.	20.3.17		We marched here today from BEAUVAL via DOULLENS.	CA
VALHUON	21.3.17		Marched here today.	CA
AUMERVAL.	22.3.17		" " "	CA
"	23.3.17		Day spent in resting.	CA
EQUEDECQUES	24.3.17		Marched to here today. Draft of 62 O.R. arrived.	CA
MERVILLE	25.3.17		" " " " + billeted N. of the town.	CA
"	26.3.17		Draft of 36 O.R. arrived.	CA
	to		Time spent in resting + training.	
	31.3.17		Strength. Officers = 23. } With Bn. O.R. = 806. }	CA

C. [illegible] Lt Col
Cmdg 12 York & Lanc R.

2353 Wt. W2544/1454 700,000 5/15 D. D. & L. A.D.S.S./Forms/C. 2118.

Confidential

Volume XVI

Vol 14

War Diary

12th Bn Yorks & Lanc Regt. 31st Division

April 1917.

Page 1

Instructions regarding War Diaries and Intelligence Summaries are contained in F. S. Regs., Part II. and the Staff Manual respectively. Title pages will be prepared in manuscript.

WAR DIARY
or
~~INTELLIGENCE SUMMARY.~~
(Erase heading not required.)

Army Form C. 2118.

Place	Date	Hour	Summary of Events and Information	Remarks and references to Appendices
MERVILLE	1/4/17 to 7/4/17	–	Battalion in training – special attention being paid to organisation in order that each individual section might, in itself, be a potent force. "Trench to trench" attack training now subordinate to training for open warfare. Battn – reserve to XI Corps.	D.C.A.
"	8/4/17	11 am	Battn marched to village of OBLINGHEM, near BETHUNE. A/Capt E.L. MOXEY, 2/Lt J. CRAWFORD, SGCLM PIRKIS, H BOOTH & 49 OR proceeded to ROBECQ to join XIII Corps Reinforcement Camp. This personnel will train future "drafts" for the Battn, as reinforcements do not receive the extensive training as heretofore.	D.C.A.
	11/4/17	2 pm	Battn moved to LABOURSE, near NOEUX-LES-MINES. Marched – 3½.	
	12/4/17 13/4/17		Reconnoitring parties sent to report on position of Assembly trenches ~~[illegible]~~ – portion of line known as MAESTRE LINE & held at this particular period by ~~[illegible]~~ 184 Brigade. The position stretched from BULLY GRENAY – CITE DE CALONNE road to the AIX-NOULETTE – ARRAS road. (Area G 25 C 22. Ref. Map. Sheet 36 B Ed. 6.)	D.C.M.

2353 Wt. W2544/1454 700,000 5/15 D. D. & L. A.D.S.S./Forms/C. 2118.

Instructions regarding War Diaries and Intelligence Summaries are contained in F. S. Regs., Part II. and the Staff Manual respectively. Title pages will be prepared in manuscript.

Page 92

WAR DIARY
or
~~INTELLIGENCE SUMMARY~~.

(Erase heading not required.)

Army Form C. 2118.

Place	Date	Hour	Summary of Events and Information	Remarks and references to Appendices
HERMIN	14/4/17	9-12 am.	Battn moved to HERMIN. Arrived 2 pm.	
	15/4/17 to 28/4/17.		Training as at MERVILLE. On 15th 2/Lts H.G. MANN & C.W. PIMM joined Battn as a draft.	DCA
			(Note: On 16/4/17. 12/481. Regt Sgt-Major C POLDEN presented with Military Cross by Lt Col. C.P.B. RIALL, the Commanding Officer. The award was made by the C-in-C under authority of ~~the~~ H.M. ~~the~~ King for conspicuous gallantry under heavy shell fire on March 1111 at PUISIEUX.)	
	29/4/17	9-40 am.	Battn marched to ECOIVRES. Billeted in NISSEN huts on high ground just outside the village.	DCA
	30/4/17.	10 am.	Battn marched to MAROEUIL. Billeted as at ECOIVRES.	DCA
			(Note: on 25/4/17. 2/Lt G.C.L.M. PIRKIS & 25 OR rejoined Bn from ROBECQ & on the 26/4/17 remainder of this ~~Party~~ moved to PERNES)	

Douglas L Allen
Major for Lieut. Colonel Comdg.
12th (S) Bn. York & Lancaster (Sheffield.)

2353 Wt. W2544/1454 700,000 5/15 D. D. & L. A.D.S.S./Forms/C. 2118.

SECRET.

CONFIDENTIAL.

12TH. SERVICE. BATTALION YORK AND LANCASTER REGIMENT.

WAR DIARY.

VOL. XVII

From 1st. May 1917.

To 31st. May 1917.

BEF June 1/17.

Instructions regarding War Diaries and Intelligence Summaries are contained in F. S. Regs., Part II. and the Staff Manual respectively. Title pages will be prepared in manuscript.

WAR DIARY

~~or~~

~~INTELLIGENCE SUMMARY.~~

(*Erase heading not required.*)

Army Form C. 2118.

Ref map 51 B N.W. 1:20000

Place	Date	Hour	Summary of Events and Information	Remarks and references to Appendices
MAROEUIL	1/5/17		The Battalion marched from the billets at MAROEUIL to the captured & vacant German trenches at G.6 Central, from which time it came under the orders of the 93rd Infy Bde. There was but little dugout accommodation & the men bivouacked in the trenches & adjacent shell holes. At about noon the C.O. attended a conference at ROCLINCOURT. In the evening he called at the H.Q.s of the 93rd Inf Bde.	[illegible]
G.6 Central	2/5/17		Company Commanders & Runners reconnoitred the route to the front line trenches held by the 93rd Inf Bde in the neighbourhood of GAVRELLE.	
		5pm	C.O. held a conference of officers to discuss the operation orders of the 93rd Inf. Bde. for the attack on the enemy trenches East of GAVRELLE, on the morning of the 3rd inst.	(93 Inf. B. Scheme)
		10.30pm	The Bn. commenced to move to H.1.b & d on those trenches being evacuated by the 18th Durham LI, the move being completed by 1.30 am 3.5.17, excepting working parties, then not found with the Bn.	

Instructions regarding War Diaries and Intelligence Summaries are contained in F. S. Regs., Part II. and the Staff Manual respectively. Title pages will be prepared in manuscript.

WAR DIARY
or
~~INTELLIGENCE SUMMARY.~~
(Erase heading not required.)

Army Form C. 2118.

Place	Date	Hour	Summary of Events and Information	Remarks and references to Appendices
G.6. Central	2/5/17		During the day officers & men of Category B returned to our Transport lines at ST CATHARINES. Working parties were supplied as shewn on the attached table.	[initials]
H.1. b & d.	3/5/17	3.30 am	C.O. reported to rear Bde. H.Qrs. of the 937 Infy. Bde. in the Railway cutting at H.1.d. to keep in close touch with the situation & to receive the Brigadier's instructions.	
"		5.45 am	Message received from C.O. ordering one Coy. to be prepared to move at once. "A" Coy accordingly detailed (C.O. 1/3)	
"		6 am	Hotchkiss Gun detachment of the Northumberland Hussars placed under our orders and O.C. detachment was instructed to send four Guns up to "HILL 80" (B.23.c) under orders from 937 Infy. Bde. (CR 2/3)	
		6.30 am	Message received from C.O. advising a further Coy. to be prepared to move at once. "C" Coy. detailed. (CR 3/3) This message also gave instructions for the remainder	

A5834 Wt. W4973/M687 750,000 8/16 D. D. & L. Ltd. Forms/C.2118/13.

Instructions regarding War Diaries and Intelligence Summaries are contained in F. S. Regs., Part II. and the Staff Manual respectively. Title pages will be prepared in manuscript.

WAR DIARY
or
~~INTELLIGENCE SUMMARY.~~
(Erase heading not required.)

Army Form C. 2118.

Place	Date	Hour	Summary of Events and Information	Remarks and references to Appendices
H.1.b.c.d.	7/8/17	6.3am	of the Bn. to be prepared to move anywhere at a moments notice. By this time the Bn. was all present working parties having all returned with the exception of one officer, 12 men of D Coy, 14 men of "C" Coy.	
"		6.8am	Orders given to "A" Coy, to proceed immediately to [illegible] (CR3/3)	
"		6.10am	Similar orders given to "C" Coy to move to [illegible] (CR4/3) Before these two Companies moved off they were issued with the Bn's mobile reserve of bombs; and this distribution was made immediately orders were received warning these Coys. to be prepared to move at short notice.	
"		6.50am	O.C. Hotchkiss gun detachment ordered to bring up the remainder of his guns & personnel to the neighbourhood of Bn. H.Qs at H.1.a.9.1, where he would hold them ready to move off at once, on receipt of orders from C.O. or Adjt. (CR5/3)	

A5834 Wt. W4973/M687 750,000 8/16 D. D. & L. Ltd. Forms/C.2118/13.

Instructions regarding War Diaries and Intelligence Summaries are contained in F. S. Regs., Part II. and the Staff Manual respectively. Title pages will be prepared in manuscript.

WAR DIARY

or

~~INTELLIGENCE SUMMARY.~~

(Erase heading not required.)

Army Form C. 2118.

Place	Date	Hour	Summary of Events and Information	Remarks and references to Appendices
H.1.6.a.	3/5/17	7.45 am	C.O. returned to Bn. H.Q. from rear H.Qrs of 93rd Infy Bde. and issued verbal orders for the remaining two Coys. ("B + D") and H.Q. Coy. personnel to move forward to reverse slope of hill behind advanced H.Qrs. of 93rd Bde, about B26d. Leaving the Adjutant in command, the C.O. then went forward to advanced Bde. H.Qrs. to report personally for instructions. Without delay the Bn. (less two Coys detached to [illegible]) moved up to the neighbourhood of B26d. On arrival there they were met by the C.O. with verbal orders that we were to move up to the support of the Bns. in the front line of the 93 Infy. Bde. Whilst moving forward in artillery formation, in compliance with that order, a message was received from the 93 Bde. to the effect that the Bde's left was being turned, and that we were to reinforce the 16th Bn. West Yorks Regt. ~~[illegible]~~	(X) unnumbered message.

A5834 Wt. W4973/M687 750,000 8/16 D. D. & L. Ltd. Forms/C.2118/13.

Army Form C. 2118.

WAR DIARY
or
~~INTELLIGENCE SUMMARY.~~

(*Erase heading not required.*)

Instructions regarding War Diaries and Intelligence Summaries are contained in F. S. Regs., Part II. and the Staff Manual respectively. Title pages will be prepared in manuscript.

Place	Date	Hour	Summary of Events and Information	Remarks and references to Appendices
"R.C.2"	3/5/17		~~[illegible]~~ A further order, timed 9.5 a.m. ("BM 80") was received from the 93rd Bde. in the neighbourhood of the German gunpits at "R.C.2" cancelling the instructions to move to the support of the 18th Bn. West Yorks. Regt., and ordering one Coy. to be sent to the support of the 15th West Yorks. Regt. on the Right flank, our fourth Coy to remain in support to the Centre (18th West Yorks & 18th Durham L.I.). Guides were furnished by the front line Bns. at R.C.2. Our "B" Coy. was ordered to the support of the 15th West Yorks, and "D" Coy remained in the neighbourhood of R.C.2, taking cover in adjacent evacuated trenches & shell holes. They were detailed to hold themselves in readiness to reinforce the Centre at a moment's notice. Bn. H.Qrs., under orders from the 93rd Inf. Bde., were	

A5834 Wt. W4973/M687 750,000 8/16 D. D. & L. Ltd. Forms/C.2118/13.

Instructions regarding War Diaries and Intelligence Summaries are contained in F. S. Regs., Part II. and the Staff Manual respectively. Title pages will be prepared in manuscript.

WAR DIARY
or
~~INTELLIGENCE SUMMARY.~~
(Erase heading not required.)

Army Form C. 2118.

Place	Date	Hour	Summary of Events and Information	Remarks and references to Appendices
"R.C.2"	7/5/17		established in the gunpits at "R.C.2". The advance across the open, within sight of the enemy's observers & within range of his guns, was made with but little hinderance from enemy shelling, which is remarkable in view of our closeness to the front-line, the fineness of the weather which gave good visibility, and the absence of cover for our men. The bearing of both officers & men during this advance was splendid, and artillery formation was maintained as though on manoeuvres. The two Coy detached to "Trace 80" were shelled fairly continuously throughout the day, but they escaped with few casualties owing to the excellent siting of the trench there.	

A5834 Wt. W4973/M687 750,000 8/16 D. D. & L. Ltd. Forms/C.2118/13.

Instructions regarding War Diaries and Intelligence Summaries are contained in F. S. Regs., Part II. and the Staff Manual respectively. Title pages will be prepared in manuscript.

WAR DIARY
or
~~INTELLIGENCE SUMMARY.~~

(Erase heading not required.)

Army Form C. 2118.

Place	Date	Hour	Summary of Events and Information	Remarks and references to Appendices
"R.C.2"	3/5/17		"R.C.2" & the surrounding places also received considerable attention from the enemy artillery throughout the day & night.	[initials]
	4/5/17		The Bn. remained under the orders of the 93rd Inf. Bde. dispositions as above, until receipt of orders from the 94th Inf. Bde. to move our Centre supporting Coy to the relief of the 18th Durham L.I. in the old German front line South of ARRAS–GAVRELLE road. Batt HQ. at B30a 54, which relief was carried out during the night of the 4/5th May. Parties were dispatched during the afternoon to take over the dumps of the 93rd Inf. Bde. according to the attached schedule. (FA27) (Copies of messages referred to are attached) Working parties were provided for the period 1st/4th May, according to the attached table. Officers & men of Category "B" rejoined the Bn. Casualties to date. 1 O.R. killed. 3 O.R. wounded.	[initials]

A5834 Wt. W4973/M687 750,000 8/16 D. D. & L. Ltd. Forms/C.2118/13.

Army Form C. 2118.

WAR DIARY
or
~~INTELLIGENCE SUMMARY.~~

(*Erase heading not required.*)

Instructions regarding War Diaries and Intelligence Summaries are contained in F. S. Regs., Part II. and the Staff Manual respectively. Title pages will be prepared in manuscript.

Place	Date	Hour	Summary of Events and Information	Remarks and references to Appendices
B.30.a.7.9.	5/5/17		Line held without incident of note. During the afternoon the Bn. was ordered to withdraw to R.C.2. with the exception of "A" Coy. which was to remain at "Hill 60". Bn. accordingly moved at dusk. Weather very fine, & much aeroplane activity on both sides. Casualties: 2 O.R. wounded.	[illegible]
"R.C.2"	6/5/17		The Bn., & "A" Coy at "Hill 60", remained at R.C.2, and nothing of note occurred. Casualties 1 O.R. killed: 3 O.R. wounded.	[illegible]
"R.C.2"	7/5/17		Bn. still at R.C.2. At about 10 pm we commenced to come back to the trenches at B.25.b.& d., having been relieved by the 15th West Yorks Regt. "A" Coy at "Hill 60" was also relieved by two platoons of the 11th East Lancashire Regt. and rejoined the Bn. at B.25. During the afternoon, the Coy. cooks who had been left at the transport rejoined their Coys. & prepared hot food for them on their arrival from the front line. Casualties. 7 O.R. wounded.	[illegible]

A5834 Wt. W4973/M687 750,000 8/16 D. D. & L. Ltd. Forms/C.2118/13.

Instructions regarding War Diaries and Intelligence Summaries are contained in F. S. Regs., Part II. and the Staff Manual respectively. Title pages will be prepared in manuscript.

WAR DIARY
or
~~INTELLIGENCE SUMMARY.~~
(Erase heading not required.)

Army Form C. 2118.

Place	Date	Hour	Summary of Events and Information	Remarks and references to Appendices
B25a	8/5/17	8.40 am	Telegram received from Bde. advising that left Bde of 5th Division, holding FRESNOY Sector had been driven out of its position, and ordering us to hold ourselves ready to move at a moments notice. So far as this order would allow the day was spent in cleaning & resting.	
		8 pm.	Ordered by Bde to move up to the Railway cutting at B21.c. Whilst marching to take up this position, a counter order was received, instructing the Bn. to return to its trenches at B.25. but to hold itself ready to move at 15 minutes notice. Bn. accordingly returned; it was not called upon to move that night.	
			Casualties:- 6 O.R. wounded.	[illegible initials]
B25a	9/5/17		Day spent in cleaning up & resting.	
		8.15 pm.	At dusk we commenced to move to R.O.2. where the Bn. was met by guides of the 14th York & Lanc. Regt., whom we relieved in the Right subsector of the 94th Bde front that	

A5834 Wt. W4973/M687 750,000 8/16 D. D. & L. Ltd. Forms/C.2118/13.

Instructions regarding War Diaries and Intelligence Summaries are contained in F. S. Regs., Part II. and the Staff Manual respectively. Title pages will be prepared in manuscript.

WAR DIARY
or
~~INTELLIGENCE SUMMARY.~~

(Erase heading not required.)

Army Form C. 2118.

Place	Date	Hour	Summary of Events and Information	Remarks and references to Appendices
"B25.a	9/5/17		night. This sector included the GAVRELLE WINDMILL. The enemy's guns were very active during the relief. One Coy ["D"] defended the Windmill, its dispositions being: two platoons in a series of strong posts on the flanks of the mill: two platoons in support to the posts, which occupied trenches in rear, ie. S.E., of the mill. Casualties:– 1 officer (2/Lt Thompson), 6 O.R. wounded (5 gassed.)	[initials]
	10/5/17		Line held. We were continuously shelled by guns of all calibres, including gas shells, and at night ration parties & visiting patrols were harassed by sniper & machine gun fire. The aerial activity of both sides was considerable, & a feature of it was the low altitudes to which the enemy machines descended at dawn & dusk. Casualties:– 5 O.R. wounded.	[initials]

A5834 Wt. W4973/M687 750,000 8/16 D. D. & L. Ltd. Forms/C.2118/13.

Instructions regarding War Diaries and Intelligence Summaries are contained in F. S. Regs., Part II. and the Staff Manual respectively. Title pages will be prepared in manuscript.

WAR DIARY
or
~~INTELLIGENCE SUMMARY.~~

(*Erase heading not required.*)

Army Form C. 2118.

Place	Date	Hour	Summary of Events and Information	Remarks and references to Appendices
RIGHT SUBSECTOR	11/5/17		Line held: dispositions unaltered. Casualties:- 1 officer wounded (2/Lt J.M. SINCLAIR) 5 O.R. killed: 27 O.R. wounded.	[illegible]
"	12/5/17		Line held. 2nd Lieut. PERKIS with a party of men bombed up a trench on our left flank, & established a series of posts up it. Casualties Killed:- 1 officer (Lieut R.D BERRY) ~~(2nd Lt [illegible] DAVIES)~~ 3 O.R. Wounded:- 2 officers (2/Lt JARVIS & 2/Lt MANN) ~~(2nd Lt [illegible] & STEVEN)~~ 23 O.R. wounded	[illegible]
"	13/5/17		Line held. Advised that we should be relieved by 1st Yorkshire that night. Major Allen, with billeting party, accordingly left trenches that afternoon, but returned later, on fresh instructions being received cancelling the relief owing to a neighbouring Bde also being in course of relief that night. Casualties: Killed:- 1 O.R. Wounded 4 O.R.	[illegible]
"	14/5/17		Line held. At dusk guides were sent down to "R.C.?" to meet	

A5834 Wt. W4973/M687 750,000 8/16 D. D. & L. Ltd. Forms/C.2118/13.

Army Form C. 2118.

Instructions regarding War Diaries and Intelligence Summaries are contained in F. S. Regs., Part II. and the Staff Manual respectively. Title pages will be prepared in manuscript.

WAR DIARY
or
~~INTELLIGENCE SUMMARY.~~

(Erase heading not required.)

Place	Date	Hour	Summary of Events and Information	Remarks and references to Appendices
Right Subsector	14/5/17		The 1/4th York & Lanc Regt, who relieved the Bn. that night. On completion of relief the Bn. returned to the rest trenches at B.25.b.a.d.	
			Casualties:- Killed:- 2 officers (2/Lt F.A. DAVIES & 2/Lt N.H. MALKIN - D of W) 1 O.R. Wounded:- 1 officer (2/Lt A.R. STEVEN) 2 O.R.	[initials]
B.25.b.a.d.	15/5/17		Day spent in cleaning up, refitting & resting. Officers reconnoitred the Corps Reserve Line in front of BAILLEUL. 2nd in Command, under Bde. orders, returned to the Transport Lines, being a reinforcement against the C.O. becoming a casualty.	
			Casualties:- Killed - nil. Wounded:- 2 O.R.	[initials]
"	16/5/17		Day spent in inspections & resting.	
			Casualties:- Killed: nil. Wounded 5 O.R.	[initials]
"	17/5/17		Day spent in training & resting.	
			Casualties: Nil.	[initials]

A5834 Wt. W4973/M687 750,000 8/16 D. D. & L. Ltd. Forms/C.2118/13.

Army Form C. 2118.

Instructions regarding War Diaries and Intelligence Summaries are contained in F. S. Regs., Part II. and the Staff Manual respectively. Title pages will be prepared in manuscript.

WAR DIARY
or
~~INTELLIGENCE SUMMARY.~~
(Erase heading not required.)

Place	Date	Hour	Summary of Events and Information	Remarks and references to Appendices
B.25.b.d.	18/5/17		The C.O., being sick, went back to Transport lines; the 2nd in Command rejoining the Bn. and taking over Command. At 8.30 pm commenced to move up to the line to relieve the 14th York & Lanc. in the Right subsector, and the Bn. was again provided with guides at "R.P.2" by the 14th Y.&L. During the relief the enemy heavily shelled our area, and owing to the shallowness of the support trenches, through which all Companies had to pass on their way to the front line, many casualties were reported by all Coys. next morning. Casualties:- nil.	[signature]
Right Subsector	19/5/17		At 10.30 am Bn. HQrs. were visited by C.O. & I.O. of the 1st Bn. H.A.C. 63rd Division. Bn's dispositions explained to him & discussed; and he went round the front line as far as possible in daylight. Casualties: Killed: 1 Officer (2/Lt C.W. Pimm), 6 O.R. Wounded:- 19 O.R.	[signature]

A5834 Wt. W4973/M687 750,000 8/16 D. D. & L. Ltd. Forms/C.2118/13.

Instructions regarding War Diaries and Intelligence Summaries are contained in F. S. Regs., Part II. and the Staff Manual respectively. Title pages will be prepared in manuscript.

WAR DIARY
or
~~INTELLIGENCE SUMMARY.~~
(*Erase heading not required.*)

Army Form C. 2118.

Place	Date	Hour	Summary of Events and Information	Remarks and references to Appendices
B.25.Cent	18/5/17		The C.O., being sick, went back to Transport lines; the 2nd in Command rejoining the Bn. and taking over Command. At 8.30 pm commenced to move up to the line to relieve the 14th York & Lancs. in the Right Subsector and the Bn. was again provided with guides at "R.C.2" by the 14th Y.&L. During the relief the enemy heavily shelled our area, and owing to the shallowness of the support trenches, through which all Companies had to pass on their way to the front line, many casualties were reported by all Coys. next morning. Casualties:- nil.	R.J.H.
Right Subsector	19/5/17		At 10.30 am Bn. HQrs. were visited by C.O. & I.O. of the 1st Bn. H.A.C. 63rd Division. Bn's dispositions explained to him & discussed; and he went round the front line as far as possible in daylight. Casualties: Killed: 1 officer (2/Lt C.W. Pimm), 6 O.R. Wounded: 19 O.R.	R.J.H.

A5834 Wt. W4973/M687 750,000 8/16 D. D. & L. Ltd. Forms/C.2118/13.

Instructions regarding War Diaries and Intelligence Summaries are contained in F. S. Regs., Part II. and the Staff Manual respectively. Title pages will be prepared in manuscript.

WAR DIARY
or
~~INTELLIGENCE SUMMARY.~~
(Erase heading not required.)

Army Form C. 2118.

Place	Date	Hour	Summary of Events and Information	Remarks and references to Appendices
Right Subsector.	20/5/17		Nothing unusual occurred during the day. Commencing at 10pm, the 1st Bn. H.A.C. relieved us in the line. On completion of relief, the Bn. assembled at an open space at G.C.d, where they were met by the field kitchens, which came up from the transport lines, and prepared a hot breakfast for the men. Casualties:- Wounded: 5 O.R.	
MAROEUIL	21/5/17		After breakfast and a short rest, the Bn. marched to MAROEUIL and occupied billets there. Although the Bn. had been in shelled trenches for twenty continuous days, their moral was very good, and march discipline was exactly maintained on the march to billets. Casualties:- Nil.	
"	22–26/5/17		This period was spent in the billets at MAROEUIL, refitting, training and resting. On the 23rd inst. officers reconnoitred	

A5834 Wt. W4973/M687 750,000 8/16 D. D. & L. Ltd. Forms/C.2118/13.

Army Form C. 2118.

WAR DIARY
or
~~INTELLIGENCE SUMMARY.~~
(Erase heading not required.)

Instructions regarding War Diaries and Intelligence Summaries are contained in F. S. Regs., Part II. and the Staff Manual respectively. Title pages will be prepared in manuscript.

Place	Date	Hour	Summary of Events and Information	Remarks and references to Appendices
MARDEUIL	22-26/5/17		the "GREEN LINE" trenches at B27.	[illegible initials]
"	27/5/17	8.45 am	The Bn marched to A28a near ECURIE, and took over the Cables bivouacks of the 18th West Yorks Regt.	
		10 pm	Commenced work on the "GREEN LINE" at B27, the Bn providing a working party of 300 OR plus officers, which worked for four clear hours.	[illegible initials]
A28a.	28-31/5/17		During this period the Bn was employed on digging & improving the "GREEN LINE" at B27 the programme being:-	
		7.45 pm	Marched from camp to trenches.	
		10 pm	Commenced work without pause until -	
		2 am	Ceased work, and returned to camp	
		4 am	Breakfast: after which the men rested until 12.30 pm, there being no movement allowed within Coy. lines during that period.	
		1 pm	Lunch	

A5834 Wt. W4973/M687 750,000 8/16 D. D. & L. Ltd. Forms/C.2118/13.

Army Form C. 2118.

Instructions regarding War Diaries and Intelligence Summaries are contained in F. S. Regs., Part II. and the Staff Manual respectively. Title pages will be prepared in manuscript.

WAR DIARY
or
~~INTELLIGENCE SUMMARY.~~
(Erase heading not required.)

Place	Date	Hour	Summary of Events and Information	Remarks and references to Appendices
A.28.a	28-31/5/17	2.30 pm	Parades under Company Commanders for training.	
		3.30 pm	Dismissed, after which the men were free for recreation until the evening parade for work.	
			Ration Strength 31.5.17:- Officers 23. O.R. 565.	[initials]
			Reinforcements for month of May:- 3 Officers: 47 O.R. (Capt R E J Moore) (2Lt A C Ridlington) (2Lt A R Turner)	

Capt & Adjt

M. Humbridge for Major

~~Lieut.-Colonel~~ Comdg.

12th (S) Bn. York & Lancs. Rgt. (Sheffield.)

A5834 Wt. W4973/M687 750,000 8/16 D. D. & L. Ltd. Forms/C.2118/13.

War Diary May/17.

The Battalion provided the following to take charge of dumps as shewn:-

Off.	N.C.Os.	Men.	Dump at.
1	2	16	H.9.a.3.9. (PONT DE JOUR) H.4.c.2.6. (emergency dump). B.30.a.3.8.
1	1	3	B.22.d.8.9.

The Battalion also provided the following working parties. :-

Date.	Off.	NCOs.	Men.	Place.	Time.	Report to.	Work required to be done.
2.5.17.	-	1	20	PONT DE JOUR	6.pm.	LT. BEEDON.	Loading T.M. amm. and sandbags on to mules.
"	4	10	200	-do-	10.pm.	LT. INESON.	Carrying R.E. material to forward dump.
"	-	1	20	H.4.central.	8.pm.		Carrying wiring material for strong point.
* "	1	-	50	Rear Bde HQ.	6.pm.		

* No orders for this party received at the time they were detailed. Officer in charge afterwards received instructions to take up T.M. ammunition to trenches and Windmill.

3rd May 1917 (X)

O C 12 Y & L.

Cancel my message re assisting right & centre.

Our left is being turned & you must assist (Col. CROYDON) 16 W. Yorks

9.20.am.

(Sd) F. Kinsman Major
BM. 93 I.B.

Copy

"A" Form.

Army Form C.2121 (in pads of 100).

MESSAGES AND SIGNALS.

No. of Message

Prefix ... Code ... m.	Words	Charge	This message is on a/c of:	Recd. at ... m.
Office of Origin and Service Instructions.	Sent		A Service.	Date
	At ... m.			From
	To			
	By		(Signature of "Franking Officer.")	By

TO OC STAY

Sender's Number.	Day of Month.	In reply to Number.	AAA
* SC 69	2		

The Brigadier General wishes you to move your Bn to Trenches in H1 B + D now occupied by DECK who are moving out at 10-30 pm tonight aaa Move to be completed by 1-30 am May 3rd aaa You yourself are to be at RENR BDE HQ not later than 3-30 am so as to take any orders that may be necessary from the BRIG GEN aaa

Please acknowledge aaa

From Staff Capt HULL

Place

Time

The above may be forwarded as now corrected. (Z) (Sd) C F Davey Capt

Censor. Signature of Addressor or person authorised to telegraph in his name.

* This line should be erased if not required.

750,000. W 2186—M509. H. W & V., Ld. 6/16.

"A" Form.

MESSAGES AND SIGNALS.

Army Form C.2121 (in pads of 100).

No. of Message ....

Prefix ...... Code ...... m.	Words	Charge	This message is on a/c of:	Recd. at ...... m.
Office of Origin and Service Instructions.			(R) Service.	Date 1
V. Urgent	Sent At ...... m. To ...... By		(Signature of "Franking Officer.")	From ...... By ......

TO: Adjutant 5 TAY

Sender's Number.	Day of Month.	In reply to Number.	AAA
* CO 1/3	3		

Order one Company A for choice to get ready to proceed at once to a destination which I shall give them shortly. Leave bombs and tell them to take half their L G panniers with them. Greatcoats to be dumped. Acknowledge.

From: Rear BHQ

Place:

Time: 5-45 am

(Sd) C Rice [?] Lt Col 5 TAY

The above may be forwarded as now corrected. (Z)

Censor. Signature of Addressor or person authorised to telegraph in his name.

* This line should be erased if not required.

750,000. W 2186 –M509. H. W & V., Ld. 6/16.

"A" Form.
MESSAGES AND SIGNALS.

Army Form C.2121
(in pads of 100).
No. of Message

Prefix .... Code .... m. | Words | Charge

Office of Origin and Service Instructions.
OHM Remsey
41 Northumberland
6 5 am

Sent
Pheasant
At .... m.
To
By

This message is on a/c of:
D
Service.
(Signature of "Franking Officer.")

Recd. at .... m.
Date
From
By

TO OC HOTCHKISS COY

Sender's Number.	Day of Month.	In reply to Number.	AAA
* CR 293	3		

I am ordered by G.O.C 93rd Inf Bde to order you to send at once 4 guns to "Hill 80" location B23 central AAA Object is to repulse any counter-attack that may come from direction of OPPY AAA On arrival at "Hill 80" send two runners to report to Advanced Bde HQrs AAA Acknowledge

From OC STAY
Place
Time 6 am

The above may be forwarded as now corrected.
(Z) (Sd.) C Riall Lt Col
Censor. Signature of Addressor or person authorised to telegraph in his name.

* This line should be erased if not required.

750,000. W 2186-M509. H. W & V., Ld. 6/16.

"A" Form. Army Form C.2121
(in pads of 100).

MESSAGES AND SIGNALS. No. of Message..............

Prefix ....Code..............m. | Words | Charge | *This message is on a/c of:* C *Service.* | Recd. at..............m.

Office of Origin and Service Instructions.

Sent
At..............m.
To..............
By..............

(Signature of "Franking Officer.")

Date..............
From..............
By..............

TO { OC A Coy STAY

Sender's Number.	Day of Month.	In reply to Number.	AAA
* CR 3/3	3		

Your Company will proceed at once to hold trenches from B18a45 to B24b21 in case of a possible counter attack AAA On arrival there you will report by runners to ADVANCED Bde Hd Qrs about H3d18 AAA

From O.C STAY
Place
Time 6.8 am

The above may be forwarded as now corrected. (Z) [signature] Lt Col

Censor. Signature of Addressor or person authorised to telegraph in his name.

* This line should be erased if not required.

750,000. W 2183–M509. H. W & V., Ld. 6/16.

Army Form C.2121
(in pads of 100).
No. of Message

"A" Form.

MESSAGES AND SIGNALS.

Prefix ..... Code ..... m. | Words | Charge

Office of Origin and Service Instructions.

Sent
At ..... m.
To .....
By .....

This message is on a/c of:
(E) Service.
(Signature of "Franking Officer.")

Recd. at ..... m.
Date .....
From (2)
By .....

TO Adjutant STAY

Sender's Number.	Day of Month.	In reply to Number.	AAA
* CR 3/3	3		

Another Company is to get ready to proceed at once AAA Send both Company Commanders to report to me here at once for instructions AAA Whole Battalion should get ready prepared to move anywhere AAA Send Morris here to assist me AAA Acknowledge AAA Is all Battalion now back?

Recd 6-15 am
(Int) N.E.T.

From OC STAY
Place
Time 6 3 am.

(Sd) C Riall Lt Col

The above may be forwarded as now corrected. (Z)

Censor. Signature of Addressor or person authorised to telegraph in his name.

* This line should be erased if not required.

750,000. W 2186-M509. H. W & V., Ld. 6/16.

"A" Form.

Army Form C.2121 (in pads of 100).

MESSAGES AND SIGNALS.

No. of Message ....

Prefix ...... Code ...... m.	Words	Charge	This message is on a/c of:	Recd. at ......m.
Office of Origin and Service Instructions.	Sent		9 ...... Service.	Date ......
	At ......m.			From ......
	To			
	By		(Signature of "Franking Officer.")	By ......

TO OC C Coy STAY

Sender's Number.	Day of Month.	In reply to Number.	AAA
* CR 4/3	3		

Your Company will proceed at once to "Spine 80" location B 23 central AAA Object to repel a possible counter attack from direction of OPPY AAA 4 Hotchkiss Guns are being sent to same place AAA

From

Place

Time

The above may be forwarded as now corrected. (Z) (Sd) C Riall Lt Col.

Censor. Signature of Addressor or person authorised to telegraph in his name.

* This line should be erased if not required.

750,000. W 2186-M509. H. W & V., Ld. 6/16.

"A" Form. Army Form C.2121 (in pads of 100).

MESSAGES AND SIGNALS.

No. of Message ....

Prefix ...... Code ...... m.	Words	Charge	This message is on a/c of:	Recd. at ...... m.
Office of Origin and Service Instructions. Copy		Sent At ...... m. To ...... By	...... Service. (Signature of "Franking Officer.")	Date ...... From ...... By ......

TO OC STAY

Sender's Number.	Day of Month.	In reply to Number.	AAA
* BM 80	3		

You will not now go to assistance of 16 W Yorks (Col CROYDON) but you will instead send 1 Company to assistance of 15 W Yorks on right & 1 Company to go to centre to be in support of 18 W Yorks and 18 D.L.I. — guides are being sent you AAA

From HULL
Place
Time 9.5 am

The above may be forwarded as now corrected. (Z)

Censor. Signature of Addressor or person authorised to telegraph in his name. (Sd) [illegible] Major

* This line should be erased if not required.

750,000. W 2186–M509. H. W & V., Ld. 6/16.

"A" Form.

MESSAGES AND SIGNALS.

Army Form C.2121 (in pads of 100).
No. of Message ....

Prefix .... Code .... m. Copy
Office of Origin and Service Instructions.
V. Urgent

Words | Charge

Sent
At .... m.
To ....
By ....

This message is on a/c of: (H) Service.
(Signature of "Franking Officer.")

Recd. at .... m.
Date ....
From ....
By ....

TO OC HOTCHKISS Coy

Sender's Number.	Day of Month.	In reply to Number.	AAA
* CR 573	3		

Under instructions from 93rd Inf Bde all your guns and personnel will report at once to my Battalion H.Q. about H1a91 and act under my orders AAA They should be prepared to move whenever ordered.

From O.C. STAY (12 York Lancs R)
Place Rear Bde HQ
Time 6-50am

The above may be forwarded as now corrected. (Z) (Sd) C Riall Capt
.... Censor. Signature of Addressor or person authorised to telegraph in his name.

* This line should be erased if not required.

750,000. W 2183–M509. H. W & V., Ld. 6/16.

"A" Form.

Army Form C.2121 (in pads of 100).

MESSAGES AND SIGNALS.

No. of Message

Prefix .... Code .... m. | Words | Charge | This message is on a/c of: .... Service. | Recd. at .... m.

Office of Origin and Service Instructions.

Sent At .... m. To .... By ....

(Signature of "Franking Officer.")

Date .... From .... By ....

TO OC 5TAY

Sender's Number.	Day of Month.	In reply to Number.	AAA
* FA 27	4		

Staff Captain HULL has received instructions from ROPE that 5TAY are to provide the following parties aaa (A) 1 Off 2 NCOs 16 men to take over Dump H 9 a 39 (POINT DU JOUR) Emergency Dump at H 4 c 26, and Dump at B 30 c 38 aaa (B) 1 Off 1 NCO 3 men to take over Dump at Cross Rds B 22 d 89 aaa Party A should report to ADV HULL HQ aaa Party B should go direct to Dump at cross roads mentioned above.

From
Place
Time

W Fenwick 2/Lt
for SC HULL

The above may be forwarded as now corrected. (Z)

Censor. Signature of Addressor or person authorised to telegraph in his name.

* This line should be erased if not required.

750,000. W 2183–M509. H. W. & V., Ld. 6/16.

Secret

Confidential

94/31

12 (S) Bn. York & Lancaster Rgt.

WAR DIARY.

Vol XVIII

From 1st June 1917
To 30 June 1917.

B.E.F. July 16/17.

Vol 16

Instructions regarding War Diaries and Intelligence Summaries are contained in F. S. Regs., Part II. and the Staff Manual respectively. Title pages will be prepared in manuscript.

WAR DIARY
or
~~INTELLIGENCE SUMMARY~~.
(Erase heading not required.)

Army Form C. 2118.

Place	Date 1917	Hour	Summary of Events and Information	Remarks and references to Appendices
A 28 a (Nᵉ ECURIE)	June 1		Major F.J.Courtenay Hood, 14th Bn,York & Lancaster Rgt,assumed command of the Battn,taking over from Major D.C.Allen.	
	"	10-0 pm	Battn supplied usual Working Party of 300 strong,plus Officers,for work on the GREEN LINE at B 27 a , a reserve line of defences on the GAVRELLE Sector. Work was for four continuous hours.	[initialled]
Do	June 2.	2-0 pm	Training under Coy Commanders,special attention being devoted to Platoon and Coy organisation and Musketry.	
		10.0 pm	Working parties,as usual. Approaching midnight hostile aircraft dropped bombs in the vicinity of the camp,but there were no casualties in the Battalion.	[initialled]
Do	June 3	10.0 pm	Working Parties,as aforementioned;also training. Hostile aircraft again active,but no material damage resulted.	
			2nd Lieut.E.L.Roberts joined Battn from Base for duty.	[initialled]
Do	June 4	10.0 pm	Working Party again provided,also afternoon training. Aerial activity by enemy in Back Areas. Working Party had 3 casualties.	[initialled]
Do	June 5	5-0 pm	No Working Party provided,this being a rest day and set apart for 94th Infantry Brigade Sports. The Sports were held at 5-0 p.m.,in splendid weather,and were very successful. There were competitors from all ~~xxxxxxxx~~ Divisions of the Corps. Location: G 5 a 17. The Battn were third in the aggregate honours with 16 points. Major F.J.Courtenay Hood assumed acting rank of Lieut-Colonel.(Auth: 31st Division 1081/58A,dated 3.6.17)	[initialled]
Do	June 6 " 7 " 8 " 9	—	Working Party as usual;nothing of note happened.	[initialled]
Do	" 10	3-0 pm	Battn moved off to relieve HOOD Battn,63rd(R N) Division,at B 25 a, in Brigade reserve. Operation Orders (marked A) attached.	
B 25 A	" 11-to 13		Battn occupied chiefly in carrying to the front line.	
	" 12		2nd Lieuts G.C.Buzzacott and HL. Judd joined Battn. for duty.	[initialled]

A5834 Wt. W4973/M687 750,000 8/16 D. D. & L. Ltd. Forms/C.2118/13.

Instructions regarding War Diaries and Intelligence Summaries are contained in F. S. Regs., Part II. and the Staff Manual respectively. Title pages will be prepared in manuscript.

Army Form C. 2118.

WAR DIARY
or
~~INTELLIGENCE~~ SUMMARY.
(Erase heading not required.)

Place	Date 1917	Hour	Summary of Events and Information	Remarks and references to Appendices
B 25 a	June 13		Battn occupied chiefly in carrying to the front line .	8c
Front Line GAVRELLE.	June 14		Battn took over FrontLine in GAVRELLE Sector, from 14th Bn, York & Lancaster R. Operation Orders (marked B) attached.	
	"		From this date to 19th, nothing outstanding occurred. Casualties : 2nd Lieut. J. Buckland. Killed. (16/6/17) " " A.R. Turner. Wounded. (19/6/17) OTHER RANKS 4 Killed; 14 wounded.	8c
ROCLINCOURT	June 19/20	12 Midnight	Battn moved to WAKEFIELD CAMP, Nr ROCLINCOURT (A 28 c Central). Billeted in Nissen huts. The Relieving Battn was the 10th Bn, East Yorks. Regt. Operation Orders (marked C) attached.	
do	June 20		R.S.M. Chas. Polden. M.C., appointed to rank of hon. Lieut & QM. Re-organisation and refitting.	8c
do	June 21	Afternoon	Battn practised attack on model trenches at BRUNEHAUT FARM, Nr MAROEUIL. Model trench of CADORNA, portion of enemy front line systemwas the objective.	8c
do	" 22	Morning	Ditto.	
do	" 23 24	" "	The attack was again practised in conjunction with the other Units of 94th Infantry Brigade.	8c
do	" 25		Rest day. Company Commanders' parades.	
do	" 26	12.30pm	Major -General R. Wanless O'Gowan, C.B., G.O.C. 31st Division addressed the Battalion and explained the objects of the attack.	8c
		9.35pm	Battn moved off to that part of the front allotted to it for the attack, and took up positions in accordance with Operation Orders No. 62(marked D) attached.	
	27	11.15pm	Battn took up position in accordance with Operation Orders No 63(marked E) attached. Heavily shelled between 5 and 6 p.m. "C" Company had 3 o r killed and 10 wounded.	8c

A5834 Wt. W4973/M687 750,000 8/16 D. D. & L. Ltd. Forms/C.2118/13.

Army Form C. 2118.

Instructions regarding War Diaries and Intelligence Summaries are contained in F. S. Regs., Part II. and the Staff Manual respectively. Title pages will be prepared in manuscript.

WAR DIARY
or
~~INTELLIGENCE~~ SUMMARY.

(Erase heading not required.)

Place	Date	Hour	Summary of Events and Information	Remarks and references to Appendices
Front Line.	June 28	5 pm	Between 5 and 6 pm, the enemy again heavily shelled our front line, supports and communications. By 6-15 pm. all Companies had reported ready in assembly trenches for the attack.	
do	do	7.10 pm	The attack started at Zero -7-10 pm - following a perfect barrage and each Company gained its objective without a casualty. The Battns on our right and left flanks, viz 14th Bn, York & Lancaster Regiment and 11th Bn, East Lancs. Regt., also reached their objectives and consolidation was proceeded with at once. The enemy retaliation shelling commenced at 7-17 p.m. but was comparatively slight except at intervals when the supports and communications were heavily shelled. Further information is given in Commanding Officer's (Lt-Col F. J. Courtenay-Hood) report (marked G) attached.	
CADORNA (now Front Line)	June 29		The day was quiet and situation normal. Consolidation was proceeded with during the night. ~~xxxxxxxxxxxxxxxxxxxxxxxxxxxxxxxxxxxxxx~~ "C" Coy front ~~was~~ taken over by "A" and "D" Coys, and "C" Coy took up position in reserve ~~support~~ in FOXEY ALLEY.	
	June 30/July 1		Battn relieved by 14th York & Lancaster Regiment and 11th Bn, East Lancs. Rgt. and took up position in support in the RED LINE in accordance with Operation Orders (marked I) attached.	
			At 7-0 pm. instructions were received frm 94th Infty Brigade for two Coys to Stand to at once and at 8-30 pm. "B" & "C" Coys were ordered to reinforce the 14th Bn, York & Lancaster Regt, in the front area. The remaining two Coys were relieved by the 13th Bn, East Yorks. and arrived at WAKEFIELD CAMP at about 1-30 a.m. "B" & "C" Coys were subsequently relieved by the 13th Bn East Yorks. Regt. and arrived back at camp about 5-30 am on the 2nd. During the whole of the operation there were no Officer casualties, but o.r. as follows:- 9 Killed; Wounded 35.	

Courtenay Hood
Lieut. Colonel Comdg
12th (S) Bn. York & Lancs. Rgt. (Sheffield.)

A5834 Wt. W4973/M687 750,000 8/16 D. D. & L. Ltd. Forms/C.2118/13.

WD – A

O P E R A T I O N   O R D E R S NO. 58   Copy No.....

Ref. Map)
51 B.N.W.)

1. The 94th. Infantry Brigade will relieve the 189th. Infantry Brigade in the line on the night of 10th./11th June.
2. The dispositions of the Battalions after relief will be as follows:-
   (a) 11th. East Lancs Regt, with 1 Coy 13th. Y & L in Left Sub-Section of the line.
   (b) 14th. Y & L in the Right Sub-Section of the line with 1 Coy 13th. Y & L at Hill 80.
   (c) 2 Coys 13th. Y & L in Railway Cutting.
   (d) 12th. Y & L in B.25.a.

3. This Battalion will relieve the HOOD Battn in B.25.a.
4. The Battalion will move to the new area in the following order:- "A", "B", "C", "D", and H.Q. Details.
5. 300 yards distance will be maintained between Platoons on the march. The 1st. platoon will move off at 4 p.m. Officer Commanding "A" Coy will furnish guide to accompany the 1st. platoon. All the following platoons will keep in touch by connecting files.
6. Dress. Fighting Order - Steel helmets to be worn.
7. Cookers of "A", "C", and "D" Companies will move independantly under the Sergt. Cook to H.1. central, leaving this Camp at 3.p.m. and take over the positions now occupied by the Field Cookers of the HOOD Battalion.
8. The Camp must be left scrupulously clean and all N.C.O's and men will be clear of tents and shelters by 3.p.m.

   The Orderly Officer and Medical Officer will inspect the Camp commencing at 3.15.p.m. O.C. Coys will each detail 1 Officer to be in the Company Lines ready to go round on this inspection.
9. Packs and Valises of Officers will be dumped near the road behind Battn H.Qrs by 10.a.m. Field Service Caps will be dumped with packs. Officers may take their packs with them.
   Coy, Mess and Medical Stores will be dumped at 2.30.p.m.
10. Lewis Gun limbers will report on the ground behind the Cookers at 2.30.p.m. and will be loaded up under Coy arrangements. Nothing is to go on these limbers except Lewis Guns, panniers, and Lewis Gun equipment.
11. 2nd. Lt. Wood with the 4 C-Q-M-Ss and one N.C.O. to represent H.Qrs will leave Camp at 1.p.m., proceeding to the new area to take over and act as guides for the Companies and H.Qrs.
12. Officers Commanding Coys will report by runner to Orderly Room when the whole of their Company has arrived in the area.
13. ACKNOWLEDGE.

Issued at ...9.15...p.m.
Copies to
No.1.....C.O.
2.....2nd. in C.
3.....Adjutant.
4.....File.
5....."A" Company.
6....."B" "
7....."C" "
8....."D" "
9.....S.O.
10.....T.O.
11.....Q.M.
12.....M.O.
13.....R-S-M.

[signature]
Captain & Adjutant,
STAY.

Amendments to Operation Order
No 58

10.6.17.

1 Para 8, second line.

For "2-0 pm" read "2-15 pm"

2. Para 8, fourth line.

For "2-15 pm" read "2-30 pm"

[signature] Captain.
Adjutant,
12th (S) Bn. York & Lancaster Regt.

STH.Y. Operation Orders No 59

Copy No ___

Ref Map 51 [illegible]
& RAILWAY COPSE }

B

14. 6. 17

1. The following reliefs will take place on the Brigade front to-night (14/15th inst)
Left Subsector 13th Yorks will relieve 11th E Lancs
Right Subsector 12th Yorks " " 14th Yorks

O.C. 11th E Lancs Regt will leave one Coy at [illegible] to under orders of O.C. 12th Yorks Regt.

2. The Battalion front will be held as follows:
HINDSALL "B" 12th Yorks relieving [illegible] Coy [illegible]
RAILWAY S. "A" " " [illegible]
" N. "D" " " [illegible]
in RESERVE "C" " " [illegible]

3. The relief will be carried out by the above order.

4. Coys will move off from [illegible] in order "B", "A", "D" and "C" [illegible] and will proceed by platoons at [illegible] to the bridge over the [illegible] B27 a 0.[illegible] [illegible] platoon [illegible] the [illegible] at [illegible]

5. The RSM and CSM's will proceed to the trenches this afternoon to take over trench stores, leaving here at 4 pm.

6. An Officer or reliable NCO per platoon will reconnoitre the route to the RAILWAY BRIDGE by daylight.

7. Rations will be issued to the men before starting for the trenches & all water bottles must be filled.

Coys will draw 15 tins of water from the Water Cpl at B29 b 92 on their way in to the trenches.

8. All surplus kit, mess stores, etc, will be dumped near the road at the end of the trench, by 8.30 pm.

OC "C" Coy will leave a NCO in charge until removed by the Transport.

9. Completion of relief will be reported by Code or runner to Battn HQ.

10. Trench Store lists will be sent in as soon as possible after relief.

11. ACKNOWLEDGE

(Sgd) R. Lambridge Captain Adjutant 6 HLI

Copies to

No		No	
1	Adjutant HLI	7	TO
2	A Coy	8	MO
3	B "	9	QM
4	C "	10	IO
5	D	11	RSM
6	SO	12	File

Copy . . STAY operation orders No 61 Copy No. . .

Ref Map RAILWAY COPSE & 51b NW } C 18.6.17

1. The 10 E. Yorks Rgt will relieve the Battn in the line tomorrow night (19/20th) June

2. Coys will be relieved as below and in the order given

10th E. Yorks Rgt		12th Y & L
D Coy	relieves	B Coy
C "	"	A "
A "	"	D "
B "	"	C "

3 Guides on the scale of 2 per Coy will be detailed by Companies and 2 per Battn HQ to meet relieving troops at the BRIDGE over RAILWAY at B27a O4 at 10pm

4 The guides for Company relieving B will lead the incoming troops via FOXY & for Coy relieving A, via RAILWAY SUPPORT and SLEEPER. A & B Coys will use these trenches for filing out respectively.

5 .. The battalion on relief will move back to NISSEN hut Camp at A28 c Central, taking over from 12 E. Yorks Rgt.

6 LG limbers and maltese Cart will await arrival of Coys at the RAILWAY BRIDGE B27a04

7 Movement E of ROCLINCOURT will be by platoons & no straggling must be permitted.

8 All SAA, Grenades, trench Stores & petrol tins will be handed over to representatives of relieving Coys, who will come up in advance by daylight.

Trench Stores lists will be sent into Orderly Room as soon as handing over is completed.

9 OC Coys will personally report completion of relief on their way out.

10 Prior to relief by 10 EYR the 18th DLI will take over that portion of the front line held by B Coy from C19c7024 to C19c6022

Relief will commence at 9pm and details will be arranged direct between Coy Commanders concerned. Completion of relief will be reported separately by runner or BAB Code

11 ACKNOWLEDGE

Issued at 6.45/pm

Copy No 1 Adjutant
2 A Coy
3 B "
4 C "
5 D "
6 IO
7 TO
8 MO

(Sd) W Trimbridge Captain
Adjutant
STAY

ADDENDUM to Battn Operation Order No 61

Ref para 3 of Operation Order No 61 C Coy will detail a NCO to take charge of party of guides and take them to the [illegible]

The guides should report to this NCO at Battn HQ at 8pm prompt

18/6/17 (Sd) W Trimbridge Captain
Adjutant
STAY

12th. S. BATTALION YORK & LANCASTER REGIMENT Copy No.....15

OPERATION ORDERS NO.63.

Ref. Map. 51.B. N.W.
and Trench Map.

25.6.17

1. The Battalion will take over that portion of the Front allotted to it for offensive purposes as per "Preliminary Instructions, etc" to-morrow night 26/27th June from Battalionsof 92nd Bde at present holding the line.

2. The Battalion front is held as follows:-
   (i) RAILWAY TRENCH from BROUGH ALLEY to its junction with track at B.24.d.68.92. by "C" Company, 11th EAST YORKS.R.

   (ii) RAILWAY TRENCH from B.24.d.68.72 to BLUE TRENCH by "C" Company 12th EAST YORKS.R.

   (iii) FAMINE and FLURRY by two platoons "D" Company, 11th EAST YORKS.R.

3. RAILWAY TRENCH from BROUGH ALLEY to BLUE TRENCH will be taken over by (No.1) Composite Company of this Battalion consisting of one platoon each from "A", "C" and "D" Companies, under the command of Captain SIMPSON, each platoon tak.ing over the Battle Front of its Company.

4. FAMINE and FLURRY TRENCHES will be taken over by Composite Company(No.2) consisting of two platoons "A" Coy and two platoons "C" Coy, under the command of Captain LEAMON.

5. "B" Company and "D" Company (less one platoon) will be accommodated in the RED LINE in B.28.b. for tomorrow night, occupying the trenches as allotted today to representatives by 2nd.Lt.ROBERTS.

6. Companies will leave Camp in the order Composite Company No.1; Composite Company No.2; "B" Company; "D" Company (less one platoon); Headquarter details, commencing at 9.55.p.m.

Companies will maintain a distance of 200 yds between platoons on the march. The leading platoon of No.1. Composite Company will pass the RAILWAY BRIDGE at B.27.a.0.3. at 11.10.p.m.

<u>ROUTE</u>. ROCLINCOURT - Road Junction G.6.d.0.2. - RAILWAY Crossing B.26.c.0.0. - along Railway embankment to B.27.a.0.3. - marked track to SUNKEN ROAD B.30.a.5.9.

7. One Lewis Gun Limber per Company will report to O.C. Companies at the Camp by 3.p.m. by which hour all Lewis Guns and equipment and full number of pans will be ready for loading. These limbers will also carry 17 tins of water per Company and will proceed to ration Dump near aeroplane in B.29.b. (No.1 and 2 Composite Coys) and to B.28.d.6.4. for "B" and "D" (less one platoon) at ~~10.30~~ 11.40 p.m. and 12.p.m. respectively.

O.C.Companies will arrange to pick up Lewis Guns and water at these points

8. The Transport Officer will arrange to send up 104 tins of water to be at ration dump B.29.b. at 12 midnight. O.C."B" Company will send a carrying party to carry forward these tins to the Battalion dump in FOGGY, after having taken over trenches in RED LINE.

9. Battalion H.Qrs will be at B.30.a.5.5. until completion of relief and reports should be sent to this place until relief is completed when Battn H.Qrs will move to Battle H.Qrs at B.24.d.15.25.

10. An N.C.O. from "A", "C" and H.Qrs will proceed to the trenches to take over trench stores, reporting to Company H.Qrs and Battn H.Qrs respectively at 6.p.m.

11. Packs, including all F.S.D.Caps , will be dumped near Guard Room by Companies by 12 noon. Officers. Valises and Medical Stores 6.p.m, Mess Stores and Orderly Room 9.p.m.
Transport Officer will arrange removal.

12. Watches will be synchronised at 9.p.m. at Orderly Room.

13. Trench stores lists will be forwarded in duplicate as early as possible after relief.

14. ACKNOWLEDGE.

N.W. [signature] Captain & Adjutant.
12th.S.Battn York and Lancaster Regt.

COPIES TO :-

No.1. C.O.
2. Sec.in Command.
3. Adjutant.
4. O.C."A" Coy.
5. O.C."B" "
6. O.C."C" "
7. O.C."D" "
8. Signl.Officer.
9. Intelligence Offr.
10. L.G.Officer.
11. Medical Officer.
12. Q.M.
13. Transport Officer.
14. R-S-M.
15 &
16 War diary.
17 &
18 File.

War Diary

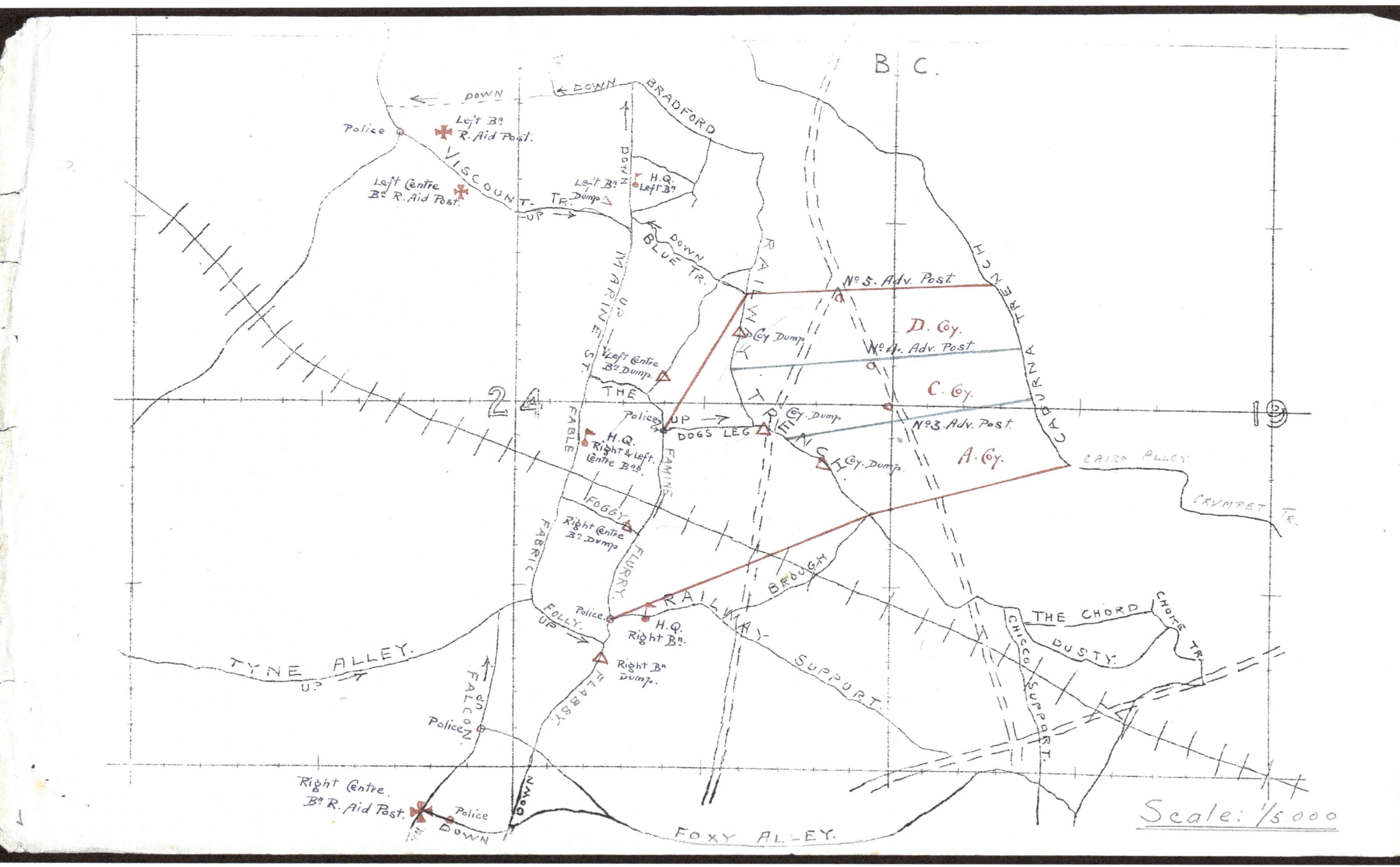
B C.
BRADFORD
DOWN
Police
Left Bn R. Aid Post.
Left Centre Bn R. Aid Post.
VISCOUNT TR.
UP
H.Q. Left Bn
Left Bn Dump
BLUE TR.
MARINE ST.
Left Centre Bn Dump.
THE
24
19
Police
DOGS LEG
H.Q. Right & Left Centre Bns.
FABLE
FAMINE
FOGGY
Right Centre Bn Dump
FABRIC
FLURRY.
FOLLY.
Police.
H.Q. Right Bn.
Right Bn Dump.
FLABBY.
TYNE ALLEY.
FALCON.
Police
Right Centre Bn R. Aid Post.
DOWN
FOXY ALLEY.
RAILWAY TRENCH
Coy Dump
No 5. Adv. Post
D. Coy.
No 4. Adv. Post
C. Coy.
No 3. Adv. Post
A. Coy.
CAPORNA TRENCH
CAIRO ALLEY
CRUMPET TR.
BROUGH
RAILWAY SUPPORT.
THE CHORD
DUSTY.
CHOKE TR.
CHICCO SUPPORT.
Scale: 1/5,000

Operation Orders No 63. Copy

Ref. Map. 57 B.N.W. & Trench Maps } E 27/6/17.

I. The Battalion will move into the areas allotted for assembly as laid down in "Preliminary Instructions etc," tonight 27/28th June.

2 Movement of Coys into Assembly Areas will be carried out as follows:—

(a) B Coy will move into FAMINE & FLURRY from B 28 b by marked track to SUNKEN Rd timing the march of its leading platoon to arrive at junction of track & SUNKEN ROAD B 30 a 59 at 11-15 pm. They will carry in water as already arranged and deposit at Batt Dump & then commence work on FAMINE & FLURRY or carrying under orders from Major Allen.

(b) The 2 platoons of "A" Coy & 2 platoons of "C" Coy at present under Capt LEAMON will commence work on FAMINE & FLURRY at dusk & work until arrival of "B" Coy, when they will hand over work to "B" Coy,

2

to move forward with RAILWAY TR. after drawing tools for Assault & any other stores not already taken up from Bath Dump.

(c) D Coy (2 pl) will follow B Coy from B28 b & move into RAILWAY TR via FOLLY & RAILWAY SUPPORT.

3 Details of moves referred to in para 2(b) will be arranged between O.C. Coys concerned.

4. ~~Plant~~ Rations referred to in Appendix E will be at the aeroplane dump about 10-30 pm & all Coys will arrange to send carrying parties to meet the Transport. All water required for Z day & Z+1 day will be drawn from Bath Dump. A special party has been arranged for carrying water coming up on the transport tonight.

5 O/C "D" Coy will arrange to draw 75 trench ladders from Bde Dump and carry them up to RAILWAY TR. & give 25 to each Coy except "B".

2

6 All ranks will be fully dressed for going over, and in their assembly positions by 4-30 pm.

7 A report will be sent by runner by each Coy as soon as the Coy is ready for the assault.

8 ACKNOWLEDGE.

9 ~~All subaltern Officers of A, C & D Coys will make a final reconnaissance of ground over which they will assault, paying particular attention to direction tonight.~~

Issued at — pm.

Copy No 1 O/c A Coy. (Sd) N. L. TUNBRIDGE.
Capt & Adjt
5 TAY

2 " B "
3 " C "
4 " D "
5 Tpt
6 T.O
7 S.O
8 M.O

9

12TH. S. BATTALION YORK AND LANCASTER REGIMENT.

PART TAKEN BY THIS BATTALION IN THE OFFENSIVE OPERATIONS OF 28TH. JUNE 1917.

POSITION IN ASSAULT.

This Battalion was the Right Centre Assaulting Battalion of the 94th. Infantry Brigade Front.

ALLOTMENT OF FRONTAGE.

The Frontage allotted to this Battalion was RAILWAY TRENCH from BROUGH ALLEY to BLUE ALLEY, B.24.b.6.3 ; FLABBY and MARINE TRENCHES from B.24.d.25.42 to B.24.d.38.93.

Battalion H.Q. at B.24.d.15.85.

ALLOTMENT OF OBJECTIVES.

The Objective of this Battalion was CADORNA TRENCH from trench junction with CAIRO ALLEY, C.19.c.4.9. to C.19.a.25.35.

The Brigade instructions were to assault with 3 Companies, keeping 1 Company in Reserve.
"A", "C" and "D" Companies were given the task of carrying out the assault, with "B" Company in Reserve.
The Objective allotted to each Company was as follows:-

"A" Coy.	(Right Coy.)	C.19.c.48.85 -	C.19.a.36.00.
"C" "	(Centre ")	C.19.a.36.00 -	C.19.a.33.17.
"D" "	(Left ")	C.19.a.33.17 -	C.19.a.25.35.

(New para) S.A.A., R.E.Stores etc.

Battalion Dump had been formed at the East end of FOGGY TRENCH during the previous tour in the trenches, and this consisted of three divisions :

One for S.A.A.
One for R.E. material, and
One for Water.

The work of filling these dumps from the Brigade Dump, was carried out by the Reserve Company and was completed by Y/Z night.

UNITS ON FLANKS.

14TH. YORK & LANC REGT were operating on the Right Flank and the 11TH. EAST LANC REGT on the Left.

POSITIONS BEFORE ASSEMBLY.

On the night of 26th./27th. June the Battalion moved from camp near LENS - ARRAS ROAD to positions in and adjacent to assembly trenches, and took over the defence of that portion of the line allotted to it for Offensive Operations.
RAILWAY TRENCH was occupied by a composite company made up of one platoon of each of the assaulting Companies and these platoons occupied that portion of RAILWAY TRENCH allotted to Companies for assembly. their

POSITIONS BEFORE ASSEMBLY. (continued).

This system was adopted as giving the best facilities for Company reconnaissance of Company Offensive Fronts. The Composite Company consisting of remaining two platoons of "C" and "A" Companies occupied FAMINE and FLURRY TRENCHES, remaining two platoons of "D" and "B" Companies occupied trenches in the neighbourhood of the RED LINE.

"Y" Day. (27th. June.)

Enemy Artilhery fairly active during the day on MARINE and FAMINE TRENCHES, also on Eastern end of TYNE ALLEY.

The Composite Company (2 platoons "C" and 2 platoons "A") suffered 11 casualties during this shelling. (3 Killed and 8 Wounded.)

ASSEMBLY.

On the night of the 27th./28th. June, all Companies moved up into their assembly positions. "A", "C" and "D" Companies in RAILWAY TRENCH and "B" Company in FAMINE.

"A" Company, 13TH. EAST YORKS REGT. reported for duty as carrying party. They were accommodated in FOGGY TRENCH. All Companies were in position by 3.a.m.

"Z" Day.

During "Z" Day the men remained in their positions, resting, and made as little movement as possible so as to escape observation from aeroplanes or balloons.

Four enemy observation balloons were up during the afternoon on the Left of this Brigade Front, and in positions from which they could observe any movement in the greater portion of RAILWAY TRENCH.

Hostile Artillery was fairly quiet during the day except between 5.p.m. and 6.p.m., when a great deal of attention was paid both to MARINE and FAMINE TRENCHES and the neighbourhood of the Battalion Dump, causing casualties to carrying company and men working at the Dump.

For the hour immediately proceeding the attack, hostile artillery was comparitively quiet. At 6.15.p.m. a report was received from each Company Commander that all men were dressed and equipped ready for the attack.

THE ATTACK.

Zero had been fixed for 7.10.p.m. and 10 minutes before this time, ladders which had previously been taken up to RAILWAY TRENCH, were placed in position. Bayonets were quietly fixed five minutes before Zero, and punctually at Zero the Artillery Barrage opened and immediately the first line of the first wave started over the top and proceeded forward at a steady pace.

They were followed at a distance of 20 yards by the second line, 50 yards behind which the second wave went over.

At the same time "B" Company emerged from FAMINE TRENCH and proceeded over the top to take up position in RAILWAY TRENCH as previously arranged.

THE ATTACK (continued).

All lines went forward at a steady pace, keeping excellent distances and intervals. There was a slight pause on the SUNKEN ROAD to get each line into rough alignment and the waves then moved steadily forward, the pace being so well regulated that there was only a very momentary pause for the barrage to lift off CADORNA TRENCH.

All three assaulting Companies reached their objectives without any casualties at all, and fifteen minutes after Zero the first runner had reached Battalion Headquarters from CADORNA, bringing back a report card with the information that Objective had been gained.

This runner was closely followed by runners from the other two Companies and from that time detailed information began to arrive at Battalion Headquarters very rapidly.

28 prisoners reported as captured, and sent back.

It was intended that these should be sent to Battalion Headquarters and thence to Brigade Headquarters, but parties were diverted by Military Police to communicators leading direct to cages.

Brief message that Objective had been gained was got through to Brigade by telephone before the wire was broken. Fuller details were forwarded by runner through forward Brigade Centre, and pigeons were despatched with messages for Brigade Headquarters with the first detailed information that came through.

Extremely useful reports were received from the Battalion Observers posted at the Battalion O.P., from which position they were able to see the whole advance on the Battalion Front.

All assaulting troops describe our artillery barrage as excellent. There was no hostile artillery reply until men had been in CADORNA for some minutes and there was practically no hostile machine gun fire on this particular sector.

CARRYING.

Forward dumps had been constructed at RAILWAY TR. for each assaulting company, and well stocked from Battalion dump before "Z" Day. One Officer and 20 other ranks of the carrying company were detailed to report to O.C.each assaulting company and these parties were in position at the company forward dump before Zero.

The first carrying party proceeded to the Objective immediately behind the second wave, their first load being mainly barbed wire and wiring material. The loads for the second and subsequent journeys had been arranged beforehand and all S.A.A. and material prepared in "one man" loads and under these arrangements the carrying was quite successfully done and the new company dumps formed in CADORNA quickly stocked with S.A.A. and material.

AFTER THE ATTACK.

1. DISPOSITIONS. The immediate dispositions after the attack, were - This Battalion was holding all the Objective allotted to it and in addition about 60 yards of CAIRO ALLEY.

At 1.a.m. the 14TH. YORK & LANCS took over part of the portion of CAIRO ALLEY held by us, including two posts which this Battalion had constructed.

AFTER THE ATTACK. (continued).

At 2.a.m. the Centre Company, "C" Company, was withdrawn from CADORNA and remaining Companies side-slipped to the Centre, taking over the ground vacated by "C" Company.

2. PROTECTION. Each Company had two Lewis Gun Posts pushed well forward, 50 to 60 yards in front of CADORNA, and held the trench itself with five posts per Company and a Strong Point at the junction of CADORNA and CAIRO ALLEY.

3. CONSOLIDATION. On arriving in CADORNA TRENCH it was found to be badly knocked about and averaging two to three feet in depth with two sections of a few yards each four to five feet deep.

Immediately Lewis Gun Posts had been put out and sentries posted , the work of consolidation was commenced.

It had been previously arranged that a Strong Point should be constructed at the ~~CABOR~~ junction of CADORNA and CAIRO ALLEY if the position was found suitable. It was found that this position gave an excellent field of fire and command, and the construction of the Strong Point was immediately proceeded with.

For the purpose of consolidation, each platoon was given a definite sector and each section a particular task.

The work was carried out in order of importance as follows :-

(a) Strong Point and Posts in CADORNA.

(b) Lewis Gun Posts in front, (work on these being carried out by section posted to them), after posts sufficiently constructed men above 1 NCO & 2 men were withdrawn.

(c) The main communicator from CADORNA to the more central of these posts.

(d) Deepening CADORNA between posts.

(e) Deepening communicator from main advanced posts communicator to other advanced posts on flanks.

(f) Constructing Machine Gun Emplacement in Strong Point and improving Lewis Gun positions in posts.

Before dawn on the day after the attack, the whole trench was in a sound defensive condition and through communication, with cover from view, was estab -lished to all points.

Immediately it was dark wiring was commenced, one section doing wiring on each Company Front.

The concertina barbed wire which had been carried over was put out and in addition a great deal of German wire was used, this German wire being transferred from the West to the East side of the trench.

By this means substantial wire entangle -ments were put up round posts each night.

OBSERVATIONS.

Battalion Headquarters. The arrangement by which two Battalion Headquarters were compelled to share one small dug-out, was very unsatisfactory and made the work of controlling operations and getting off the necessary reports, extremely difficult.

In addition to the normal Battalion H.Qrs, each Battalion had an Artillery Liaison Officer and an Infantry Liaison Officer with necessary signal terminals, orderlies and runners, and the resulting conditions were such as to be almost impossible to work under.

Signal Services. The Telephone Service did not hold out as well as had been hoped, and one of the reasons of this was that the three cables laid between Battalion and Brigade H.Qrs were all put along trench and consequently only required one shell to sever all three.

It is unfortunate that ~~that~~ the runner services from the Forward Brigade to Brigade H.Qrs was not more regularly carried out.

Battalion runners took communications repeatedly and without hesitation from Battalion H.Qrs to Forward Brigade Centre through that part of the trenches which suffered most from hostile shell-fire, namely MARINE TRENCH, and with Battalion runners unhesitatingly taking these ~~messages~~ risks, it is unfortunate that reports were held up at Brigade Forward Centre.

Dump Filling. It is suggested that for similar operations in the future, Battalions should be allowed to fill their dumps from supplies in the back area instead of having to fill from Brigade Dump, which in this case, necessitated considerable duplication of journeys.

If the Battalion/dump could have been filled from the back area in this case, the Battalion Transport could have been made much use of, and a lot of carrying considerably lightened and expedited.

Disposal of Prisoners. Any arrangements made by the A.P.M. for the disposal of prisoners, the selection of routes allotted to them and instructions given to Military Police in the Battle Area, should be communicated to Battalion Commanders so that they do not make arrangements for the disposal of prisoners which will clash with other arrangements and lead to confusion.

Contact Aeroplanes. The flares issued for communication with contact aeroplanes, were found to be quickly rendered useless by damp. The rain which came on while the men were in CADORNA put quite a lot of these flares out of action.

It is difficult for the men to keep them dry, without some special arrangement, and it is suggested that a small waterproof cover to be opened in a similar way to a shell dressing or in a similar manner to which the present cap of a flare is removed, might be of advantage.

Artillery. The 18 pr Barrage was in every way excellent. The firing of the Heavies, particularly the 6" was most erratic, and appeared to be very difficult to control.

Far too much talking in clear was carried on, on the telephone between liaison Officers and Batteries

Artillery (continued).

and on several occasions liaison Officers had to be checked for making statements on the 'phone which overheard by the enemy could not fail to acquaint them with what was going on and that an attack was impending.

It seems essential that some sort of code should be adopted between liaison Officers and the Batteries of Artillery Brigades to which they talk.

Copy

Operation Orders No 64.

30/6/17

Copy No

I

1 The Battn will be relieved in the line to night & proceed to EAST BAILLEUL Post & REDLINE in B28b.

2 The 14 Bn Y+L will take over that portion of the line now held by A Coy south of new communicator between RAILWAY TRENCH & CADORNA

3 11th East Lancs will take over portion of line held by A & D Coys, north of above communicator.

4 Relief will commence at midnight.

5 Front line Coys will move out in the following order A Coy, D Coy.

6 Support & Reserve Coys will move out on receipt of instructions to move from Battn HQ & will not leave their present trenches until these instructions are received by them

7 One guide from each platoon Coy HQ & two from Bn HQ details will report to 2nd Lt TONGE at Bn HQ at 5pm to proceed to new area. They will afterwards report to their Coys & act as platoon guides on relief. In addition there will be

one guide per Coy & one from Bn HQ to conduct ration carrying party to Coy & Bn HQ sector in new area.
These ration party guides will report to OC C Coy by 9pm

8 Front line Coys will report relief complete by runners to Bn HQ as early as possible. Support Coys will acknowledge by runner the order sent to them to move out.

9. The Battalion on arriving in new area will be in Brigade Support.

10. A sketch shewing dispositions of Coys will be forwarded to Battn HQ by 10 am tomorrow morning.

11 Rations & water will be brought to dumping place used by B & D Coys on X Y night. OC "C" Coy will furnish a party of 30 men under an Officer to carry rations from dump to Coy sectors. These parties will be guided by guides detailed under para 7. Carrying party will be at new ration dump at 11pm.

Add para 7. The ration guides will also report to 2nd Lt TONGE at Battn HQ at 5pm

(Sd) G Crawford 2nd Lt
Asst Adjutant
5 TAY

Copy ETAY Operation Orders No 65
Copy No...

1-7-17

1. 94 Inf Bde less Machine Gun Coy will be relieved in the line by 92nd Inf Bde 1/2nd July.
2. 13 East Yorks R will relieve 12 Y&L in RED LINE.
3. On Completion of relief, 12 Y&L will move back to WAKEFIELD CAMP.
4. Order of Coming in of 13th EYR:-
D, C, B, A, HQ.
The incoming Coys will take over the same dugouts now occupied by same Coys of this Battn.
5. Coys will detail one guide per platoon and one for Battn HQ to report to 2nd Lt TONGE at 10.30 pm at No 16 dug out (B Coy 13EYR, 2 platoons only, other Coys 3 platoons).
6. Lewis Gun limbers will be at ration dump REDLINE at 11 oclock tonight Coys will arrange to have their Lewis + panniers dumped there by this hour. One man per team will be left to load guns + accompany limbers back to camp. A Coy will detail a NCO

to be in charge of this party.

7 Coy Commanders' horses & those of CO 2nd in C. & MO will be at the Bosch Cemetery at 11·30 pm

8 Platoons will march at 300 yds interval in order of relief

9 OC Coys will arrange for 1 guide from each platoon to reconnoitre the route from these dugouts to white post track which will be the route back to Camp.

10 D Coy will move off at 10·45. C Coy will stand to in trench in front of dug out & will commence to move off as soon as the head of D Coy 13 EYR arrives at dug out.

11 A & B Coys will each stand to in trench at 11 pm & will file out as soon as first platoon of Coys of incoming unit arrives

12 Hot tea will be provided for the men when they arrive in Camp.

Copies to

1 A Coy
2 B "
3 C
4 D
5 2nd in Comd
6 IO
7 MO
8 File

(Sd) J Crawford
2nd Lt
Asst Adjutant
STAY.

SECRET.

COPY NO.....14

12TH (S) BATTALION, YORK AND LANCASTER REGIMENT.

PRELIMINARY INSTRUCTIONS
FOR ATTACK ON GERMAN TRENCHES FROM
TRENCH JUNCTION C.19.c.4.9. (exclusive)
TO BEND C.19.a.25.35.

Ref. Map. Sheet 51.B.N.W.
1/20,000 and Special
Map attached.

22.6.17.

SECTION 1.

1. 94th Infantry Brigade will attack the German Trenches on the front from WINDMILL to B.18.d.3.0. in conjunction with the 5th Division, to the North.

2. Troops detailed for the attack will be distributed as follows:
   (a) Right Assaulting Battn.............14th Bn. York & Lanc.R.
   Right Centre Assaulting Battn....12th Bn. York & Lanc.R.
   Left " " " ...11th Bn. East Lanc.R.
   Left Assaulting Battn.............13th Bn. York & Lanc.R.

   One Battn in Brigade Reserve
   (attached from 92nd Inf. Bde)...10th Bn. East Yorks.R.

   Battn for carrying duties
   (attached from 92nd Inf. Bde)...13th Bn. East Yorks.R.
   One Company attached to each Battn.

   Troops for holding the line......2 Coys 11th. Bn. E. Yorks.R.

   (b) Two Vickers Guns from 94th Machine Gun Company and one Trench Mortar from 94th Trench Mortar Battery are allotted to this Battalion.

3. Distribution of the Battalion on X/Y night will be:

   One Company: RAILWAY TRENCH.
   One Company: FLURRY & FAMINE TRENCHES.
   Two Companies: TRENCHES in B.28.b. and B.29.a.
   Battn. H.Qs: B.24.d.15.85 (Shared with 11th Bn. East Lanc.R.)

4. Allotment of Frontages.

   (1). For assembly
   RIGHT CENTRE BATTN: RAILWAY TRENCH from Junction with BROUGH ALLEY B.24.d.92.70 to trench Junction B.24.b.61.30 - FLURRY and FAMINE TRENCHES from B.24.d.25.40 to B.24.d.38.93.
   FOGGY and MARINE: B.24.d.15.75.

   (2). Objective.
   RIGHT CENTRE BATTN: CADORNA TRENCH from Trench Junction C.19.c.48.85 to C.19.a.25.35.

5. The Battalion will attack with three Companies, "A", "C" & "D" Assaulting, and one Company ("B") in Reserve.

6. The Battalion frontage will be allotted to Companies as follows:

   (1) For Assembly: RAILWAY TRENCH.

   Right to Left: "A" Coy (B.24.d.93.70 - Trench Junction BROUGH ALLEY and RAILWAY TRENCH - to B.24.d.73.88. 30 yds South West of track crossing RAILWAY TRENCH.

6. Battalion Frontage (Cont).

Right to Left (cont) "C" Coy: (B.24.d.73.88 to B.24.b.
(57.10.

"D" Coy: (B.24.b.57.10 to B.24.b.
(61.30. junction of BLUE
(TRENCH and RAILWAY TRENCH.

"B" Coy: MARINE and FAMINE.

Carrying Coy, "B" Coy 13th. E.Y.R. FOGGY and FLURRY.

(2). Objective: CADORNA TRENCH.

Right to Left: "A" Coy: C.19.c.48.85 - C.19.a.36.00.
"C" Coy: C.19.a.36.00 - C.19.a.33.17.
"D" Coy: C.19.a.33.17 - C.19.a.25.35.

7. Advanced Posts.

The following Advanced Posts will be occupied on Y/Z night by Lewis Gun Detachments of one N.C.O and three men. (These will be Reserve Lewis Guns with Companies).

NO. OF POST.	LOCATION.	HELD BY.
No.3.	C.19.a.0.0.(approx).	"A" Coy, 12 Y & L.
No.4.	B.24.b.90.12. "	"C" Coy, "
No.5.	B.24.b.85.30. "	"D" Coy "

8. Communication Trenches.

(1) Main Trenches: In and Out before Assault.

(a) Main Trenches IN to Battle Front:

1. TYNE ALLEY,

2. NORTH TYNE ALLEY - VISCOUNT Tr. to MARINE - MARINE southward as far as the DOG'S LEG - DOG'S LEG.

(b) Trenches OUT from Battle Front:

1. THAMES ALLEY,

2. BLUE ALLEY - MARINE TRENCH. from BLUE ALLEY to B.24.b.30.85 - New Communication Tr. to VISCOUNT Tr. - OUSE ALLEY. (OUSE ALLEY for evacuation of wounded only)

(c) Trenches IN and OUT:

1. MARINE Tr. from TYNE ALLEY to DOG'S LEG.

2. FOLLY Trench.

3. BROUGH ALLEY.

(d) BLUE Tr. may be used as an IN Trench by Left Centre Assaulting Battn at Zero when moving its Reserve Company from MARINE Tr. to RAILWAY.

8. Communication Trenches (Cont).

(2). After Assault.
Communication Trenches will be dug or opened up as follows:

1. New Trench from about B.24.d.9.7. to C.19.c.4.9. — By "B" Coy, 12 K.O.Y.L.I.

2. Open up old trench from B.24.b.65.70 to B.24.b.95.70. — By 11 E.Lanc.R.

3. Open up WOOD TRENCH B.24.b.65.70 to B.24.b.75.85. — By 13 Y & L.R.

4. Open up OPPY Tr. from B.24.b.3.9 to B.18.d.32.05. — By 13 Y & L.R.

9. Dumps.

(a) Brigade: B.23.a.5.1.
(b) Battalion: B.24.d.2 5.65. (In FOGGY)
(c) Companies:
"A" Coy. B.24.d.82.85.
"C" Coy. B.24.d.65.95.
"D" Coy. B.24.b.6.2.

(b)–(c): For contents see Administrative Supplement.

10. Regimental Aid Post. B.30.a.80.95.

-----------0-----------

SECTION 2.

1. Troops will take up positions laid down in Section 1. para.3. on X/Y night, and Section 1. para.6 & 7 on Y/Z night, under orders to be issued later.

2. The Attack will be delivered at a date and hour to be notified later and the "Jumping Off" line will be RAILWAY Tr.

3. Formations for the Attack.

The Attack of the Assaulting Companies will be delivered in two Waves; two platoons in the first Wave, one platoon in the second.

1st WAVE: (1st Line: Rifle Section.
Bombing Section.
(2nd Line: Lewis Gun Section.
Rifle Grenadier Section.

2nd WAVE: One platoon: Four Sections in Line.

Diagram shewing positions of Units at Zero is being issued herewith.

4. Action at Zero.

(i) Garrisons of Advanced Posts as laid down in Section 1, para.7. will first try and locate position of any hostile machine gun which may open fire after our barrage starts at Zero, and engage the same; and second, traverse the enemy's trenches and ground in front. They will maintain their fire until the leading line of the first Wave reaches them. The garrisons will remain at their posts until receipt of orders after Zero.

4. Action at Zero (Cont).

(ii) First Line of the First Wave leaves Front Line Trenches.

(iii) Second Line leaves Trenches, so as to be 20 yds behind First Line.

(iv) Second Wave leaves Trenches, so as to be 50 yds behind Second Line.

(v). One Vickers Gun, 94th Machine Gun Company, detailed for Strong Point moves forward with the Second Wave of "C" Company.

(vi) Carrying Parties from attached Company of 13th Bn. East Yorks.R. move forward with loads as laid down in Administrative Supplement, Appendix N.

(vii) "B" Company moves forward across the open into Front Line Trenches, vacated by Assaulting Companies.

5. Action after capture of Objective.

1. When the barrage has moved sufficiently far from the Objective, (about 100 to 150 yds), small advanced Lewis Gun Posts (strength 1 N.C.O and 2 men) will be established in shell holes about 50 yds in advance of the Objective. These Posts will be well supplied with water, rations, and ammunition. They will remain out and form an outpost line. Their positions must be strengthened and well wired, and they must be connected with front line by communication trenches.

2. Contact aeroplanes will fly over the line after Zero. Flares will be lighted by troops immediately they are called for on the Klaxon Horn or by the firing of a white light. The flares will be lit by the troops occupying the objective.

3. Consolidation of Captured position: - - Consolidation will commence immediately the objective has been seized, the enemy occupants of the trench disposed of and Lewis Gun Posts established in advance of the New Line. A Strong Point will be constructed by the Assaulting troops at approximately C.19.a.4.0. to contain a garrison of ½ platoon to be found by "C" Company and one Vickers Gun from 94th Machine Gun Company.

The ½ platoon will consist of Lewis Gun Section and Rifle Section. The emplacement for the Vickers Gun will be constructed by its own team.

6. Re-organisation after consolidation.

When the consolidation of the position is completed and there is no sign of an impending counter-attack, and in any case before dawn on Z plus 1 day, the defence of the position will be re-organised and Companies distributed in depth. This will be effected under orders to be issued later.

On completion of the re-organisation, Companies will submit to Battalion H.Qs with the least possible delay, maps shewing their dispositions and the position of posts of neighbouring units on each flank. The posts on the flanks are to be within five yards of Battalion Boundaries.

7. <u>Carrying Parties</u>. See Administrative Supplement, Appendix N.

8. <u>Liaison</u>. 2nd.Lt.F.TONGE will act as Liaison Officer, and keep in touch with Battalions on the flanks.

9. <u>Situation Reports</u>.

A situation report will be rendered to Battalion H.Q as soon as possible after Zero, not later than Zero plus 15 minutes, and a further report at Zero plus 45 minutes, and hourly onwards. Important information should not however, be with-held for the regular situation report, but sent immediately.

10. <u>Observation</u>.

The Intelligence Officer will post Battalion Observers in suitable positions for watching operations. A runner will be attached to the Observers and any information obtained should be sent through as soon as possible.

11. <u>Ground gained, to be held</u>.

Once ground is gained, it must not be given up, and every garrison is to hold out to the last in the place where it has been posted or in the position it has taken up.

12. These Orders supersede "Proposals for Attack &c" issued 18th inst.

H. Tunbridge Captain and
Adjutant,
12th. S. Battn. York & Lancaster Regt.

Copies to:-

No.1.....Commanding Officer.
2.....Second in Command.
3.....Adjutant.
4.....O.C. "A" Company.
5.....O.C. "B" "
6.....O.C. "C" "
7.....O.C. "D" "
8.....Signalling Officer.
9.....Intelligence Officer.
10.....Lewis Gun Officer.
11.....Medical Officer.
12.....Quartermaster.
13.....Transport Officer.
14.....Regtl. Sergt. Major.
15.....94th Machine Gun Company.
16.....94th Trench Mortar Battery.
17.....O.C. "B" Coy, 13th Bn. East Yorks.R.
18.....94th Infantry Brigade.
19.....) War Diary.
20.....)
21.....) File.
22.....)

ADMINISTRATIVE SUPPLEMENT
to
PRELIMINARY INSTRUCTIONS FOR ATTACK ON GERMAN TRENCHES.

1. DRESS. All Officers taking part in the attack will be dressed and equipped exactly the same as the men.

(a). Clothing. As issued, except greatcoats.

(b). Arms. As issued. The No.1 of a Lewis Gun team will carry a revolver.

(c). Equipment. As issued, except pack and entrenching implements. Water bottle filled, and haversack ration. (Haversack on back).

(d). Tools. One shovel or one pick per man,
65% shovels, 35% picks.
To be fastened on to equipment at left side, or on the back, so as not to impede movement.
Wire-cutters as available. To be attached to the man's shoulder-strap by string, and cutter tucked in belt.

(e). Box Respirator. (in "Alert" position), and Tube helmet.

(f). Ammunition. 120 rounds per man, except runners and signallers who will carry 50 rounds only and No's.1. of Lewis Gun teams; who will carry 36 rounds P.W.A. each.

(g). Iron rations, Mess tins, solidified alcohol, water proof sheet under flap, (all carried in the haversack).

(h). Aeroplane flares. Two carried, one in each bottom pocket, by all N.C.Os below the rank of Sergeant.

(i). S.O.S. Signals. One set to be carried by each Officer and Sergeant.

(j). Sandbags. 3 per man, carried under the braces.

(k). Very Pistols. Two per Company.

(l). Rifle grenades. Rifle Grenadiers, six each.

(m). Mills Grenades. Each bombing section, four buckets; 15 bombs in each.

(n). Lewis Gun Ammunition. 20 filled pans per gun.
The remaining 22 pans per gun to be kept filled in Reserve in our own front line trench, where carriers know where to find them.

(o). Signalling equipment.
As considered necessary by Battalion Commander.
One power buzzer will be taken to the objective by the Left Centre Battalion.

(p). Distinguishing marks. A coloured tape will be worn, tied on each shoulder-strap, to denote the line or wave to which a man belongs. Three different colours will be supplied:

1st LINE.
2nd LINE.
2nd WAVE.

1. DRESS (Cont).

(q). Officers and N.C.Os will carry with them note-book and pencil, several tracings of enemy trenches opposite our lines,(supplied under Battalion arrangements) and report cards. No other maps, documents, or letters, except A.B.64, are to be taken East of our present front Line.

2. POLICE ARRANGEMENTS.

1. Brigade Police Posts will be established at the following trench junctions:-

	By whom found.	No.of men.
(a) Junction of THAMES ALLEY with TOWEY.	Right Battn.	2.
(b) Junction of TYNE ALLEY with MARINE Tr.	Right Battn.	2.
(c) Junction of VISCOUNT Tr. and MARINE Tr.	Left Battn.	2.

2.. Battalion police Posts consisting of a Lance Corporal and one man found by "B" Company will be established at the junction of DOG's LEG and FAMINE TRENCHES and the junction of RAILWAY SUPPORT and FLURRY; and in addition post to be found by the Regtl Police at Regtl Aid Post.

These posts will be under the orders of the Battn. Police Corporal, and will be posted and withdrawn under his orders only.

DUTIES.
1. To stop stragglers and return them to their Coys.
2. To direct walking wounded to Regtl Aid Post.
3. To see that traffic regulations are complied with. i.e. IN and OUT Trenches are used as such only.
4. Give information to isolated parties or individuals as regards whereabouts.
5. To stop any lightly wounded man who is capable of carrying rifle and equipment and has not got such, and ~~them~~ send him back to get them.

3. Advanced posts, rations, etc.

1. Each of the Advanced posts mentioned in Section 1, para.7, will be provided with rations for Z day,2 two-gallon petrol tins filled with water,and will have 20 filled pans per gun in the Posts.

Companies finding the posts will be responsible that this is done.

2. Posts mentioned in Section 2, para.5. (i) will be provided with rations for Z plus 1 day, 2 tw o-gallon petrol tins filled with water, and two boxes S.A.A. before dawn on ~~the~~ Z plus one day, and the responsibility for doing this rests with Company Commanders furnishing the Posts.

4. Dumps.

(a) Brigade Dump. B.23.a.5.1.
(b) Battalion Dump. B.2 4.d.25.65.

Reference Administrative Supplement, para 4 (c) Dumps.

	A	C	D
S.A.A. (boxes)	10	10	10
Bombs.	16	8	8
Rifle Grenades. (boxes)	4	2	2
Concert inas	25	25	25
Coils, barbed.	6	6	6
Screw pickets.	50	50	50
Hairpins.	80	80	80

	A	C	D
Sandbags.	1000	1000	1000
Very Lights.			
1"	50	50	50
1½"	15	15	15
Tracing Tape.			
Hedging Gloves.	6	6	6
Gas gongs.			

Dumps (Cont).

The following quantities of Ammunition, Stores, etc, will be maintained at the Battalion Dump.

R.E. Material.

300 Shovels.
200 Picks.
500 yds Tracing tape.
~~100~~ 150 Screw pickets.
25 coils barbed wire
5000 Sandbags.

~~40~~ 80 Barbed wire Concertinas.
2 Coils plain wire.
1 Box hairpains.
25 prs hedging gloves.
6 Gas Gongs.
10 Improvised Stretchers.

Ammunition.

50,000 Rds. S.A.A.
50 Boxes Bombs.
50 " Rifle Grenades.
2 " White Very Lights 1".
2 " " " " 1½"
40 Sets S.O.S. Signals.
1 Box P.W.A.
50 Stokes Mortar Shells.
50 Green Cartridges.
100 Ringed Charges.

Water.

50 Petrol Tins, Filled.

(c) Company Dumps.

"A" Company. B.24.d.82.85.
"C" " B.24.d.65.95.
"D" " B.2 4.b.6.2.

All material to be carried over to CADORNA must be tied up in loads of normal weight.

Companies are responsible for establishing their dumps to above establishment and will each detail an N.C.O to take charge of their dumps before and during operations.

5. Instructions will be issued on the following points in the form of Appendices to Administrative Supplement.
(a) Artillery Plan and Liaison;
~~(b) Machine Gun Barrage with Map;~~ JWW
(c) Signal Communications;
(d) Collection of, escorting and disposal of prisoners;
(e) Ration and water supply;
(f) Medical arrangements;
~~(g) March of troops to position of Assembly.~~ JWW
(h) Clearing the Battle Field.
(i) Arrangements for holding the line on Z Day.
(n) Carrying parties.

Dumps (Cont).

The following quantities of Ammunition, Stores, etc, will be maintained at the Battalion Dump.

R.E. Material.

300	Shovels.	~~40~~ 80	Barbed wire Concertinas.
200	Picks.	2	Coils plain wire.
500	yds Tracing tape.	1	Box hairpains.
~~100~~ 150	Screw pickets.	25	prs hedging gloves.
25	coils barbed wire	6	Gas Gongs.
5000	Sandbags.	10	Improvised Stretchers.

Ammunition.

50,000 Rds. S.A.A.
50 Boxes Bombs.
50 " Rifle Grenades.
2 " White Very Lights 1".
2 " " " " 1½"
40 Sets S.O.S. Signals.
1 Box P.W.A.
30 Stokes Mortar Shells.
50 Green Cartridges.
100 Ringed Charges.

Water.

50 Petrol Tins, Filled.

(c) Company Dumps.

"A" Company. B.24.d.82.85.
"C" " B.24.d.65.95.
"D" " B.2 4.b.6.2.

All material to be carried over to CADORNA must be tied up in loads of normal weight.

Companies are responsible for establishing their dumps to above establishment and will each detail an N.C.O to take charge of their dumps before and during operations.

5. Instructions will be issued on the following points in the form of Appendices to Administrative Supplement.
(a) Artillery Plan and Liaison;
~~(b) Machine Gun Barrage with Map;~~ JW
(c) Signal Communications;
(d) Collection of, escorting and disposal of prisoners;
(e) Ration and water supply;
(f) Medical arrangements;
~~(g) March of troops to position of Assembly.~~ JW
(h) Clearing the Battle Field.
(i) Arrangements for holding the line on Z Day.
(n) Carrying parties.

ADMINISTRATIVE SUPPLEMENT.

APPENDIX "C".

SIGNAL COMMUNICATION.

1. TELEPHONE AND TELEGRAPH. Two telephone lines will be laid from Battalion Headquarters to a point about the centre of the Battalion Sector in RAILWAY TRENCH (No.1. via BOYNTON; No.2. via RAILWAY Line and BROUGH ALLEY). From this point they will be carried forward under Battalion arrangements across No. Man's Land, by slightly different routes to Objective, and a station established in "C" Company's Sector (Call L.B.).

The point where lines leave RAILWAY TRENCH will be made a test point V.B. (i.e. existing Signal Station near C.H.Q. in RAILWAY TRENCH) which can be used by Reserve Company ("B").

If possible laterals will be run overland between BOYNTON and the Railway.

2. VISUAL.

(a) "D" Company will take a daylight lamp and work to Brigade O.P. (Call D.I.) in OUSE B.29.b.7.9. which will be in telephonic communication with Brigade Headquarters.

(b) All Company Signallers will take discs.

(c) A receiving station will be established near Battalion. O.P. B.24.d.1.5. by Battalion Signallers.

3. RUNNERS.

(a) Runner Relay Posts will be established by Brigade at Brigade Forward Signal Station F.S. B.24.c.9.3. and at all linesmen test points: T.J. B.23.d.8.5.;
B.P. B.23.a.9.2.;
S.K. B.22.b.4.8.;
I.M. B.16.c.1.3.:

Messages may be handed in at any Signal Office or Relay Post.

(b) The Battalion Signalling Officer will establish a relay Post in RAILWAY TRENCH at Test Point V.B.

(c) Messages for transmission to Battalion Headquarters may be handed in at V.B.

"PRELIMINARY INSTRUCTIONS, &C"

AMENDMENTS AND ADDENDA. 25.6.17.

1. Section 1, para. 2. b.

For "2 Vickers Guns" read "1".

2. Section 1, para. 6. (i)

For "'B' Coy MARINE & FAMINE" read "FAMINE & FLURRY"

For "Carrying Coy, 'B' Coy, 13 E.Y.R. FOGGY & FLURRY" read "FOGGY & MARINE".

3. Section 2, para. 3.

For "2nd. WAVE: One platoon: Four Sections in Line" read "2nd. WAVE: Two Sections and Coy. H.Q. in line".

Add "Remaining two sections of the platoon forming the 2nd. WAVE will assemble in FAMINE & FLURRY Trenches."

4. Section 2, para. 4. (vii).

For "'B' Company moves, etc" read "The Two Sections of the platoon of each Company forming the 2nd. WAVE assembled in FAMINE & FLURRY and 'B' Coy move forward across the open into RAILWAY TRENCH."

5. Section 2, para. 4. (v).

Delete this section.

6. Section 5, para. 3.

Delete " and one Vickers Gun from 94th Machine Gun Company" and "The emplacement for the Vickers Gun will be constructed by its own team".

7. For "DOG'S LEG" read "BOYNTON TRENCH" whenever referred to.

ADMINISTRATIVE SUPPLEMENT.

APPENDIX "E".

RATIONS AND WATER.

The arrangements regarding rations and water are as shewn in Table below.

1. Rations. Two days rations to be drawn on Y day for consumption on Z and Z plus 1 days. The rations will be bagged up before leaving the Q.M. Stores and those for Z plus 1 day will be distinguished by dab of white paint.

2. Water. (i) Reserve of 50 tins of water will be held in the Battalion Dump in FOGGY.

(ii) Other arrangements are as shewn in Table.

	DETAILS.	TO BE TAKEN UP. ON	BY	TO BE DUMPED AT.	HOW DISPOSED OF	REMARKS.
Rations Y day	Ordy.	XY night	Coys, on the man		–	–
Z " Z+1 "	" Preserved	YZ night	Regtl. Transport.	Nr aeroplane. B.29.b.	Ration parties to meet Transpt at 10.30pm from ea. Coy & carry both days ratns to Coy dumps.	Ratns for Z+1 day will be dumped at Coy & HQ dumps.
Water. Y day	17 per Coy 13 Bn H.Q	XY night	Regtl. Transport.	B.28.d.64 (approx) for B & D Coys; at aeroplane for A, C, HQ.	Coys will arrange to send carryg parties to meet Transpt & pick up tins on way in to trenches	Each Coy's water will be loaded on their LG limbers with their guns & pans, etc
Z day Z+1 "	90 tins 90 " 180 "	104 XY night.	-do-	At aeroplane. B29b.	B Coy will arrange to send sufficnt men to carry 104 tins to meet Transpt at 11pm and carry to Battn Dump after arr. at B.28.b. trs.	
		76 YZ night	-do-	-do-	B Coy will pro-vide carrying party to meet Transpt. at 10.30pm. & carry to Battn Dump.	All empty tins taken up XY night must be retd to Transpt. on YZ night by carrying parties.

N.B. Coys will draw water from Battn. Dump on YZ night for consumption on Z and Z plus 1 day and deposit tins in their own dump. "B" and H.Q. will construct separate dumps for rations and water.

ADMINISTRATIVE SUPPLEMENT.

A P P E N D I X "I".

ARRANGEMENTS FOR HOLDING THE LINE ON "Z" DAY.

1. The following arrangements are made for holding the line on Z day after the Assault.

2. Two Companies, consisting of two platoons only of 11th Bn. EAST YORKS.R. are available for holding the Line. They will be disposed as follows:-

(i) After the Assault.

1 Platoon: CHOKE TRENCH. 1 Platoon: Remainder of WINDMILL Defences.

4 posts: Strength: ½ Platoon each.

No.1. C.19.c.30.45.
2. B.24.d.95.70.
3. B.24.b.7.0.
4. B.24.b.60.35.

(ii) Assembly Position.

The WINDMILL garrison will move into its Assembly position as below, by 1.0.a.m. on Y/Z night and the garrison for the Posts by 5.0.p.m. on Z day.

Assembly Positions:

1 platoon, the WINDMILL Garrison will occupy CHOKE Tr.
1 " " " " " assemble in DUSTY Tr.

No.1.Post. Northern Portion of CHICO Support.
No.2. " In RAILWAY SUPPORT Tr. immediately E. of BROUGH Tr.
No.3 " The Eastern end of BOYNTON) No.4.Post
No.4 " -do- -do-) leading.

Garrisons of the Posts will use TYNE ALLEY and will dribble forward in very small parties, each post concentrating in MARINE TRENCH, before moving to Assembly place.

Garrisons of No.4 and No.3 Posts will file up RAILWAY TRENCH into position at ZERO plus 2 minutes.

ADMINISTRATIVE SUPPLEMENT.

APPENDIX "N".

25.6.17.

CARRYING PARTIES.

The arrangements for carrying parties are as follows:-

1. "B" Company, 13th Bn. East Yorks. R. is placed at the disposal of this Battalion for carrying.

2.. Carrying parties from this Company: strength: 1 Officer and 20 carriers, will be attached to "A", "C", and "D" Companies for carrying forward from Company Dumps to the Objective.

3. The Company referred to in para. 1. will join the Battalion on Y/Z night and be accommodated in FOGGY and MARINE, as shewn in diagram attached, being in position by 3.0.a.m.

4. The Carrying Parties referred to in para. 2. will join Companies the afternoon of Z day, by an hour to be notified later. They will assemble in RAILWAY TRENCH in the immediate vicinity of their respective Company Dumps.

5. These Carrying Parties will move forward close behind the 2nd. WAVE and will carry loads as follows:-

	Quantities.		No. of Men.
1st journey.	Barbed wire Concertinas, 12.		12 men in pairs with pole.
	Screw pickets, small,	54.)	6 men in loads of 9 pickets and 10 hair-pins.
	Hairpins.	60.)	
	Sandbags,	200.	2 men.
		Total.	20 "

2nd journey. According to list in possession of N.C.O i/c of Dump.

Other journeys. As required.

6. O.C. Companies will arrange for R.E. Stores mentioned in para. 5. to be made up into loads as above.

7. One Officer and the remainder of "B" Company, 13 East Yorks. R. will remain at Battalion Dump in FOGGY and await orders.

8. The Regtl. Sgt. Major will be held responsible that all stores in the Battalion Dump are made up beforehand into suitable 1 man loads.

1

ADMINISTRATIVE SUPPLEMENT .- APPENDICES
REFERRED TO IN PARAGRAPH 5.

26.6.17.

APPENDIX "A". Already issued.

" "B". Will not be issued.

" "C".- Already issued.

APPENDIX "D".- DISPOSAL OF PRISONERS.&C.

All prisoners taken will be sent to Battalion H Qs at once. O/C "B" Company will furnish escort from RAILWAY TRENCH to Battn H Qs. Escort will not exceed 10 % of the number of prisoners and should, where possible, be taken from Walking Wounded cases.

All Officer prisoners should be searched at the earliest opportunity and any maps or other documents found on them will be sent to Battn H Qs immediately.

APPENDIX "E".- Already issued.

APPENDIX "F".- MEDICAL ARRANGEMENTS.

Stretcher bearers will remain with their Companies up to an hour (to be notified later) shortly before Zero, as in ordinary trench routine.
Special Medical arrangements will be notified to Companies direct by the Medical Officer.

APPENDIX "G".- Will not be issued as such, but will be incorporated in Operation Orders.

APPENDIX "H".- CLEARING THE BATTLEFIELD.

(i) Search Parties will be organised as soon as possible after dark under Battalion arrangements and all bodies conveyed to the Cemetery, near the wire N. of SUNKEN ROAD, about B 30 a.8.9.
(ii) All Red Identity Discs and personal effects must be removed from all bodies buried, and handed in to the Orderly Room.
(iii) All graves will be marked by a special disc and personal effects placed in ration bags, a supply of which will be kept at Battn. H Qs.
(iv) Each disc will be numbered and any not returned after the operation must be accounted for.

PRELIMINARY INSTRUCTIONS &C.- AMENDMENTS & ADDENDA .

Section 2.para.5.(ii).-

Add: Contact Aeroplane will carry 4 long black streamers.
A Contract aeroplane may call for flares in the early morning of Z plus 1 day, and flares will be reserved for this purpose.
Care will be taken that flares are only lighted in answer to an aeroplane which has a British marking.

Administrative Supplement.

1.Dress. (p) Distinguishing Marks: After "supplied" read as follows:-
"1st Line: RED.
2nd " : YELLOW.
2nd WAVE: BLUE. "

Appendix "E":

Water for Z and Z plus 1 day. Times given in column 6 should be deleted. They will be notified later.

66

PRO document reference: WO 95/2365 ② END

The item(s) described below have been extracted from this document for reasons of preservation.

map based on 1:10,000 trench map, with added title: '31st Division Barrage Map Attack on Cadorna Tr'

Please order as: MF 1/53

Date: 12 March 2003

Signed: G L Beech

Name: G. L. BEECH

SECRET

C O N F I D E N T I A L.

WAR DIARY.

12TH. S. BATTALION YORK AND LANCASTER REGT.

PERIOD.

July 1st 1917
to
July 31st, 1917.

VOLUME 19.

Date 1, 8, 17.

B. E. F.

WO 17

Army Form C. 2118.

WAR DIARY
or
INTELLIGENCE SUMMARY.
(Erase heading not required.)

Instructions regarding War Diaries and Intelligence Summaries are contained in F. S. Regs., Part II. and the Staff Manual respectively. Title pages will be prepared in manuscript.

Place	Date	Hour	Summary of Events and Information	Remarks and references to Appendices
	2/2/17		The Battalion moved from WAKEFIELD CAMP handing over to the 63rd R.N Division & proceeded to new quarters at Bray. Operation orders attached.	[illegible]
Bray	3/2/17		Battalion occupied in cleaning up & re-organisation. Major General O'Gowan addressed Bn & congratulated them on their great success in taking CADORNA TRENCH. Congratulatory messages (attached hereto) were read out to the Bn	[illegible]
〃	4/2/17		Reorganisation of the Bn & Training. Owing to the weakness in numbers it was decided to have three Coys of 2 Platoons each & a Company H.Q.	[illegible]
〃	5/2/17		Battalion carried on Training. During the period of stay in BRAY Sports were held during each evening also Concerts, when the times for night training permitted.	[illegible]

A5834 Wt. W4973/M687 750,000 8/16 D. D. & L. Ltd. Forms/C.2118/13.

Army Form C. 2118.

Instructions regarding War Diaries and Intelligence Summaries are contained in F. S. Regs., Part II. and the Staff Manual respectively. Title pages will be prepared in manuscript.

WAR DIARY
or
~~INTELLIGENCE SUMMARY.~~
(*Erase heading not required.*)

Place	Date	Hour	Summary of Events and Information	Remarks and references to Appendices
Bray	6/7/17		Bn. Training	
"	7/7/17			&c.
"	8/7/17		Sunday:- Church service & observed as a day of rest. appointments:- Extract from London gazette supplement dated 6-7-17 Temp Captain (acting major) D.C. Allen to be temp major (Jan. 21) " 2nd Lieut (acting Captain) V.S. Simpson " " " Captain (Jan 21) Posting:- Captain K.R. Davies joined the Bn. for duty, was temporarily attached to C. Co. as supernumerary.	&c.
"	9/7/17		Bn. re-organised again following a Brigade conference. It was decided to have three companies of three Platoons each	&c.

A5834 Wt. W4973/M687 750,000 8/16 D. D. & L. Ltd. Forms/C.2118/13.

Army Form C. 2118.

WAR DIARY
or
INTELLIGENCE SUMMARY.
(Erase heading not required.)

Instructions regarding War Diaries and Intelligence Summaries are contained in F. S. Regs., Part II. and the Staff Manual respectively. Title pages will be prepared in manuscript.

Place	Date	Hour	Summary of Events and Information	Remarks and references to Appendices
Bray	10/2/17		Training & Coy Re-organised. The G.O.C 31st Division has approved the grant of Tempy rank to the undermentioned officers as stated against their names.	G.G.B.
			Temp Lieut (actg Capt) E.L. Moxey to be Temp Capt. Feb: 23	
			" " T.L. Ward " " " March 13	
			" 2nd Lieut M.B. Wallace to be Temp Lieut Feb. 23	
			" " F.G. Morris " " " " " "	
			" " C.A. Jackson " " " " " "	
			" " F.H. Westby " " " " " "	
			" " G.L.M.L. Pirkis " " " " March 13	
			" " S. Crawford " " " " May 13.	
			No 12/1565 L/c Osborn H. "H.2" Comp promoted corpl as from this date. Vice Peet (to England 4.6.17).	
Bray.	11/2/17		Standing by all the morning prepared to move. Eventually moving at 3 p.m. to forward area. Resting in Paisley Camp for night.	G.G.B.
Paisley Camp N 35 Vaast	12/2/17	10pm	Relieved 14th Canadians in front line & support T.24 & 30 & T.29. Operation orders attached.	G.G.B.

A5834 Wt. W4973/M687 750,000 8/16 D. D. & L. Ltd. Forms/C.2118/13.

Instructions regarding War Diaries and Intelligence Summaries are contained in F. S. Regs., Part II. and the Staff Manual respectively. Title pages will be prepared in manuscript.

WAR DIARY
or
~~INTELLIGENCE SUMMARY.~~
(Erase heading not required.)

Army Form C. 2118.

Place	Date	Hour	Summary of Events and Information	Remarks and references to Appendices
	12/7/17 to 17/7/17		During this period the Battalion held the line & nothing of importance occurred. No casualties.	G.G.B.
	17/18	night	The Battalion was relieved by the 14th Y & L & took over Area occupied by them in Railway Embankment & Ridge line in A 6. Operation orders attached. Nothing to report. No Casualties.	G.G.B.
	19/7/17		Capt Davies assumed command of C Co. as from 15-7-17. 2nd Lieut Judd attached to H.Q. Co for course with Signals. The following officers were struck off the establishment. Capt D.E. Grant with effect as from 11-3-17 2nd Lieut E.N.M. Butterworth " " " " 1-7-17. The Corps Commander has awarded Military Medals for gallantry in the field as follows. 18582 Sgt Jarvis R.A. 235226 L/Cpl Mantonfield C. 14/1464 Pte Briggs J. 24251 Pte Clark J.W.	G.G.B.

A5834 Wt. W4973/M687 750,000 8/16 D. D. & L. Ltd. Forms/C.2118/13.

Instructions regarding War Diaries and Intelligence Summaries are contained in F. S. Regs., Part II. and the Staff Manual respectively. Title pages will be prepared in manuscript.

WAR DIARY
or
~~INTELLIGENCE SUMMARY~~.

(Erase heading not required.)

Army Form C. 2118.

Place	Date	Hour	Summary of Events and Information	Remarks and references to Appendices
	20/7/17		The Field Marshall Commanding-in-chief has awarded the decoration as follows. dated 16-7-17. The Military Cross to Capt V. S. Simpson. The Corp Commander awarded military medals to the folling N.C.O.s for gallantry in the field 17385 Pte (A/corpl) W. Burrell A Co. 13/147 L/Sergt J. Breathwick A Co.	G.b.B.
	21/7/17		The undermentioned officer is struck off the strength on transfer to R.F.C. 21-7-17. Capt. E.L. Moxey.	G.b.B.
	21/22	night	The Battalion was relieved by the 18th D.L.I. & marched back to Camp in Neuville St Vaast A.9.a. Camp taken over from 15th W. Yorks. Operation orders attached.	G.b.B.
	22/7/17		Sunday:- church service. Clothing & Kit Inspections.	G.b.B.
	23/7/17		Training (Co programme) & M.O. Inspection. 2nd Lieut W. H. Rowlands is struck off the establishment of the Battalion with effect from June 1st 1917.	G.b.B.
	24/25	night	Bn commenced working parties to carry wire & materials from Neuville St Vaast up to forward area.	

A5834 Wt. W4973/M687 750,000 8/16 D. D. & L. Ltd. Forms/C.2118/13.

Instructions regarding War Diaries and Intelligence Summaries are contained in F. S. Regs., Part II. and the Staff Manual respectively. Title pages will be prepared in manuscript.

WAR DIARY
or
~~INTELLIGENCE SUMMARY.~~
(Erase heading not required.)

Army Form C. 2118.

Place	Date	Hour	Summary of Events and Information	Remarks and references to Appendices
25-7-17 [illegible]			Posting:– 2nd Lieut G.W. Jones joined the Battalion for duty & was posted to A Co. dated 24-7-17.	G.B.
	25/26	night	Bn Working parties commencing at 9 pm & returning to Camp at 5 am. work as for 24/25.	G.B.
	26/27	night	Bn Carrying wire etc to B.H.Q. & to forward area 9 pm to 5.0 am.	G.B.
	27/28	night	Bn Carrying Party to forward area	G.B.
	28/29	night	Transport of Wire Pickets etc. to Bde dump & forward dump.	G.B.
	29/7/17		Lieut Jackson proceeded to take up the duties of Bde Pioneer Officer	G.B.
	29/30	night	Bn Relieved the 18th W. Yorks in Bde support near the Beehive. Operations orders attached.	G.B.
	30/31	night	Bn Working parties for Front Area.	G.B.
	31/7/17		2nd Lieut O.H. Green joined the Batt for duty & was posted to B. Co. – – – D.O. Browning – – – – – C. Co. Capt R.E.J. Moore rejoined Bn from Hospital & was posted to C. Co. Acting second in Command Vice Capt Y.S. Simpson. M.C. gone on leave.	G.B.
	–	10 pm	Bn Working parties started for Front Area.	

A5834 Wt. W4973/M687 750,000 8/16 D. D. & L. Ltd. Forms/C.2118/13.

[illegible] Allen Major Cmdg 12. S. Bn York & Lancs Regt.

~~Copy~~

STAY. Copy No ____

Operation Order No 66.

2.7.17.

Ref Map 51B & 51C }
1/40,000 }

1 The Battalion will move to BRAY today 2-7-17 by march route.

2 Companies will leave camp in the following order.

H.Q. & Band & A Coy
B "
C "
D "

Commencing at 3 pm. and 100 yards being maintained between Coys.

Starting Point Junction of track from ROCLINCOURT behind cookers, with ARRAS LENS Road.

3/ Transport will march 200 yds behind rear Company.

4 2nd Lt. C L Roberts & billeting N.C.Os as for today, will proceed to BRAY, leaving Camp at 10. am. to take over billets from 63rd R.N. Divn. Report to Town Major on arrival.

5 Officers Valises, Mess Stores, Medical

Stores, Orderly Room stores will be
[illegible] and ready for removal by
transport at the [illegible] by
1/2 [illegible]
Transport Officer will arrange to
collect.

6. ACKNOWLEDGE

Time of [illegible]

Copy No 1 to File
" " 2 " "A" Coy
" " 3 " "B" "
" " 4 " "C" "
" " 5 " "D" "
" " 6 QM & T.O.
" " 7 I.O.
" " 8. M.O.

Sd. N.L. TONBRIDGE
Capt
Adjt.
STA 4.

STAY

Operation Order No. 67 — Copy No. 1

Ref map 51.B N.W.
$\frac{1}{20,000}$ & special
map of forward area

SECRET — 12-7-17

1. The 94th Inf Bde will relieve the 3rd Canadian Infy Bde in the line tonight 12/13th July.

2. The 12th & 13th York & Lancs Regt will take over the line from the 14th Royal Montreal Canadian Regt. The 12th York on the right and the 13th York on the left.

3. This battalion will take over the front line from No 3 Coy 14th Canadians & and will relieve No 1 Coy in support in NEW BRUNSWICK TR & WINNIPEG TR.

4. Dispositions after relief will be as follows

"B" Coy 12th York relieves Right half of No 3 Coy 14th Canadians in front line NOVA SCOTIA.

"C" Coy " relieves LEFT half No 3 Coy as above.

"A" Coy " relieves No 1 Coy 14th Canadians in support in NEW BRUNSWICK & WINNIPEG

HQ Coy " relieves HQ 14th Canadians in New BRUNSWICK & WINNIPEG with Batt HQ at T 29 b 2·1.

5. Coys will leave present area in the order B, C, A, H.Q. commencing at 9. pm with 100 yds between platoons. Platoons will pick up guides at the 3rd Canadian Brigade H.Q. at A 6 C 75.75 ~~at 9~~ en route.
Guides will be provided on the scale of 3 per coy & 2 for H.Q.

6 Lewis guns & 4 panniers per gun will be carried in by the teams together with spare part bags, remaining 4 panniers per gun are ~~will be dumped by coys near the workers and~~ will be brought up on the transport with ~~was~~ water.

7 16 tins of water per company will be brought up on the transport to the advanced ration dumps and will be there about 1.30 am.
O.C. H.Q. Coy will send a carrying party of 1 Officer & 32 carriers to meet the transport & O.C.s A B C & H.Q. will each send 2 men per L.G. team to be at Batt H.Q. at 1.15 am to go with this party to bring up Lewis gun panniers. They should all report to Lieut. JACKSON

8 Trench store lists will be forwarded to H.Q. as soon as possible after relief.

9 Completion of relief to be reported by runner to Batt. H.Q. immediately relief is complete.

10 Sketch showing dispositions to be forwarded to Batt. H.Q. as early as possible on morning following relief. Sketch to shew exact garrison & position of each post.

11 All surplus kit not required for trenches should be dumped ~~at~~ near cookers by 4 pm & mess stores by 8 pm.

12 ACKNOWLEDGE.

Issued at pm.

Copy No. 1 to Adjt.
" 2 – A Coy
" 3 – B "
" 4 – C "
" 5 – H.Q. "
" 6 – I.O. "
" 7 – T.O.
" 8 – Q.M.
" 9 – 2nd in C.
" 10 – M.O.

C.N. Cambridge Capt. & Adjt.
12th York & Lancaster

Adjutant

SECRET Copy

Operation Orders No 68

Ref Map 17-7-17
PETIT VIMY 1/20,000

1. The Battn will be relieved in the line on the night of the 17/18th by the 14th York & Lanc Regt and this will be carried out as follows.

"A" Coy STAY relieved by "C" Coy BLOCK
B " " " A "
C " " " B "

2. This Battn will take over the area now occupied by BLOCK.
A Coy in RAILWAY EMBANKMENT and B. C. HQ in Ridge Line in A6.

3. Each Coy will detail 4 guides & HQ Coy 3 guides to meet relieving Coy at the LONE TREE at 10 pm. These guides will report at Battn HQ at 8.30 pm. LIEUT. F.H. WESTBY will report at same time to proceed out in charge of guides.

4. 2nd Lt WILSON will take over from B Coy BLOCK on RAILWAY EMBANKMENT during the afternoon & arrange for

three guides to meet the Coy at LONE TREE

5. 2nd Lt MCNAMARA will proceed to new area on afternoon of 17th inst to take over billets of B & C Coys & HQ. He will take with him, one man per Coy & these men will be at LONE TREE at 12 midnight to guide Coys in. C.Q.M.S.s will report to 2nd Lt MCNAMARA during the afternoon.

6. Four limbers will be at Battn Ration dump at 1 am, one for the Lewis Guns, pans etc of each Coy. O.C. Coys will arrange for all L.G. material to be carried to Ration dump on way out. Two Lewis Gunners from each Coy will proceed with the limbers which will unload at nearest point to new Battn area. A Coy limber will unload at Railway. O.C. A Coy will make the necessary arrangements.

7. All water tins now in the line will be carried out &

S E C R E T. COPY NO. 1

STAY OPERATION ORDER. NO 69.

Ref. Map:
51 B.N.W. 1/20,000) 20/7/17.

1. The 93rd Infantry Bde will relieve the 94th Infty Bde in the Right Section of the line on the night of the 21/22 July/17.

2. The 12th York & Lancaster Regt., will be relieved by the 18th Durham Light Infantry, the relief of "B","C" and "HQ" Coys commencing about 5-0 p.m. on the 21st inst.,and "A" Coy as soon after dusk as possible.

3. The 12th York & Lancaster Regt.,on completion of relief will proceed to camp NEUVILLE ST VAAST A 9 a , and take over from 15th Bn,West Yorks. Regt.
Movement to take place by platoons at 200 yds distance.

4. A Billeting party consisting of 2nd Lieut BUZZACOTT and the 4 Coy Q M Ss will proceed to the new camp on the 20th July to take over huts and storesetc.

5. Trench Stores,including petrol tins,trench maps,taken over etc., will be handed over on relief and receipts obtained.

6. O C "A" Coy.will detail two guides to report to relieving Coy - "D" Coy.18th Durham Light Infantry - at Battn H Qs at 8-0 pm. 21st July.

7. Completion of relief will be notified by Coy Commanders,who will call personally at Battn H Qs for this purpose and also hand in trench store lists,if any.

8. Officers' valises,Mess Stores and Medical Stores will be at Ration Dump ,Battn H Qs at 4-30 p.m.21st inst.
Os C "B","C" and "HQ" Coys will arrange for 1 N.C.O and 2 men to remain behind to act as loading party.

9. O C "A" Coy will detail Lewis Gun Sergt and 2 men per gun to load limber and proceed with same to new camp.

10. Transport Officer will arrange for :-
(a) A limber for "A" Coy's Mess Stores,Lewis Guns and panniers to be at "A" Coy's HQs at 11-0 p.m. July 21st.
(b) Limbers and Maltese Cart for "B","C",and "HQ" Coys Officers valises,Mess,Medical and Orderly Room Stores,to be at Ration Dump,Battn H Qs. at 10-30 p.m.
(c) Eighty empty water tins to be dumped at Transport lines of 15th Bn,West Yorks.Regt., at A 8 b 4.4., before 6-0 a.m. on 21st July.
(d) The ration limbers on the night of the20th July to take back all surplus mess and Orderly Room stores.
(e) ~~Off~~ Limbers for Officers' valises,mens packs and cookers to be taken to the new camp.
(f) The transport lines and Q M Stores will remain where they are.

11. The R Q M S will arrange for the Band,Cobblers and Tailors to proceed to the new camp on the 21st inst.
12. The C Q M Ss of "B","C" and "HQ" Coys will arrange to meet the Coys at PAINSLEY (old Battn H Qs) about 8-0 p.m. and C Q M S of "A" Coy at about 11-30 p.m.
13. ACKNOWLEDGE.

E Crawford
Lieut &
A/Adjutant.
STAY.

Copies to: 1. C.O. 4 to 7 Coys.
2. 2nd in C. 8 M.O.
3. Adjt. 9 T.O.
10. Q M. 11. RSM. 12 File.

placed on the LG limbers of B & C Coys. & HQ. OC Coys will take steps to ensure that every tin is carried out. Any tins arriving at Ration dump before limbers reach there will be left in charge of 1 man who will accompany limbers out.

8. Completion of relief will be notified by Coy Commanders who will call personally at Battn HQ for this purpose & also hand in Trench Store lists

9. ACKNOWLEDGE

Copies to:
No 1 CO
2 2nd in C
3 A Coy
4 B
5 C
6 HQ
7 MO
8 File

(Sd) G Crawford
Lieut
A/Adjutant
5 TAY

SECRET. **12th. S. BATTALION YORK AND LANCASTER REGT.**

OPERATION ORDERS NO. 70.

Ref. Map.)
51b. N. W.)

28. 7. 17.

1. The 94th Inf. Bde (less M.G. Coy) will relieve 93rd Inf. Bde (less M.G. Coy) in the Right Section of the Line on the night of the 29/30 July 1917.

2. The 12th. S. Bn. York & Lanc. R. will relieve the 18th. Bn. West Yorks. R. in the support line, near the BEEHIVE and will be in Bde Support. Companies will relieve corresponding Companies of the 18th. W. Y. Rgt, thus:-

"A"	Coy,	12 Y & L	relieves	"A"	Coy	18 W.Y.R.
"B"	"	"	"	"B"	"	"
"C"	"	"	"	"C"	"	"
H.Q.	"	"	"	H.Q	"	"

3. The Battalion will move by march route, leaving camp at 9.45.p.m.

4. Order of march: "A", "B", "C", & "H.Q". 200 yds distance to be maintained between platoons. Coys will reach their place independently in the column.

5. ROUTE. Via PAYNESLEY CAMP, Duck board track and Bde H.Q, A.6.c.75.75.

6. Dress. Fighting order. Water bottles will be filled.

7. Coys on leaving the present quarters will hand them over to representatives of 92nd. Inf. Bde.

8. Coys will send 1 Officer and 1 N.C.O. per Coy to Support Bn. H.Q. at 4.p.m. to take over Trench Stores, etc.

9. All trench stores, water tins, etc., will be taken over on relief.

10. All Band, shoemakers and pioneers stores will be dumped opposite Guard Room by 2.30.p.m. and Officers' Valises, Mess Stores, Medical Stores, etc will be dumped at the same place by 8.30.p.m.

11. Q.M. and Transport Sgt will be responsible forall stores being transferred to Transport Lines in accordance with above given times.

12. One limber will report at each Coy. H.Q. at 8.30.p.m. for taking of Lewis Guns, panniers etc, to the line and each Coy will detail one N.C.O. and 3 men per Coy to act as loading and unloading parties. These men will accompany the limbers. The Mess cart will report at Bn. H.Qs at 8.30.p.m. and 3 H.Q. Officers' Servants will be detailed to accompany the Mess Cart to act as loading and unloading party.

13. Completion of relief will be notified to Bn. H.Qs. Code words - RATIONS ISSUED.

14. Maps shewing dispositions of Coys, and locations of nearest posts of neighbouring units on the flanks, will be forwarded to Bn. H.Qs 12 hours after completion of relief.

15. Usual personnel will stay behind with Transport and 1 N.C.O Musketry Instructor per Company.

16. ACKNOWLEDGE.

S Crawford.
Lieutenant,
A/Adjutant,
12th. S. Battn. York & Lancaster Regiment.

Copies to

No. 1. C.O.	4 to 7 Coys.	10. Q.M.
2. 2nd. in. C.	8. M.O.	11. R.S.M.
3. Adjutant.	9. T.O.	12. File.

SPECIAL ORDER OF THE DAY

By

Brigadier-General G. T. Carter Campbell, D.S.O.,
Commanding 94th Infantry Brigade.

I desire to express to all Ranks my very high appreciation of the manner in which the operations on the 28th June were carried out.

I attribute success to the zeal displayed by all commanders in the training and practice for the Attack, to the able handling by Commanding Officers and subordinate commanders of their respective units, to the determination of all ranks to succeed, and to the excellence of the barrage given us by our comrades of the Royal Field Artillery.

I look forward to the day when we shall again be given an opportunity of coming to close quarters with the enemy.

G. Carter Campbell

Brigadier-General,
Commanding 94th Infantry Bde.

3 July, 1917.

COPIES.

CONGRATULATORY MESSAGES.

Congratulations, of Commander-in-Chief.

S.O.13/175
1.7.17.

13th. York & Lancaster Regt.

The following from Division is forwarded :-

"A.430. 30.
First Army Wire as follows aaa The Army Commander has received the following from the Field Marshal Commanding in Chief aaa I congratulate you and all concerned on the successful operations carried out yesterday aaa Ends "

(Sd.) W.CARTER, Captain, Brigade Major,
94th. Infantry Brigade.

1.7.17.

S.O.13/168
30.6.17.

13th. York and Lancaster Regt.

The following ffom Division are forwarded :-

1. "A.A.1001 30. Following wire received from Advd First Army aaa Begins aaa Army Commander has received following message. From H.R.H. Duke of Connaught aaa Begins aaa I congratulate you on the complete success of the operations aaa Please convey to the troops my congratulations aaa Connaught aaa Ends aaa"

2. "A.A.1002 30. Following wire received from Advd. First Army aaa Begins aaa Army Commander has received the following message from Commander Second Army aaa Begins aaa Second Army Offer hearty congratulations on your most successful operations aaa Ends."

(Sd.) W.CARTER, Captain, Brigade Major,
94th. Infantry Brigade.

30.6.17.

~~Confidential~~

WAR DIARY

12th S. Bn York & Lancaster Regt

Period

August 1st 1917
to
August 31st 1917

Volume 20.

Date 1.9.17

B.E.F.

Army Form C. 2118.

Instructions regarding War Diaries and Intelligence Summaries are contained in F. S. Regs., Part II. and the Staff Manual respectively. Title pages will be prepared in manuscript.

WAR DIARY
or
~~INTELLIGENCE SUMMARY.~~
(Erase heading not required.)

Place	Date	Hour	Summary of Events and Information	Remarks and references to Appendices
Support Trenches ACHEVILLE Sector	1-8-17	MN[ight] to 3 a.m.	Battalion continued work in front areas, also improvement of Support trenches. Capt. W.L. Tunbridge returns from Rest Camp.	G.b.B.
	1/2nd	night	Battalion continued work in the Front Area 10 P.m. —— 3.a.m.	G.b.B.
	2nd/3rd	night	Battalion working in forward area 10 pm — 3. a. m. Capt Simpson M.C. proceeded on leave	G.b.B.
	3/4	night	The Battalion relieved the 14th Y & L in the Front line. Left Section. Casualties:- 1 man Wounded. Lieut Col. F.L. Hood resumed command, from leave.	G.b.B.
	6/8/17	1.30am.	The Enemy heavily bombarded our Trenches; using gas shells mixed with smoke, machine guns & Trench mortars also taking part. This lasted until 1.45 a.m. Total Casualties including men coming in for the next 3 days were:- 2 officers & 58 O/R's from gas. (2/Lt J THOMPSON & F.B. WILSON) 5 men Wounded. one officer (Mr Wilson) died on the 7th inst as the result of the gas.	G.b.B.
	—	afternoon.	Two men reported missing.	G.b.B.
	6th/7th	night	nothing of importance occurred on these two days. The usual work & wiring of Trenches were carried on.	G.b.B.
	7th/8th	—		

A5834 Wt. W4973/M687 750,000 8/16 D. D. & L. Ltd. Forms/C.2118/13.

Army Form C. 2118.

Instructions regarding War Diaries and Intelligence Summaries are contained in F. S. Regs., Part II. and the Staff Manual respectively. Title pages will be prepared in manuscript.

WAR DIARY
or
~~INTELLIGENCE SUMMARY.~~
(Erase heading not required.)

Place	Date	Hour	Summary of Events and Information	Remarks and references to Appendices
	8/9	night	nothing of importance occurred.	[initials]
	9/10	–	Bn. was relieved in the line by the 14th Y & L & moved back into support in the BEEHIVE.	[initials]
	10/11	–	The Battalion moved back into Bde reserve at Thelus, relieving the 11th E. Lancs	[initials]
	11/8/17		Major Allen proceeded on leave.	[initials]
	11/12	night	Battalion working parties to Front Area	[initials]
	12/8/17		Officers postings:-	
			Capt R.E.J. Moore. rejoined the Bn. from Hospital. 30.7.17 and assumed command of C. Co. 5.8.17 vice	
			Capt K.R. Davies to XIII Corps Draft Training depot.	
			2nd Lieut. E.N. Taylor rejoined the Bn. from Hospital 2.8.17. and is posted to "A" Company.	[initials]
			" " O.H. Green joined the Bn. for duty from the Base 30.7.17 and is posted to "B" Coy.	
			" " D.O. Browning " " " " " " " " " " " "C" "	
			" " G.W. Todd " " " " " " " " 2-8-17 " " " "A" "	
			Lieut & actg Capt. R.W. Leamon relinquished the acting rank of Capt on ceasing to command a Coy. 15.7.17.	

A5834 Wt. W4973/M687 750,000 8/16 D. D. & L. Ltd. Forms/C.2118/13.

Instructions regarding War Diaries and Intelligence Summaries are contained in F. S. Regs., Part II. and the Staff Manual respectively. Title pages will be prepared in manuscript.

WAR DIARY
or
~~INTELLIGENCE SUMMARY.~~

(Erase heading not required.)

Army Form C. 2118.

Place	Date	Hour	Summary of Events and Information	Remarks and references to Appendices
VIMY RIDGE.	12/13	night.	The Battalion found Working parties to the Front Area.	[initials]
	13/14	night	The Battalion found working parties for Front line.	[initials]
	14/15	"	Working Parties provided for improvement of Front Line system & its defences, as on previous nights.	[initials]
	15/16	"		
	16th.	After noon.	Battn on being relieved by the 18th Bn West Yorkshire Regt, marched via NEUVILLE ST VAAST to hutments at MONT ST ELOI in the ACQ area. WINNIPEG CAMP The Battn strength at this time was lower than it had been at any time since July 1916 & Coys were forced to re-organise on the basis of 2 Platoons per Company. Details of the strength were as follow:- Effective Strength 31 Officers 559 Other Ranks. Detached from unit for various employments 10 Officers 132 Other Ranks. Ration strength 21 " 437 "	[initials]
MONT ST ELOI	17th.	-	Rest day for the troops.	

A5834 Wt. W4973/M687 750,000 8/16 D. D. & L. Ltd. Forms/C.2118/13.

Instructions regarding War Diaries and Intelligence Summaries are contained in F. S. Regs., Part II. and the Staff Manual respectively. Title pages will be prepared in manuscript.

WAR DIARY
or
~~INTELLIGENCE SUMMARY.~~
(*Erase heading not required.*)

Army Form C. 2118.

Place	Date	Hour	Summary of Events and Information	Remarks and references to Appendices
MONT ST ELOI	18/8/17.	—	Day devoted to general cleaning up & sports. The Sports were very successful, but heavy rain compelled a premature finish at 5-30 pm. Brigadier Gen. G.T. Carter-Campbell D.S.O., Commanding 9th Infty Bde, was an interested spectator.	JHW
"	19/8/17 to 23/8/17.		These five days were spent in general training which comprised nearly all subjects. At 9-0 am daily the Battn fell in in Mass & performed "setting up" drill for ½ hour. Coys were then placed at the disposal of Coy Commanders. Riflemen & Snipers fired on the Rifle Range, & Specialists had special "refresher" courses. An interesting feature was rehearsals of a small raid by Fighting Patrols, live Bangalore Torpedoes being used. On one occasion special instruction was given by the R.Es in Revetting work. Owing to the increasing use of poisonous gases, necessitating almost constant use of Box Respirators, & the importance of troops maintaining their sense of direction when wearing the mask, the men were practised nightly in marching short distances, whilst wearing their masks.	JHW
	24/8/17	1-15pm.	Battn entrained at LAUREL Light Railway Siding en route for Front line trenches ACHEVILLE Sector there to relieve 15th Bn West Yorks Regt. Tea was taken at NEUVILLE ST VAAST (Transport lines) Bn marching off at 7-30 pm. Weather fine.	JHW

A5834 Wt. W4973/M687 750,000 8/16 D. D. & L. Ltd. Forms/C.2118/13.

Instructions regarding War Diaries and Intelligence Summaries are contained in F. S. Regs., Part II. and the Staff Manual respectively. Title pages will be prepared in manuscript.

WAR DIARY
or
~~INTELLIGENCE SUMMARY.~~
(*Erase heading not required.*)

Army Form C. 2118.

Place	Date	Hour	Summary of Events and Information	Remarks and references to Appendices
Trenches. Front Line. ACHEVILLE. Sector.	25/8/17		For this period hostilities were very quiet, but during	[illegible]
	26/8/17		the nights much active patrolling was done. For the first time Camouflage suits were	[illegible]
	27/8/17		used by this Battn for daylight reconnoitring patrols.	[illegible]
	28/8/17		Still little activity. In a patrol encounter in NO MAN'S LAND, a "C" Coy Private failed to return to our lines, & though search was afterwards made he could not be found.	[illegible]
	29/8/17	9.30 pm	Very quiet all day. An Enterprise Patrol, consisting of 1 Officer & 16 OR proceeded into NO MAN'S LAND with object of locating hostile patrol & securing identifications. No hostile patrol was seen. On the way out the enemy apparently observed our party & opened Machine Gun fire. One of the patrol (Sgt FOOTITT) dropped first in front of our wire. As the N.C.O. was the last man of the party this was not noticed except by a N.C.O. in the Front Line, who mentally marked the place where the soldier fell. But when search was made the Sgt was missing. He may possibly have been wounded & lost his way.	[illegible]
Brigade Support. BEEHIVE & CANADA TR.	30/8/17	10.30 pm	Battn relieved by the 1/4th Bn, York & Lancs Rgt. Battn moved back to Brigade Support at the BEEHIVE & CANADA TRENCH. There were no casualties. No trace has been seen of Sgt FOOTITT, although several parties have been out, including men in camouflage suits during the day.	[illegible]
	31/8/17		Uneventful.	

Nauman Hood Lieut Col
Commanding
12 S. B. York & Lancaster Rgt.

A7092 Wt. W128 9/M1293 750,000. 1/17. D. D & L. Ltd. Forms/C2118/14.

Copy
STAY
Operation Order No 42.

Ref Map PETIT VIMY French Map 8.8.17

1 The Battn will be relieved in the line on the night of 9/10th Aug by BLOCK & will move into support on completion of relief taking over accommodation in CANADA TR & the BEEHIVE from BLOCK

2. The Battn will move into Bde Reserve on the night of 10/11 Aug taking over accommodation from GUY on the VIMY RIDGE & Railway Embankment.

3. The Relief referred to in para 2 will be carried out as follows –

B Coy BLOCK	relieving	B Coy STAY	–	Left front
C "	"	A "	"	Right "
B "	"	B "	"	WINNIPEG
HQ "	"	HQ "		BRANDON

B Coy STAY will remain in WINNIPEG RD after being relieved in front line until arrival of B Coy BLOCK. The relief will take place in above order commencing at dark.

4 A & B Coy with details of C Coy attached will take over accommodation in CANADA TR from B & C Coys BLOCK respectively after relief.

5 2nd Lt Burgess 1 NCO + 2 Signallers from HQ together with 1 Officer, 1 NCO + 1 Signaller per Coy will report at HQ BLOCK at BEE HIVE at 2 30pm + take over accommodation trench stores etc.

6 1 Officer 1 NCO + 2 Signallers from HQ + each Coy of BLOCK will be sent forward to take over trench stores etc in the line arriving 2 30pm.

7 Trench store lists will be made out by 2 30pm forwarded to Bn HQ as soon as possible after stores have been handed over.

8 All empty water tins must be returned to Bn Dump by 8pm + OC HQ Coy will arrange to carry them out + hand them over to Transport of BLOCK at the ration dump.

9 Rations will be delivered tomorrow night to Coy HQ in the new area by Transport.

10 Completion of relief to be reported to Battn HQ by Coy Commanders personally on the way out

11 The move referred to in para (1) above will be carried out as follows.
C Coy STAY will relieve X Coy GUY in RAILWAY EMBT.
A+B " " remaining Coys of GUY in trenches on VIMY RIDGE, A Coy taking over trenches nearest Battn HQ. Coys will move at dusk.

12 Guides at the rate of 1 per Coy will report at Battn HQ at BEEMIE at dusk & Coys will pick them up in passing

13 2nd Lt Pring with 1 NCO per Coy will report to HQ GUY at 11 am on the 10th inst to take over accommodation etc.

14 OC. Coys will report when all men of their Coy are settled in new area

15 Coys will re-organise into the original 3 Coys during the morning of the 10th inst

16 ACKNOWLEDGE

(Sd) NL Lumbridge Capt
Adjt
5TA

Copies to No 1 File
2 A
3 B
4 C
5 HQ
6 QM
7 MO
8 BLOCK
9 GUY
10 TACKLE
11 WAR DIARY
12 P Coy BLOCK.

S E C R E T. Copy No. 12

STAY OPERATION ORDER NO.73. 15.8.17.

Ref Maps:-
Sheet 36.c.S.W.)
57.b.N.W.)
51.c.N.E.)

1. The 94TH.INFANTRY BRIGADE will be relieved in the line by the 93RD.INFANTRY BRIGADE on 16th/17th. August and will move into Divisional Reserve on relief.

2. The Battalion will be relieved by the 18TH.WEST YORKS RGT on the afternoon of the 16th inst, and will take over accommodation at WINNIPEG CAMP (F.1.d.8.3.) from the 18TH.DURHAM LIGHT INFANTRY on relief.

3. The relief will be carried out by daylight, the relieving troops commencing to arrive at Battn.H.Qrs about 5.15 p.m., and the Embankment at 6.15 p.m.

4. The Coys at the Embankment will wait until both relieving Companies have arrived on the spot, and will then file off along the embankment from the Right and will move out by the trench over the ridge.
H.Q.Coy and "B" Coy will move off on receipt of orders from H.Qrs.

5. Route. Companies will march out by the following route :-

LES TILLEULS Cross Roads,
NEUVILLE ST VAAST,
LA TARGETTE Cross Roads,
Cross Roads, F.12.a.,
" " F.10.b.,
" " F.15.a.0.6.,
WINNIPEG CAMP.

Coys will rendezvous at A.8.a.2.7 on the Left side of the road, where hot tea will be served to the men.

6. Guides on the scale of 1 per Coy, and 2 for H.Qrs, will report at Battalion Orderly Room at 1.45pm O.C."B" Coy will detail a N.C.O. to take charge of this party of guides and to be at LA TARGETTE Cross Roads at 3.45pm. They will conduct relieving troops via mule track running past PAYNSLEY CAMP. N.C.O. will reconnoitre route earlier in morning.

7. 18TH WEST YORKS REGT will send one Officer per Coy and one for Battn H.Qrs, and one N.C.O. per platoon to report at Battn H.Qrs at 9.a.m. tomorrow. They will proceed to respective Coys on arrival to take over stores, accommodation, etc.

8. All Trench Stores, except petrol tins on ridge will be handed over on relief and Trench Store Lists forwarded to Battn H.Qrs as soon as possible after relief.

9. Completion of relief will be wired to Battn H.Q., Code Word "WIRE" being used.

10. ACKNOWLEDGE.

A.P. Trenbridge
Captain & Adjutant,
STAY.

Copies to :-

No.1.	C.O.	9.	R-S-M.
2.	Adjutant.	10.	2nd.Lt.Tonge.
3/6	All Coys.	11.)	
7.	M.O.	12.)	War Diary.
8.	Q.M.	13.	File.

ADMINISTRATIVE INSTRUCTIONS ISSUED WITH OPERATION

ORDER NO. 73.

1. Regimental Transport and Q.M. Stores will not move to WINNIPEG CAMP with the exception of
   1 limber,
   1 watercart,
   Messcart,
   Officers' Riding Horses.

2. All baggage, stores, etc, of Headquarters and "B" Coy will be sent down by rail to TERRITORIAL EASTSTATION. Tractor and truck will be at Battalion H.Qs at 4.30.p.m. for this purpose. The Q.M. will arrange Transport from TERRITORIAL EAST STATION.

3. All trench Stores with H.Qs and "B" Coy will be collected in a Dump under the supervision of the R.S.M. and handed over to Brigade and not to the relieving Unit.

4. All petrol tins at Headquarters and "B" Coy will be sent down by rail and not handed over.

5. O.C.Coys at the Embankment will arrange to point out to the relieving troops the exact spot their rations are dumped from the trucks.

6. 2nd.Lieut TONGE will proceed in advance to WINNIPEG CAMP to take over accommodation etc, leaving Battalion H.Qs at 9.0.a.m. andpicking up C.Q.M.Ss at Transport Lines.

Captain and Adjutant,
STAY.

Addendum to Operation Order No 14

The 15th West Yorks Regt are holding 20 posts only. New numbering of posts has been altered since the Battalion was in the line.

B Coy will take over posts 1 to 10

A " " " " 11 to 20

according to new numbering.

23/8/17

[illegible signature] Capt & Adjt 1 BEF

S E C R E T.

Copy No. 12

IBEX OPERATION ORDER NO. 74.

Ref Maps :-
Sheet 36.c.S.W.
51.b.N.W.
51.c.N.E.

23.8.17.

---

1. The 94TH INFANTRY BRIGADE will relieve the 93RD INFANTRY BRIGADE in the ACHEVILLE SECTION on the night of 24th/25th August.

2. Dispositions after the relief will be as follows :-

12th. YORK & LANC R.	L.1. Sub-section.
13th. YORK & LANC R.	L.2. -do-
11th. EAST LANC R.	Brigade Support.
14th. YORK & LANC R.	Brigade Reserve.

3. This Battalion will relieve the 15th WEST YORKSHIRE REGT in L.1 Sub-section. The relief will be carried out as follows :-

"C" Coy, 12th Y & L relieves "A ½ B" Coy, 15th W Y Rgt in Right Front Sub-section.
"A" Coy 12th Y & L " "½ B + C" 15th W Y Rgt in Left Front Sub-section.
"B" Coy 12th Y & L " "D" " 15th W Y Rgt in Support in WINNIPEG.
H.Q.Coy 12th Y & L " H.Q. " 15th W Y Rgt in BRANDON TR.
The relief will take place in the above order.

4. The Battalion will entrain at LAUREL SIDING at 1.15.p.m.24th. inst.,10 trucks of the train being available. Companies will entrain in the order laid down in para 3 above, and will detrain at TERRITORIAL WEST SIDING and will proceed to A.8.a.2.7 on the Left side of the road where Tea will be served. The Battalion will remain at the above place until 7.30.p.m. at which hour it will move off for the trenches in the order indicated in para 3.
No guides will be provided.

5. One Officer, one N.C.O. and two signallers from each Company, together with C-S-M BROWN and two signallers from H.Qrs will proceed to the trenches from the Transport Lines at 9.a.m. tomorrow, to take over stores, etc, of their respective Companies.

6. Trench Store Lists will be handed in to Orderly Room as soon as possible after stores have been taken over.

7. Completion of relief will be notified to Battalion H.Qrs by Wire,- Code Word - MONEY.

8. Sketch shewing dispositions and locations of nearest posts of Units on the flanks will be ~~reported~~ submitted to Battalion H.Qrs by 10.a.m on the morning after relief.

9. ACKNOWLEDGE.

(Sd.) N.L.TUNBRIDGE, Capt & Adjutant,
IBEX.

Copies to :-

No.1.	C.O.	9.	T.O.
2.	Adjt.	10.	R-S-M.
3/6.	All Coys.	11.	War
7.	M.O.	12.	Diary.
8.	Q.M.	13.	File.

ADMINISTRATIVE INSTRUCTIONS ISSUED WITH OPERATION ORDER No. 74, dated 23.8.17.

---

1. The Transport Officer will arrange Transport for all Lewis Guns, Panniers, etc., from TERRITORIAL WEST STATION to LEVIS DUMP.
   Officers Commanding Companies will arrange to be at LEVIS DUMP at 10.p.m. and pick up their Lewis Guns etc on their way to the trenches.

2. Water. All water bottles will be filled before moving off for the trenches. The usual water supply will be sent up on the Lewis Gun Limbers.
   O.C. "B" Company will arrange carrying parties to distribute this to Companies after completion of relief.

3. Rations. Rations will be issued to Companies at A.8.a.2.7 on the Left side of the road and carried in on the man.

4. Packs will be dumped at A.8.a.2.7 and Transport Officer will arrange for transport to Q.M.Stores.

5. Baggage. All Officers' Valises, Orderly Room Stores, Mess Stores and other surplus stores will be dumped outside the Guard Room by 1.p.m.

(Sd.) N.L.TUNBRIDGE, Capt & Adjutant,
IBEX.

Copy No. [illegible]

[illegible] York & Lancaster Regt.

Operation Order No 75

Ref Maps:-
[illegible] {
[illegible] {

---

1. The Battalion will be relieved in the line by the 14th York & Lancaster Regt on the night 30/31st Aug. and will move into Brigade Support in CANADA TRENCH on completion of relief.

2. The relief will be carried out as follows:-
"D" Coy. 14th Y&L relieves "C" Coy 12th Y&L in left front line
"B" " " " "A" " " " Right "
"C" " " " "B" " " " Support.
HQ " " " HQ " " "
Relieving Companies will arrive in above order commencing at about 10.15pm.

3. 1 Officer, 1 N.C.O. and 2 Signallers per Coy and HQ of 14th Y&L will report at Bn. HQ at 3pm proceeding to respective Coys on arrival to take over trench stores etc.

4. All water tins in possession of A, B & C Coys will be dumped at

WINNIPEG ROAD by 6 pm. [illegible] O.C.
B Coy will arrange to take them down to the ration dump before relieving troops commence to arrive.

R.Q.M.S. will arrange to take all [illegible] in his possession to the ration dump as above. The R.Q.M.S. will arrange to hand these over to the 11th [illegible] at the dump.

5. Trench store lists will be handed in to Orderly Room signed by both parties by 12 pm.

6. Completion of relief in the line, to be reported in writing [illegible] as well as by [illegible] [illegible] being used.
A Battalion runner will wait at junction of HUDSON C.T. and BRANDON from 11.30 pm until completion of relief and reports may be handed to him for conveyance to Battalion H.Qrs.

7. On completion of relief the Battalion will take over accommodation in CANADA TR and the BEEHIVE from 13th York & Lanc Regt as follows:-

C Coy 12th Y+L from C Coy 13th Y+L
D " " " B " "
B " " A " "
HQ " " HQ " "

Companies of 13th Y+L are situated as follows:-

D Coy (HQ at T.28 b 7.2) in CANADA TR.
S of HUDSON C.T.
A Coy (HQ at T22 c 5.3.) in CANADA TR
from HUDSON C.T. to junction of GRAND TRUNK
and CANADA.
B Coy (HQ at T21 d 4.6) in CANADA TR
junction of GRAND TRUNK & CANADA TR
to Brigade Northern Boundary.

6. Coys will each detail 1 officer, 1
N.C.O and 1 signaller and 1 Runner
to report at Batt HQ at 2pm to
proceed under 2nd Lt McNAMARA to
H.Q. 13th Y+L at the BEEHIVE to take
over stores & accommodation. C.S.M
BROWN and 2 signallers from HQ will
accompany this party.
Coys will also detail one N.C.O and 5
men to leave the trenches at 6pm and
proceed to their new area to assist in
unloading rations etc.

9. The [illegible] [illegible] in new position will furnish a guide for each Coy from junctions of HUDSON and SASKATCHEWAN.

10. Companies will report completion of move by wire to Batt. H.Q. code word – "SANDBAG" being used.

11. Rations will be delivered by transport to Coy H.Qrs in the new area about 9.30 pm.

12. ACKNOWLEDGE.

[signature]
Capt & Adjutant.
[illegible] Bn York & Lancaster Regt

Copies to:–

No 1.	C.O.	No 6.	Q.M.
2	O.C. A	" 7	T.O.
3	B	" 8	[illegible]
4	C	" 9	[illegible]
5	HQ	10.	File

Confidential

Volume XXI

Vol 19

War Diary.

12th (S) Bn. York & Lancaster Regt — 31st Division

September 1917.

Army Form C. 2118.

Instructions regarding War Diaries and Intelligence Summaries are contained in F. S. Regs., Part II. and the Staff Manual respectively. Title pages will be prepared in manuscript.

WAR DIARY
or
~~INTELLIGENCE SUMMARY.~~

(*Erase heading not required.*)

Place	Date	Hour	Summary of Events and Information	Remarks and references to Appendices
BEEHIVE & CANADA TRENCH. Area: T 27 d.	1/9/17	–	In the evening the Battalion provided Working Parties in forward trenches.	
	2/9/17	9-0 AM	Capt. H. L. TUNBRIDGE proceeded to 94th Infantry Brigade HQrs for temporary duty as Brigade Major. Information received that Captain R.E.J. MOORE on account of defective eyesight had been declared "P.B." at Base Depot. Working Parties provided in the evening as on previous day.	B.
In front of Railway Embankment & Petit Vimy & Vimy.	3/9/17		Quiet day with increased aerial activity. 2/Lieut. R. MARSDEN joined the Battn for duty. Usual evening Working Parties provided.	
	4/5-9/17	Midnight onwards	Quiet day. The area in the rear: VIMY (T 10 c & d, T 20 c & d, T 25 A & b, T 26 a & b) was subjected to gas shell bombardment, 7.7 cm & 4.2 cm being the type of shell used. Between the hours 12 midnight to 12-30 AM and 1-25 AM to 2-20 AM, over 5000 shells were fired by the enemy. "Yellow Cross" marks were seen on shell fragments denoting the kind of gas used. The battalion suffered no casualties.	B.
Front Line ACHEVILLE	5/9/17	8 pm.	The Battalion commenced to relieve the 14th K. S. Bn. York & Lancaster Regt in Front Line – ACHEVILLE Sector. There were no casualties. (0076)	B.
	6/9/17 & 7/9/17		The 31st Divn extended its right to include the Left and Centre Battn fronts of the 5th Divn, handing over the Left Brigade front, MERICOURT Section, to 2nd Canadian Division. The 94th Infantry Brigade will now hold the ACHEVILLE Section permanently. The Battalion ~~[struck out]~~ extended its frontage taking over the frontage ~~[struck out]~~ held by the 13th Bn York & Lancaster Rgt, one Company of the 13th York & Lancaster Rgt being attached as local reserve. (0077)	B.

A7092. Wt. W123 9/M1293 750,000. 1/17. D. D & L. Ltd. Forms/C2118/14.

Instructions regarding War Diaries and Intelligence Summaries are contained in F. S. Regs., Part II. and the Staff Manual respectively. Title pages will be prepared in manuscript.

WAR DIARY
or
~~INTELLIGENCE SUMMARY.~~
(Erase heading not required.)

2

Army Form C. 2118.

Place	Date	Hour	Summary of Events and Information	Remarks and references to Appendices
–	–	–	The under mentioned appointments appeared in the "London Gazette" Supplement, dated August 27th/17 "York & Lancaster Regt.– Temp. Lieuts. to be Temp. Captains: E.L. MOXEY (Actg Capt) (Feby 23) T.L. WARD (March 12) To be Temp. Lieuts. 2 Lieut (Actg Capt) M.B. WALLACE. (Leo. Rif. T.F.) 2 Lieut. F.G. MORRIS. (from York & Lancaster R–attd) 2 Lieut C.A. JACKSON. 2 Lieut. F.H. WESTBY. – All four dated Feby 23 – 2 Lieut. G.C.M.L. PIRKIS (March 12) 2 Lieut S. CRAWFORD (Spec. Res.) (May 13)." "	B.
Front Line	8/9/17	–	Battalion transport lines were moved from NEUVILLE ST VAAST to ECURIE, the lines of 1st Bn, EAST SURREYS being taken over. A/Captain R.W. LEAMON proceeded to XI Corps School, MERVILLE as instructor.	B.
	9/9/17 10/9/17 11/9/17		Hostilities continued to be normal for this period of duty in the line, but the value of camouflage suits was further proved by the success of Daylight patrols. These patrols were able to approach the enemy lines to within 50 yds. without being discovered & brought back useful information concerning the enemy wire, posts, & locations of snipers posts. The Intelligence	

A7092 Wt. W128 9/M1293 750,000. 1/17. D. D & L. Ltd. Forms/C2118/14.

Instructions regarding War Diaries and Intelligence Summaries are contained in F. S. Regs., Part II. and the Staff Manual respectively. Title pages will be prepared in manuscript.

WAR DIARY or ~~INTELLIGENCE SUMMARY.~~

(*Erase heading not required.*)

3

Army Form C. 2118.

Place	Date	Hour	Summary of Events and Information	Remarks and references to Appendices
ACHEVILLE	–	–	Depot reported the relief of the 6th BAVARIAN Division by the 11th Reserve GUARDS Division on the 9th, in this particular section of the line. On the 10th 2Lt D.O. BROWNING & 3 O.R. were gassed owing to one of our gas cylinders being perforated by enemy shelling.	[initials]
ROCLINCOURT	11/9/17	2pm	Battalion ~~[struck out]~~ relieved by the 13th S. Bn York & Lancaster Regt & moved back to hutments at SPRINGVALE CAMP, ROCLINCOURT, the relief being complete by 6 0 pm. No casualties (0079)	
			2nd Lieut C.E. BLAD. and 2nd Lieut D. HARRISON joined the Battn for duty & were posted to "C" Company.	[initials]
	12/9/17		Capt N.L. TUNBRIDGE rejoined Battn from Brigade H.Q. 2/Lt A.L. TAYLOR proceeded to XIII Corps Musketry & Reinforcement Camp to relieve Capt K.R. DAVIES. The Battalion had rest day.	[initials]
	13/9/17 14/9/17 15/9/17		Training on usual lines, special attention being given to patrol work by day and night. "A" Coy did special training in connection with the Company Raid they will make when in the line next time.	
			Two Officers joined the Battn for duty. Lieut NOAKES. T.L., from 6th Entrenching Battn & 2Lieut. LAYCOCK. H.R., also from the 6th Bn. Capt DAVIES rejoined the Bn on the 15th.	[initials]
	14/9/17		GHQ List No 151, dated 1st Sept/17 contained the following:–	

A7092 Wt. W128_9/M1293 750,000. 1/17. D. D & L. Ltd. Forms/C2118/14.

4

Army Form C. 2118.

WAR DIARY
or
~~INTELLIGENCE SUMMARY.~~
(Erase heading not required.)

Instructions regarding War Diaries and Intelligence Summaries are contained in F. S. Regs., Part II. and the Staff Manual respectively. Title pages will be prepared in manuscript.

Place	Date	Hour	Summary of Events and Information	Remarks and references to Appendices
			"York & Lancs. R. – 12th Bn. Lieut. M. B. WALLACE, 5th Bn. [illegible] to be actg Capt whilst commanding a Co. 3rd July, 1917	
			The under mentioned to be actg Capts (Additional) dated 20th July/17 – Lieut. R. W. LEAMON (S.R.) Temp. Lieut. G. C. M. L. PIRKIS.	[illegible]
ROCLINCOURT	16/9/17	9-30 am	Draft of 132 O.R. joined the Battalion from XIII Corps Musketry & Reinforcement Camp, where they had been training for some 6 weeks. This draft was composed of men transferred from 1/6th Bn NORFOLK Regt. Army Cyclist Corps.	[illegible]
		2-0 pm.	Battn Practised attack (See attached)	
	17/9/17	9-0 am.	Battn again practised the attack as per scheme for previous day. The Battn is now re-organised on the basis of 3 Fighting Coys each consisting of 3 platoons, & the actual Trench Strength is approximately 475. The Bn Ration strength is 595 O.R.	[illegible]
BROWN LINE VIMY RIDGE	18/9/17	10-0 am.	Battn moved off to relieve the 11th [illegible] Bn East Lancs Regt in Brigade "B" Support Line or BROWN LINE, a system of trenches running over the crest of VIMY RIDGE & to the SOUTH of THELUS area. Working parties were provided in the evening. (OO 80)	
	19/9/17	–	Working Parties during day & night. "A" Coy sent patrols to front line & to reconnoitre the point of entry for the coming raid.	[illegible]
	20/9/17	–	A similar programme of work prevailed as on the 19th. The Battn,	

A7092 Wt. W128 9/M1293 750,000. 1/17. D. D & L. Ltd. Forms/C2118/14.

Instructions regarding War Diaries and Intelligence Summaries are contained in F. S. Regs., Part II. and the Staff Manual respectively. Title pages will be prepared in manuscript.

WAR DIARY
or
INTELLIGENCE SUMMARY.
(Erase heading not required.)

Army Form C. 2118.

5

Place	Date	Hour	Summary of Events and Information	Remarks and references to Appendices
	20/9/17		however, had an officer casualty, Captain V. S. SIMPSON M.C., the Officer Commanding "A" Coy, being wounded in the left arm by a bullet [whilst on patrol work.]	S.
	21/9/17 22/9/17		Quiet days. Usual working parties. The Raiding Party left for transport lines to complete their training, under the personal supervision of the Commanding Officer.	S.
	23/9/17		Nothing to report.	
	24/9/17		Battn moved up to Bde "A" Support Line, viz RED LINE in front of WILLERVAL at 10 AM, relieving the 11th Bn East Lancs Rgt, the 13th Bn York & Lancaster Rgt, taking over the BROWN LINE. "B" Coy were moved up in close support to 11th S. Bn, EAST Lancs. Rgt & came under orders of C.O., of that Battn. Artillery activity was above normal, the enemy intermittently shelling WILLERVAL & FARBUS. No casualties. (O.O. 81)	S.
	25/9/17		Very quiet & spell of good weather still unbroken. At 12 Noon O/C "B" Coy reported 6 casualties owing to enemy shelling: 2 O.R killed & 4 O.R. wounded. Strangely enough, all with the exception of 1 O.R. wounded, were men of the new draft. Later one died of wounds in Aid Station.	S.

(A7092). Wt W12839/M1293. 75,0.0. 1/17. D. D. & L., Ltd. Forms/C.2118/14.

WAR DIARY
or
~~INTELLIGENCE SUMMARY.~~
(Erase heading not required.)

6

Army Form C. 2118.

Instructions regarding War Diaries and Intelligence Summaries are contained in F. S. Regs., Part II. and the Staff Manual respectively. Title pages will be prepared in manuscript.

Place	Date	Hour	Summary of Events and Information	Remarks and references to Appendices
RED LINE ACHEVILLE	26/9/17	–	Very quiet. Usual Working Parties provided. 2/Lieut. H.G. MANN, "B" Coy, was transferred to the 2nd Bn York & Lancs Regt, his original Battn. The G.O.C. Division granted Lieut S CRAWFORD sanction to wear the badges of Acting Captain vice Capt MOORE, pending notification in the "London Gazette".	
do	27/9/17		Quiet day, & usual W.Ps. Capt K R DAVIES having been certified unfit physically for front line work proceeded to join the Infantry Base Depot for duty. The Coy Commanders now are:- "A" Coy Lieut. T.C. NOAKES. "B" " A/Capt. M.B. WALLACE. "C" " A/Capt. G.C.M.L. PIRKIS. "D" (HQ) A/Capt. S. CRAWFORD.	
do	28/9/17	–	Quiet day & Working Parties as on previous days. Considerable aerial activity.	
do	29/9/17	–	do do do do	
		7.0pm	Raiding Party rejoined the Battn from Transport Lines.	
FRONT LINE ACHEVILLE	30/9/17	10 AM	Battalion moved from the RED LINE to relieve the 11th Bn EAST LANCS. R. in the Front Line the 13th Bn YORK & LANCS taking over the RED LINE. The relief was completed without any casualties. (O.O. 80)	

Instructions regarding War Diaries and Intelligence Summaries are contained in F. S. Regs., Part II. and the Staff Manual respectively. Title pages will be prepared in manuscript.

WAR DIARY

or

~~INTELLIGENCE SUMMARY.~~

(Erase heading not required.)

Army Form C. 2118.

Place	Date	Hour	Summary of Events and Information	Remarks and references to Appendices
FRONT LINE. ACHEVILLE	30/9/17	9-0pm	In the evening ~~[illegible]~~ the enemy has bombarded the Battn frontage with gas shells and despite precautionary measures we have suffered considerable casualties, the full extent of which will not be known until tomorrow. Oct 1/17.	[illegible]

[illegible signature] Lieut. Colonel Comd., 12th (S) Bn. York & Lancs. Rgt. (Sheffield)

A7092 Wt. W128_9/M1293 750,000. 1/17. D. D & L. Ltd. Forms/C2118/14.

IBEX OPERATION ORDER No.76. Copy No.13.

Ref.Map.
PETIT VIMY 1/20,000. 4.9.17.

1. The Battalion will relieve IMBIBE in the front line on the night of the 5/6th September.

2. The relief will be carried out in the following order, commencing as soon after dusk as possible
"A" Coy IBEX relieve "A" Coy IMBIBE on the Right Front.
"B" " " " "B" " " " " Left "
"C" " " " "C" " " in Support.
H.Q " " " H.Q " " .

3. 1 Officer, 1 N.C.O and 2 Signallers per Coy and H.Q. will report at IMBIBE Battn H.Q. at 3.p.m. on the 5th, proceeding to respective Coys on arrival to take over trench stores, etc. Similar parties from IMBIBE will report to us for the same purpose at 3.p.m.

4. The Transport Officer will arrange for ration limber to call at the BEEHIVE on the way back to pick up Officers' valises and surplus stores.

5. Completion of relief to be notified to Battn.H.Q. by code word "BERM", and trench Store lists signed by both parties to reach H.Q by 9.a.m. on the 6th inst.

6. A sketch shewing dispositions and positions of neighbouring posts to be sent in to Battn.H.Qs by 9.a.m. on the 6th.

7. ACKNOWLEDGE.

S Crawford
Lieutenant.
A/Adjutant.
IBEX.

Copies to

No.1	C.O.
2.	2nd.in.C.
3.	Adjutant.
4.	O.C."A" Coy.
5.	"B" "
6.	"C" "
7.	H.Q. "
8.	M.O
9.	Q.M:
10.	T.O.
11.	R.S.M.
12.& 13.	War Diary.
14.	File.

trench store lists to Battalion H.Qs as soon as possible.

7 Completion of relief to be notified to Batt. HQ by code word "COTTON"

8 Transport Officer will arrange for four limbers to be at LEVIS Dump at 9 pm to convey L.G. panniers, MO's & other stores to new camp.

9 Coys will each detail two men from their L.G. teams to remain at LEVIS Dump to act as loading party & they will proceed with the limbers. C Coy will detail one N.C.O to be in charge of this party.

10 An Officer & N.C.O from HQ & each Coy of IMAGE will report to take over trench stores & dispositions at 11-0 AM.

11 The QM will arrange for hot meals to be provided for each Coy on arrival in camp.

12 The T.O. will arrange for horses for the C.O, Adjutant & M.O, to be at LES TILLEULS X RDS at 5-30 pm.

13 A guide will be at LES TILLEULS X Rds to direct Coys to the Camp & the QM will arrange for guides to meet each platoon at ECURIE.

(C7)

Operation Orders No 77

Ref. Map. PETIT VIMY 6/9/17
1/20,000

I. The Battn will today, the 6 Sept, take over in addition to their present frontage, the frontage at present occupied by IMAGE. One Coy of IMAGE being attached as local reserve and accommodated in WINNIPEG Rd.

2 Dispositions of Coys. "A" Coy will take over Posts Nos 8 to 18, both inclusive, Nos 1–7 being evacuated. The remainder of platoon to be in close support in TRIUMPH TR. South of HUDSON TR. HQ to remain as before:

B Coy will take over the front at present occupied by A Coy, IMAGE plus posts 19 & 20. Same dispositions & strength of posts to be observed. The remainder of Coy to be in close support in TRIUMPH TR, North of HUDSON TR. Battn HQ to remain as before.

C Coy will take over the front line at present occupied by B Coy IMAGE. Same dispositions & strength of posts to be observed. Remainder of Coy to be in close support in QUEBEC TR in old Coy HQ evacuated by IMAGE.

2

Coy HQ will be in NOVA SCOTIA . N. of TICKLER .

3 HQ Lewis gunners will be attached to Coys as follows:-

1 N.C.O & 10 to A Coy.
5 to B "
1 " & 5 to C "

4 Relief to take place at following times.
A Coy — as soon as possible.
B " 4-30 pm.
C " 5-30 pm.

5 Trench Store lists to be sent in to Bn HQ on completion of relief — Completion of relief to be notified to Batt HQ by code word BOTTLE.

6 A sketch showing new dispositions, including AA Lewis guns & neighbouring posts to reach Batt HQ by 9-0 AM 7th inst.

7 B & C Coys will each send an Officer & also 1 N.C.O per platoon in advance to take over trench stores & fix up accommodation.

8. ACKNOWLEDGE.

Copies No1 A by (Sd) S CRAWFORD
2 B " Lieut
3 C " A/Adjt
4 Files IBEX

1BEX

Operation Orders No 78

1. The following Coy boundaries in the front line will be arranged as follows:
Right Coy (A) From old No 5 Post to HUDSON (incl)
Centre Coy (B) from HUDSON to TICKLER (both excl).
Left Coy (C) from TICKLER to ACHEVILLE Rd (both incl)

2. B Coy will take over the left post of A Coy.
C Coy will hand over their left post NORTH ~~Road~~ of ACHEVILLE Rd to the 43rd CANADIANS & will take over the 2 left posts of B Coy. These two posts will consist of Rifle section + 1 NCO + 7 and L.G. post of 1 + 6 respectively.

3 Arrangements to be made between Coy Commanders & Completion of relief notified to Bn HQ by codeword TRENCH.

4 The necessary Changes in dispositions to be made tonight

Copies to 1 A Coy
2 B "
3 C "
4 File
5 } War Diary
6 }

[illegible]
1BEX

31/1/17

Copy II IBEX Operation Order No 79. No X

Ref Map.
PETIT-VIMY }
1/20,000 11/9/17

I. The Bn will be relieved by IMAGE today & will proceed to SPRINGVALE Camp, ROCLINCOURT.

2 A Coy IBEX will be relieved by A Coy IMAGE.
B " " " B " "
C " " " C " "
Support Coy IMAGE " " " Support " IMAIBE
HQ IBEX " " HQ " IMAGE.

3 Time of relief A.B. & HQ about 3pm & C Coy as soon after dusk as possible.

4 Route to new camp will be as follows: HUDSON – CANADA – RED LINE – TIRED ALLEY. Movement will be carried out through the trenches named only. On no account will any movement be allowed on the top until after dusk.

5 The following distances will be maintained – Between front line & TIRED ALLEY – 100x between platoons & 50x between sections. Between TIRED ALLEY & SPRINGVALE Camp 100x between platoons.

6 All trench stores to be handed over to incoming Bn & Coys will render

3.

Gds Rds & conduct them to their proper quarters.

(Sd) S CRAWFORD
Lieut
A/Adjt
IBEX

Copies to –

1 A Coy
2 B "
3 C "
4/5 HQ "
5 A A IMAGE.
6 File
7 OM & T.O.
8 ~~War Diary~~ File.
9 IMAGE.

SECRET. Copy No....15

13th. S. Battalion York and Lancaster Regiment.

OPERATION ORDER NO. 80.

Ref. Map. MAROEUIL, Sheet. 17.9.17.

1. The 13th. S. Battn. York and Lancaster Regiment will relieve the 11th. S. Battalion East Lanc. Rgt, in Brigade "B" Support Line tomorrow.

2. The relief will be carried out as follows:-

"A"	Coy	13th	Y & L	will	relieve	"W"	Coy	11th	E.L.Rgt.
"B"	"	"	"	"	"	"X"	"	"	"
H.Q	"	"	"	"	"	Y(HQ)	"	"	"
"C"	"	"	"	"	"	"Z"	"	"	"

3. Battalion will parade in Mass at 9.30.a.m. in fighting order for necessary inspections and will be ready to move off in the above order at 10.a.m. From the Camp to the BROWN LINE, 100 yds distance will be maintained between platoons.

4. ROUTE. A guide will proceed with the first platoon of "A" Coy to direct the way to the BROWN LINE.

5. 1 Officer, 1 N.C.O. and 2 Signallers per Coy and H.Q. will report at Orderly Room at 7.a.m. and will then proceed to H.Q. 11th. S. Bn. East Lanc. Rgt, to take over trench stores etc. from their respective Companies on arrival.

6. Trench Store list will be handed in to Orderly Room as soon as possible after stores have been taken over.

7. Completion of relief will be notified to Battalion H.Qs by wire, code word CONCERTINAS.

8. A sketch shewing dispositions will be sent to Battalion H.Qs by 9.p.m., 18.9.17.

9. ACKNOWLEDGE.

S. Crawford

Lieutenant,
A/Adjutant,
13th. S. Battalion York and Lancaster Regt.

Copies to

1. C.O.
2. 2nd. in. C.
3. Adjutant.
4 to 7. Coys.
8. M.O.
9. T.O.
10. Q.M.
11. R.S.M.
12. 11th. E.L.R.
13. File.
14 } War
15 } Diary.

ADMINISTRATIVE INSTRUCTIONS ISSUED WITH OPERATION ORDER NO.80. DATED 17.9.17.

---

1. The Transport Officer will arrange the Transport for all Lewis Guns, panniers, etc., from SPRINGVALE CAMP to OUSE ALLEY. Two men per Coy will proceed with the limbers to act as guard on arrival. Companies will make their own arrangements for collecting ~~preventing~~ the guns and panniers.

2. All water bottles will be filled before moving off for the trenches.

3. Sgt.Cook and Coy Cooks except one who will be detailed by the Sgt Cook to remain behind to look after Company cookers, will proceed with their Companies. Quartermaster will arrange for camp kettles to be taken up by the Transport.

4. Packs will be dumped near the guard room by 7.30.a.m. in order of Companies.

5. Any Officer who wishes, can have his valise taken up to the line. These will be dumped at Orderly Room by 8.30.a.m. Valises not to be taken, Mess Stores, or other surplus baggage will be dumped opposite the guard room by 8.30.a.m.

6. Transport for baggage detailed in para 4 and 5, will be arranged by Transport Officer.

7. Rations (but not water) will be sent up as usual, and a guide will meet limbers at Cross Roads near Commandant's House.

8. Transport Officer will arrange to send up two watercarts nightly; one water man to go up with the Battalion and remain in the line.

9. The 2nd.in.Command, Medical Officer, and Quartermaster, accompanied by the Orderly Officer and Area Commandant's representative, will inspect the Camp at 9.30.a.m. The Orderly Officer will obtain from the last named, a certificate of cleanliness for the Camp.

10. The Quartermaster will arrange to hand over SPRINGVALE CAMP to representative of the 13th.S.Bn.York and Lanc.Rgt.

SECRET

Copy No. 3 .....

12TH.S.BATTALION YORK AND LANCASTER REGIMENT.

Ref Maps, MAROEUIL, 1/20,000 & Trench Maps.

OPERATION ORDER No. 81.

23.9.17.

1. The Battalion will relieve the 11TH.EAST LANCASHIRE REGT in "A" Support tomorrow, 24th September, and will be relieved by the 13TH.YORK AND LANCASTER REGT in "B" Support.

2. The relief will be carried out as follows :-

"B" Company, 13th Y & L relieving "W" Company, 11th East Lanc Rgt, in TRIUMPH TRENCH and WINNIPEG RD, coming under orders of O.C. 11th East Lanc Rgt on relief.

"A" Company, 12th Y & L relieving "X" Company 11th E.Lanc Rgt in CANADA TRENCH, (T.28.b.)

"C" Company, 12th Y & L relieving "Z" Company, 11th E.Lanc Rgt in OTTAWA TRENCH.

"HQ"Company, 12th Y & L, relieving "HQ"Company 11th E.Lanc Rgt in RED LINE in B.4.c.

3. Companies will move off in the above order, using TIRED ALLEY and maintaining 100 yds between platoons, and 50 yds between sections, leading platoon moving off at 10.a.m.

4. 2nd.Lieut.McNAMARA, the R-S-M and 2 Signallers from "HQ", together with 1 Officer, 1 N.C.O. and 1 Signaller per Company will parade at the Orderly Room at 8.a.m. and proceed to H.Qrs 11th East Lanc Rgt at B.4.c.6.4 reaching there at 8.45.a.m., to take over accommodation trench stores, etc.

5. The Assistant Adjutant and 1 N.C.O. per Company will be left behind to hand over accommodation, trench stores, etc., to 13th Y & L Rgt, rejoining the Battalion in "A" Support on completion.
1 Officer, 1 N.C.O. and 2 Signallers per Company from 13th Y & L will arrive at Battalion H.Qrs at 9.a.m. to take over accommodation, stores, etc.

6. Trench Store Lists for both reliefs will be handed in to the Orderly Room by 6.p.m. on day of relief.

7. Sketches, shewing dispositions and location of Anti-aircraft Lewis Guns to reach Battalion H.Qrs by 6.p.m. on day of relief.

8. Completion of relief will be reported to Battalion H.Qrs by wire or runner - Code Word, DETONATOR.

M Tunbridge
Captain & Adjutant,
12th S.Battalion York and Lancaster Regiment.

Copies to :-

No.1. C.O.
2. 2nd in C.
3. Adjt.
4. to 7. Coys.
8. M.O.
9. T.O.
10. Q.M.
No.11. R-S-M.
12. 11th E.Lanc Rgt.
13. 13th Y & L Rgt.
14.) War
15.) Diary.
16. File.

ADMINISTRATIVE INSTRUCTIONS ISSUED WITH OPERATION ORDER NO81.

1. Rations and water will be delivered nightly to the following places.

	Rations.	Water.
"C" Coy.	To ration dump S. of WILLERVAL - ARLEUX Rd. at B.4.c.5.5.	Brought nightly in petrol tins with rations.
"B" Coy.	Brought up to LEVIS Ration Dump.	Same as for rations.
"A" Coy.	To point where limber track crosses CANADA TRENCH in T.28.b.	Tanks filled nightly by water carts at same place.
H.Q.	Same as for "A" Coy.	Tanks near Battalion H.Q filled nightly by water carts.

2. All water bottles must be filled before starting from present trenches.

3. All Coys except "B" Coy will take their cooks and dixies forward with them, as cooking can be carried out in the trenches to be occupied by them. "B" Coy's cooks will be sent back to Transport Lines.

4. Baggage. 1. All Officers' kits and other Company stores not required to be taken forward will be dumped near the canteen by 9.a.m.

   2. Officers' valises, Orderly Room stores, dixies (if desired), etc., will be dumped at the same time and place, but separate from stores mentioned in 1.

   Transport Officer will arrange for removal after dark.

   Each Company will leave an N.C.O. in charge of their dump, who will be responsible for the correct distribution of stores.

5. The Quartermaster will arrange to take over petrol tins from the Q.M. of the 11th E.Lanc.R. for the use of "C" and "B" Companies.

SECRET. COPY NO. 13

13TH (SERVICE) BATTN, YORK & LANCASTER REGIMENT.

Ref. Maps: MAROEUIL 1/20,000 & Trench Maps.

OPERATION ORDER. NO 82.

29.9.17.

1. The Battalion will relieve the 11th S.Bn, EAST LANCASHIRE REGT. in L 3 Sub-section tomorrow, September 30th, and will be relieved in "A" Support by the 13th S.Battn, YORK & LANCASTER REGIMENT.

2. Companies will relieve as follows :-

"A" Coy. 12 Y & L relieving "Z" Coy, 11 E.L., in RIGHT Front Line, relieved by "C" Coy, 13th Y & L.
"B" Coy. 12 Y & L relieving "W" Coy, 11 E.L. in CENTRE Front Line, relieved by "B" Coy, 13th Y & L.
"C" Coy. 12 Y & L relieving "X" Coy, 11 E.L., in LEFT Front Line, relieved by "A" Coy, 13th Y & L.
"HQ" Coy. 12 Y & L relieving "HQ" Coy. 11 E.L. relieved by "HQ" Coy. 13th Y & L.

"B" Coy, 13th Bn, York & Lancaster Regt will relieve "B" Coy, 12th York & Lancaster Regiment attached 11th Bn, East Lancs, at present in Support, coming under orders of O.C., this Battn on relief.

3. Companies will take over the existing dispositions of the 11th Bn, East Lancashire Regt in the Front Line, remainder of the Coy going into Support in TRIUMPH or NOVA SCOTIA, as the case may be.

4. The relief will be carried out in the order:

"B" Coy, "A" Coy, "C" Coy, "HQ" Coy.

The leading platoon of "A" Coy will pass junction of MONTREAL and CANADA at 10-0 a.m. Remaining platoons of "A", "C" and "HQ" will follow at 100 yds interval between platoons, 50 yds between sections.

5. Captain Crawford, the R.S.M, and two signallers from HQs, together with one Officer, one N.C.O and two signallers per Coy, will parade at the Orderly Room at 8-0 a.m. to proceed to HQs, 11th East Lancs. Regt, in BRANDON TR. to take over Trench Stores, etc.

6. One Officer, 1 N.C.O and 2 Signallers per Coy. of 13th Bn, York & Lancaster Regt., will report at Battn. H.Q. at 9-0 a.m. to take over Trench Stores and accommodation. 2nd Lieut. McNamara, one N.C.O from HQs and 1 N.C.O per Coy will be detailed to hand over Trench Stores, Accommodation etc, to 13th Bn, York & Lancaster Regt. and will, if necessary, remain behind to do so, rejoining their respective Coys in Front Line on completion.

7. Trench Store Lists and disposition sketches to reach Bn HQs by 6-0 p.m. on day of relief.

8. Completion of relief to be reported to Battn H Qs by Fullerphone or runner. Code Word TASK being used.

9. ACKNOWLEDGE.

A. G. Tumbridge
Captain.
Adjutant.
12th. S. Bn, York & Lancs. R.

Copies to:

No 1. C.O.
2. 2in C.
3. Adjutant.
4-7 All Coys.
8. M.O.
9. T.O.
10. Q. M.
11. R.S.M.
12 & 13 War Diary.
15 File.
16 13 Bn, Y & L.R.
17 11th Bn, East Lancs.

ADMINISTRATIVE INSTRUCTIONS ISSUED WITH OPERATION ORDER NO. 83.

1. Valises, Dixies and other stores not required for the trenches will be dumped by 9-0 a.m. tomorrow, near junction of RED LINE with the WILLERVAL - ARLEUX RD, at a place which will be pointed out by the Regtl Sergt-Major, a N.C.O being left in charge by each Company until arrival of the Transport. Any H Qs kit or stores to go up the line will be dumped in the same place, only separately.
   Transport Officer will arrange removal after dark.

2. All Lewis guns and pans will be carried into the Front Line by Lewis Gun Sections.

3. (a) Rations for H Qs will be delivered nightly to Battn HQs in BRANDON and for "A", "B" and "C" Coys, WINNIPEG ROAD.

   (b) Water. The Transport Officer will arrange to send one Water Cart to fill the tanks at WINNIPEG ROAD and the tanks in BRANDON TR. nightly.

   (c) The Quartermaster will arrange to take over water tins from Q.M. 11th Bn, East Lancs. Regt. Twenty-five tins of water (full) will be handed over to each Coy by 11th Bn, East Lancs. Regt, in the Line.

4. The Sergt-Cook and Coy Cooks will return to the Transport Lines after breakfast tomorrow.

Reference scheme for Tactical Exercise.

The last paragraph but one, relating to artillery barrage, refers only to the Brigade Orders referred to in the preceding paragraph..

12TH S BATTALION YORK AND LANCASTER REGIMENT.

OPERATION ORDER FOR BATTALION TACTICAL EXERCISE 18.9.17.

Ref Map :-
MAROEUIL,
1/20,000

1. Information has been received that the enemy is withdrawing from the front of the Brigade sector referred to in "GENERAL IDEA".

2. This Battalion will carry out the pre-arranged bounds in the Right Sub-sector, passing through the Battalion now holding the Line.

3. For the advance,

   "A" Company on the Right,
   "B" " " " Left,
   "C" " in Support,
   H.Q. " in Reserve, with Battalion H.Qr details.

4. The following formation will be adopted, as far as any hostile resistance permits :-

   (a) 1st Line. One platoon from each front line Company in line of section columns at 100 yds interval, protected by screen of scouts 150 to 2 00 yds in advance.

   (b) 2nd Line. Remaining platoon of front line Companies in line of small groups of 3 or 4 men in file, at about 12 yds interval, for "Mopping-up" work. 300 yds distance from first line.

   (c) 3rd Line. Platoons of Support Company - ½ platoons in artillery formation. 500 yds distance from 2nd Line.

   (d) Battalion H.Qrs with Battalion H.Qrs Company.

5. When enemy strong points are encountered they will be dealt with without altering general direction of line or affecting troops on the flanks.

6. On reaching first objective, the two front Companies will hold and consolidate, pending orders for 2nd bound.

7. It may be possible that the enemy are holding the MONT ST ELOY - ARRAS ROAD, in which case orders will be issued to attack and capture same.

8. Dress. Fighting Order, without steel helmets.
   Time of moving off etc, will be notified to O.C.Coys later.

M. Trowbridge
Captain & Adjutant,
12th S Battn York and Lancaster Regt.

Copies to :-

No.1. C.O.
2. 2nd in C.
3. Adjt.
4. O.C."A".
No.5. O.C."B".
6. O.C."C".
7. O.C."HQ".
8. I.O.
No.9. Brigade.

12TH.S.BATTALION YORK AND LANCASTER REGIMENT.

T A C T I C A L   E X E R C I S E.

Ref Map :-
MAROEUIL
1/20,000

GENERAL IDEA.

British Front Line runs from BERTHONVAL WOOD to ST CATHERINE (G.15). Enemy holds corresponding line West of this and withdrawal is expected.

Line held by Right Battalion of Brigade Sector is from Cross Tracks, A.13.b.3.4 to A.13.d.5.5.

SPECIAL IDEA.

This Battalion is at SPRINGVALE CAMP in "A" Support. Information has been received that the enemy is withdrawing. Orders are received from Brigade that this Battalion is to carry out pre-arranged bounds, passing through the Battalion holding the line in Right Sub-sector. Other Units are co-operating on flanks.

The pre-arranged bounds are as follows :-

1st Bound. Cross Roads F.17.d.7.0. to F.24.a.2.2.

2nd Bound. MONT ST ELOY - ARRAS ROAD from Cross Roads F.22.d.6.1 to F.29.a.2.4.

MAROEUIL Rd exclusive

Two points offering determined Machine Gun resistance will be encountered. These will be marked by White flags.

Special attention to be paid to "Mopping-up" whole area covered, and leaving no possible place where enemy can remain concealed.

Before moving forward from 1st Bound objective, information is received that MONT ST ELOY - ARRAS ROAD is being held by enemy and Brigade orders that this is to be taken, consolidated and held as Front Line.

Artillery Barrage has been arranged for, this to commence on a line approximately 300 yds East of Objective and to creep forward at rate of 50 yds a minute, Zero hour being notified.

Time of assembly in our own Front Line system - 3.p.m.

C O N F I D E N T I A L.

W A R   D I A R Y.

12TH.S.BATTALION YORK AND LANCASTER REGIMENT.

Period - October 1st 1917

to

October 31st 1917.

VOLUME XXII

Date of despatch.

November 1st 1917.

B E F.

WO 20

Instructions regarding War Diaries and Intelligence Summaries are contained in F. S. Regs., Part II. and the Staff Manual respectively. Title pages will be prepared in manuscript.

WAR DIARY
or
~~INTELLIGENCE SUMMARY.~~
(Erase heading not required.)

Army Form C. 2118.

Place	Date	Hour	Summary of Events and Information	Remarks and references to Appendices
FRONT LINE. ACHEVILLE Sector.	1/10/17.	—	Full details of last nights gas attack are now to hand and are as follows:- Commencing at about 8-0 pm the enemy fired salvoes of gas bombs, evidently from some form of Trench Mortar, on to our front line, HUDSON and SOUTH TRIUMPH trenches. The shells were fired in salvoes from 5 to 12 shells in each, and at intervals of about 10 minutes from 8-0 pm to 9-30 pm. The enemy fired the first salvoes on our left Coy front and then worked southwards. As the wind was in a N.E. direction the Centre and right Coys (B & A) were not at first affected, the gas drifting behind the salient and passing over the Support Coy area to Batt. H.Qs. The gas appeared to be Phosgene with a mixture of lachrymatory gas of some sort. The eyes were immediately affected and also coughing & choking sensations were experienced. The later gas bombs are reported to have been fired from the direction of FRESNOY PARK and could be traced in flight by the burning fuse. Several direct hits were obtained in TOTNES Trench between posts 16 and 17, and the eastern part of HUDSON. At first it was thought that the gas was further to the North than our front, as only our left Coy ("C") was affected, The Alarm was given at once by means of Gas Rattles and Box Respirators	S.L.

(A7092). Wt. W12839/M1293. 75,0.0. 1/17. D. D. & L., Ltd. Forms/C.2118/14.

Instructions regarding War Diaries and Intelligence Summaries are contained in F. S. Regs., Part II. and the Staff Manual respectively. Title pages will be prepared in manuscript.

2

WAR DIARY
or
~~INTELLIGENCE SUMMARY.~~
(*Erase heading not required.*)

Army Form C. 2118.

Place	Date	Hour	Summary of Events and Information	Remarks and references to Appendices
FRONT LINE ACHEVILLE.	1/10/17		were immediately put on. The majority of the casualties were due to direct hits in the trench, and the suddenness with which the salvoes were fired. All possible precautions were taken.	
			The casualties were:- 1 Officer (2/Lt. R. MARSDEN) 74 other ranks of this Battn, 24 other ranks of the 15th York Lancs & 16 O.R. of other units.	
			The day passed quietly little work being done in order to enable the men to recover & to prevent slight "cases" developing seriously. Hostilities were normal.	
Do	2/10/17.		Situation normal and ordinary trench routine work resumed. During the day delayed effects of the gas caused further casualties 27 additional men having to be evacuated up to 12 noon, and 7 more later. The total Gas casualties for this Battn thus amounted to 1 Officer & 108. Other ranks. Of the latter 1 died in the 92nd Field Ambulance.	
			Unfortunately the Raiding Party of "A" Coy suffered severely and the Party had to be re-organised, being altered to one consisting of (approx) 30 volunteers from each Company – A. B. & C. with Capt. G.C. M.L. PIRKIS in command of party, & his subalterns being 2/Lt A C. RIDLINGTON & 2/Lt C.V. BURGESS the latter in place of 2/Lt E.N. TAYLOR. evacuated sick.	

(A7092). Wt. W12839/M1293. 75,0.0. 1/17. D. D. & L., Ltd. Forms/C.2118/14.

Instructions regarding War Diaries and Intelligence Summaries are contained in F. S. Regs., Part II. and the Staff Manual respectively. Title pages will be prepared in manuscript.

3

WAR DIARY
or
~~INTELLIGENCE SUMMARY.~~
(Erase heading not required.)

Army Form C. 2118.

Place	Date	Hour	Summary of Events and Information	Remarks and references to Appendices
FRONT LINE ACHEVILLE.	3/10/17	–	Hostilities still normal but the Trench Mortar fire of the enemy caused annoyance. The Raiding Party returned to Transport lines for further training, under supervision of the C.O. **NOTES**:- The fire of the enemy Trench Mortars is on the increase on the Brigade Front, resulting in our suffering casualties and doing considerable damage to the Trench system. Efforts are to be made to reduce this fire & the following instructions have been issued:- (a) On the enemy Heavy or Medium T.M's opening fire, a call for retaliation will at once be made on the Artillery, & this call will be made each time the enemy T.Ms fire their first rounds. (b) If the enemy opens fire with Granatenwerfer or Rifle Grenades, Stokes Guns will open fire on the enemy's front line trench in the direction from which the projectiles came, and will fire 10 shells for every one sent over by the enemy. (c) This will be repeated each time the enemy opens fire.	
Do	Night of 3/4/10/17.	→	Our troops projected 50 tons of gas on this Divisional front, causing the enemy heavy casualties. The retaliation by the enemy was fairly heavy but erratic, and we suffered no casualties.	
Do	4/10/17		Quiet day. Heavy rain NOTES:- Preparations for the winter campaign are rapidly being completed & both in Forward & Rear areas splendid work has been accomplished.	

(A7092). Wt W12839/M1293. 75 ,0.0. 1/17. D. D. & L., Ltd. Forms/C.2118/14.

Instructions regarding War Diaries and Intelligence Summaries are contained in F. S. Regs., Part II. and the Staff Manual respectively. Title pages will be prepared in manuscript.

WAR DIARY
or
~~INTELLIGENCE~~ SUMMARY.
(Erase heading not required.)

Army Form C. 2118.

Place	Date	Hour	Summary of Events and Information	Remarks and references to Appendices
FRONT LINE. ACHEVILLE.	4/10/17	–	Practically all the trenches in the Forward Area have been trench-boarded, and an efficient drainage system instituted; thus reducing the future dangers of "Trench Feet" owing to flooded trenches to a minimum. Formidable belts of wire have also been put out in front of our line as a protection against surprise attacks & raids. In the rear hutments are being erected — old ones repaired — & winter standings for the transport animals have been completed. The stone and rubble ~~were~~ obtained from the [illegible] ruins of NEUVILLE ST VAAST and ECURIE. In all these directions of activity the 12th Batt^n Y & L Regt has taken its share of labour.	
	5/10/17	–	Owing to the heavy rain of yesterday the proposed raid on the enemy posts was postponed 24 hours. Day very quiet & nothing to report. Usual patrolling done.	
	6/10/17	10 AM.	Batt^n were relieved by the 13th S. Bn. York & Lancaster Regt moving back to Brigade reserve at ROCLINCOURT (Springvale Camp) Heavy rain all day.	(0.0.84 att)
	Night of 6/7/10/17.	9-30pm.	In accordance with 94th Inf^y Bde Order No 183 (attached) the Raiding Party, which had moved up from the Transport Lines, attempted to raid the enemy's posts at T 24 a. 40.35 & T 24 a 40.55, for the purpose of securing identifications & inflicting casualties. The 1st post was believed to be a Rifle or Bombing Post, the 2nd a Machine Gun post.	

(A7092). Wt. W12839/M1293. 75,000. 1/17. D. D. & L., Ltd. Forms/C.2118/14.

5

Instructions regarding War Diaries and Intelligence Summaries are contained in F. S. Regs., Part II. and the Staff Manual respectively. Title pages will be prepared in manuscript.

WAR DIARY
or
INTELLIGENCE SUMMARY.

(*Erase heading not required.*)

Army Form C. 2118.

Place	Date	Hour	Summary of Events and Information	Remarks and references to Appendices
FRONT LINE. ACHEVILLE.	6/7 Oct 1917.		HUDSON TRENCH West of the Aid Post was the Assembly place for the Raiding Party & they arrived here at 6.0 pm, & then proceeded to TINY Trench. The original idea was to fire the Bangalore Torpedoes in the front line but owing to the heavy rainfall all morning, it was found impossible to do this & keep them dry. They were, therefore, filled in WINNIPEG ROAD, some distance from the front line. The Bangalores could not be taken away from WINNIPEG ROAD until after dark as owing to their length — 40 ft — they had to be carried over the top. This meant considerable delay. Another alteration made in the arrangements, owing to the wet weather & wet state of NO MANS LAND was, that the Bangalores were detonated before leaving our front line, 50 yds, of electric cable being attached to the detonator ready to be joined to the remainder of the cable after the Bangalore was in position.	
		10pm	At 10 pm when both Bangalores were being taken across, some of the 18 pounders suddenly opened with apparently rapid fire, and the T.Ms and machine guns thinking this was the signal for Zero also opened out. The artillery and the 9th Infantry Brigade HQ were at once communicated with and informed that no message had been sent through stating that the bangalores were ready, and the guns were then stopped. Owing to their various positions, it was difficult to stop quickly all the Trench Mortars and machine guns until they had been firing for some time.	

(A7092). Wt W12839/M1293. 75 ,0.0. 1/17. D. D. & L., Ltd. Forms/C.2118/14.

Instructions regarding War Diaries and Intelligence Summaries are contained in F. S. Regs., Part II. and the Staff Manual respectively. Title pages will be prepared in manuscript.

6/

Army Form C. 2118.

WAR DIARY
or
INTELLIGENCE SUMMARY.
(Erase heading not required.)

Place	Date	Hour	Summary of Events and Information	Remarks and references to Appendices
NO MAN'S LAND — ACHEVILLE	6/7 Oct 1917	–	The Left Party were not worried by this premature opening by the artillery, but the right party stated that the lights thrown up by the enemy when the guns opened resulted in their being seen and fired at.	
		10-35 pm.	At 10-35 pm the Left Bangalore was reported in position and the report stated that it was well through the wire at a point a few yards to the Left of the machine gun post which was one of the objectives. There was considerable delay with the right party and replies to messages sent out to them for information, stated that they were being occasionally bombed and fired at and could only move with great difficulty.	
		11-30 to 12 midnight	Between 11-30 pm & midnight the state of affairs in NO MAN'S LAND seemed particularly quiet and at midnight a message was received back from the right party that the Bangalore was then being placed in position and should be ready very shortly. A message was sent to the Left Party who had been lying waiting for an hour and a half that the right party had been delayed but was expected to be ready at any time.	
		12-30 AM	At 12-30 AM. there was still no news from the right party that everything was ready. By this time the Left Party had been lying waiting for 2 hours and the CO was afraid they would be getting cold and stiff, while from the report ~~that~~ the Bangalore was very well placed and almost in front of the post to be attacked, there seemed an excellent chance of success with the Left party provided things could be got moving.	

(A7092). Wt. W12839/M1293. 75 ,0.0. 1/17. D. D. & L., Ltd. Forms/C.2118/14.

Instructions regarding War Diaries and Intelligence Summaries are contained in F. S. Regs., Part II. and the Staff Manual respectively. Title pages will be prepared in manuscript.

WAR DIARY
or
~~INTELLIGENCE SUMMARY.~~
(Erase heading not required.)

Army Form C. 2118.

Y

Place	Date	Hour	Summary of Events and Information	Remarks and references to Appendices
NO MANS LAND ACHEVILLE	6/7 Oct 1917.		The Commanding Officer, therefore, went out to the two Raiding Groups of the Right party to investigate what was causing the delay. He found both these Raiding Groups lying out in what seemed to him a position far too much to the right & where they appeared to be opposite the thickest part of the wire. It was, of course, too late to attempt to alter the direction of the Right party at this stage & they were instructed to carry on in the hope that they might still get through there. It seemed very doubtful ~~whether they would be~~ [illegible] able to join up with the Left Party in the enemy trench, even if the wire was cut successfully, and the Left Party were informed accordingly. They were instructed to carry on as they would for a single entry raid if the Right Party failed to join up.	
		1-10 AM	At 1-10 AM, everything was reported ready on the Right and the artillery opened 5 minutes later. On the exploder being operated it was reported that both Bangalores had been fired but shortly afterwards word came back that only the right one had gone off. Later reports from the right stated that there was still a lot of wire left uncut, and they were still unable to get through. Reports from the left confirmed that their Bangalore had not gone off, that it could not be fired and that the party were withdrawing. The whole party subsequently reached our trenches having had 4 casualties, all wounded, two very slightly.	
			Remarks:- The failure of the right party to get its proper direction was due	

(A7092). Wt. W12839/M1293. 750,000. 1/17. D. D. & L., Ltd. Forms/C.2118/14.

Instructions regarding War Diaries and Intelligence Summaries are contained in F. S. Regs., Part II. and the Staff Manual respectively. Title pages will be prepared in manuscript.

8

WAR DIARY
or
~~INTELLIGENCE SUMMARY.~~
(Erase heading not required.)

Army Form C. 2118.

Place	Date	Hour	Summary of Events and Information	Remarks and references to Appendices

to the fact that practically the whole of this party including the Officer in charge had been selected to carry out this work only three days previously owing to 42 other ranks of the original party being gassed and the Officer then in charge of the raid being evacuated sick.

As the better part of these three days were taken up in training behind the lines there was little opportunity for special reconnaissance, though most of the men had been on patrol in this part at one time or other. As an additional help small patrols were sent out on each night that the party were behind the lines to reconnoitre the situation etc, and these acted as guides on the night of the Raid.

The Left Bangalore party being nearly all men of the original party, were very quick in getting their Bangalore in position and in the right place, and had this Bangalore exploded there is no doubt the object of the Raid would have been achieved by this Left Party.

The difficulties of getting the Bangalores properly fixed in the existing weather conditions were very great indeed, and it seemed quite possible that the ammonal might be damp and thus be inefficient in firing them. For the preparation of the Bangalores the weather could not have been worse.

[illegible initials]

(A7092). Wt. W12839/M1293. 75 ,0 0. 1/17. D. D. & L., Ltd. Forms/C.2118/14.

Instructions regarding War Diaries and Intelligence Summaries are contained in F. S. Regs., Part II. and the Staff Manual respectively. Title pages will be prepared in manuscript.

9

WAR DIARY
or
~~INTELLIGENCE SUMMARY.~~
(Erase heading not required.)

Army Form C. 2118.

Place	Date	Hour	Summary of Events and Information	Remarks and references to Appendices
ROCLINCOURT Springvale Camp	7/10/17. 8/10/17 9/10/17 10/10/17 11/10/17		This period was devoted to "Refresher" Training, such as Setting Up Drill, Bayonet Fighting, Musketry, Lewis Gunnery, Revetting work & Wiring. There were Rabbit Practices by day and night and short night marches with Box Respirators. Company attacks were also practised. "B" & "C" Coys commenced to train special Fighting Patrols one platoon of each Coy being selected. [On 11/10/17 a limited number of Officers & N.C.Os were conveyed on motor bus to BETHUNE — an appreciable pleasure trip. 2/Lt E.L. ROBERTS rejoined Bn from UK. 8/10/17	
BROWN LINE	12/10/17	10 AM	Battalion moved to BROWN LINE, Brigade "B" Support Line, relieving the 11th S. Bn EAST LANCASHIRE Regt who moved to A Line. The 13th S. Bn York Lancaster Regt occupied Springvale Camp. In the evening Working Parties were provided in the Forward Area.	(O.O. 85 att'd) S.
	13/10/17 14/10/17 15/10/17		Nothing of note to report. Working Parties were continuously provided as on the 12th. In the day time troops were engaged in making barbed wire concertinas for Brigade wire defences.	S.
	16/10/17	5.10 am.	The enemy attempted a raid in the sector & the Battn was held in readiness to move within 30 minutes on receipt of orders. The 14th S. Bn York & Lancs. Regt were in the front line. Despite heavy preparatory bombardment	

(A7092). Wt W12839/M1293. 75,0,0. 1/17. D. D. & L., Ltd. Forms/C.2118/14.

Army Form C. 2118.

Instructions regarding War Diaries and Intelligence Summaries are contained in F. S. Regs., Part II. and the Staff Manual respectively. Title pages will be prepared in manuscript.

10

WAR DIARY
or
INTELLIGENCE SUMMARY.
(*Erase heading not required.*)

Place	Date	Hour	Summary of Events and Information	Remarks and references to Appendices
			The enemy raiders, consisting of 250 men of the 6th Sturm Batt (BAVARIANS) were driven off without getting through our wire by rifle & Lewis Gun fire. One wounded prisoner was captured. The enemy suffered heavy casualties a Daylight Patrol counting 40 German dead in the wire. The 11th Bn casualties were: Killed 1. OR, Wounded 1 Officer and 6. OR.	
	17/10/17	–	Quiet day. Nothing to report, save the completion of the task of making 600 Barbed Wire concertinas whilst in this line.	
RED LINE	18/10/17	10 AM	Battalion relieved the 11 S. Bn EAST LANCS Rgt in RED LINE being relieved in turn by 13. S. Bn York & Lancs Rgt. "A" Coy went forward as Support Coy to 11. E. Lancs. Nothing of note to record.	(O.O. 86) att
	19/10/17 20/10/17 21/10/17		Very quiet. Usual Working Parties provided. 2/Lt. J. BROWN joined the Battn for duty from the Base (20/10/17). "C" Coy, on the 20th, moved from OTTAWA TR to NEW BRUNSWICK TR, relieving portion of 6th Bn ROYAL WARWICKS on the left of the Brigade front. The Coy will be under the orders of the O/c 11 E. Lancs. Rgt in case of an attack by the enemy.	(O.O. 87 att)
	22/10/17 23/10/17		Quiet. Usual working parties provided.	
FRONT LINE	24/10/17	10 AM	Battn commenced to relieve the 11th Bn East Lancs Rgt in front line, the 13th Bn York & Lancs Rgt taking over the RED LINE. Hostile artillery was more active than usual whilst relief was in progress but no casualties were caused.	(O.O. 88) att.

(A7092). Wt W12839/M1293. 75,0.0. 1/17. D. D. & L., Ltd. Forms/C.2118/14.

Instructions regarding War Diaries and Intelligence Summaries are contained in F. S. Regs., Part II. and the Staff Manual respectively. Title pages will be prepared in manuscript.

11

Army Form C. 2118.

WAR DIARY
or
~~INTELLIGENCE SUMMARY.~~

(Erase heading not required.)

Place	Date	Hour	Summary of Events and Information	Remarks and references to Appendices
FRONT LINE.	24/10/17	4-15 to 5-0pm	At 4-15 pm, the enemy, apparently in retaliation for our Artillery fire, opened up a sudden bombardment on our front line from ALBERTA ROAD to right of the Battalion front and continuing from there to top of ARLEUX crest. The bombardment consisted of 10 c.m. & 77 m.m. H.E. and medium T.M's. The Right Coy (A) front trench was blown in, in 4 places. The Centre Coy (B Coy) had only one direct hit in their trench. The parapet of No 7 Post (garrisoned by "A" Coy) was knocked in for 4 or 5 yds. There were only two casualties — both wounded. The majority of the shells intended for the Front Line fell from 20 to 30 yds behind, and except in the one instance referred to men in the Front Line posts were quite safe.	
	25/10/17	9-0am	Patrol Reports disclosed the fact that the neighbourhood of the unoccupied area by junction of trenches NOVA SCOTIA & BRANDY was still the object of some curiosity on the part of the enemy as two enemy parties were seen there. It was decided to concentrate on this point for the next night or two, [Enterprise Patrols] with object of capturing some members of the hostile parties referred to. Enemy T.M's were again aggressive.	
	26/10/17	—	Hostilities continued to be very lively. Though the Battn suffered no casualties the trench system was damaged in several parts.	
	27/10/17		The hostile T.M fire this morning appeared to come from a position in FRESNOY SUPPORT TR. about T.24 b 9.5. or somewhere between T 24 b 9.9 and U 19 A 0.2. Artillery replied on T24 b 9.9 & T 24 b 7.1 but without stopping the Trench Mortars.	

(A7092). Wt. W12839/M1293. 750,000. 1/17. D. D. & L., Ltd. Forms/C.2118/14.

Instructions regarding War Diaries and Intelligence Summaries are contained in F. S. Regs., Part II. and the Staff Manual respectively. Title pages will be prepared in manuscript.

WAR DIARY

or

~~INTELLIGENCE SUMMARY.~~

(*Erase heading not required.*)

Army Form C. 2118.

12

Place	Date	Hour	Summary of Events and Information	Remarks and references to Appendices
Front Line.	27/10/17		A hostile aeroplane was over our lines most of the morning & possibly was observing for hostile T.M's. It was engaged by Lewis Gun fire and occasionally turned off. NOTES – "The hostile bombardment during the last few days on the front line and support, and the T.M. work this morning was quite possibly the result of our recent wire-cutting from which the enemy might be anticipating some form of operation on our part. On the other hand if the enemy had been preparing for some minor operation against this sector his preparations would be very much the same, except that there would probably be more evidence of some attempt at wire cutting. "In order to take all precautions should this latter view be the correct one each Company will from and including tonight have 2 Listening Posts of 2 men each in shell holes in front of our wire and preferably near one of our gaps. These posts will be occupied from "Stand To" at night till as near "Stand Down" in the morning as light permits. In the event of any alarm one man from the Listening Post will return to the Front Line to pass the alarm while the other will at once open rapid fire, and this in itself should also cause the alarm to be taken up along the line. "Steps should be taken to see that all S.O.S. sets are in a dry and useable condition, also that the ammunition in bays is clean. "In the case of an enemy bombardment opening on our Front Line it should be known by now from recent bombardments, at what points the shells fall well behind and at what points the Front Line is likely to be more or less untenable	

(A7092). Wt. W12839/M1293. 750,000. 1/17. D. D. & L., Ltd. Forms/C.2118/14.

Army Form C. 2118.

Instructions regarding War Diaries and Intelligence Summaries are contained in F. S. Regs., Part II. and the Staff Manual respectively. Title pages will be prepared in manuscript.

13

WAR DIARY
or
~~INTELLIGENCE SUMMARY.~~
(*Erase heading not required.*)

Place	Date	Hour	Summary of Events and Information	Remarks and references to Appendices
Front Line	27/10/17		"In the latter places, ie in places where the enemy gets direct hits on the Front Line the garrison or posts in the neighbourhood should move forward and occupy shell holes near our wire.	
			" These instructions are sent through for you to take the action referred to as a precautionary measure from tonight and are not to be considered as expressing the opinion that some form of attack is by any means imminent." —	
			The above sent to Coy Commanders by the Commanding Officer, displays the keenness of hostilities at this period.	
	28/10/17	-	During the morning there was a concentrated heavy shoot on known group of T.M. positions namely —	
			JERRY M. T 24 b 9.9.	
			NEW YORK T 24 b 7.1.	
			LOCK U 19 a 0.2.	
			PIPE. U 19 a 60.15	
			HILL U 19 a 4.1	
			JERRY .P. T 30 d 8.9.	
			BLAST U 25 a 55.30.	
			In the evening three American Officers were attached to the Battn for training whilst in the Line.	
			Recent Officer reinforcements have been:	
			2/Lt P CRAGGS. (25/10/17)	
			" T W LEWIS do	
			" A DRURY (26/10/17)	

(A7092). Wt W12839/M1293. 75,0.0. 1/17. D. D. & L., Ltd. Forms/C.2118/14.

Instructions regarding War Diaries and Intelligence Summaries are contained in F. S. Regs., Part II. and the Staff Manual respectively. Title pages will be prepared in manuscript.

14

WAR DIARY
or
~~INTELLIGENCE SUMMARY.~~
(Erase heading not required.)

Army Form C. 2118.

Place	Date	Hour	Summary of Events and Information	Remarks and references to Appendices
Front Line.	29/10/17	–	Nothing abnormal to record.	
	night of 29/30/10/17.		Bursts of Lewis Gun & Rifle Fire into a gap in the enemy wire at T 24 d 35.60, were carried out at 6 pm, 9 pm, 11 pm, 1 AM, 3 AM 5 AM. The L.T.M's co-operated in all of them and the Artillery in 2 of them.	(OO 59 [illegible])
ROCLINCOURT Springvale Camp.	30/10/17	10 AM	Battn relieved by 13th Bn York & Lancaster Rgt, & moved back to Springvale Camp.	
	31/10/17	–	Day devoted to inspections and cleaning up.	

[illegible signature] Hood
Lieut. Colonel Comd
12th (S) Bn. York & Lancs. Rgt. (Sheffield.

(A7092). Wt. W12839/M1293. 75 ,0.0. 1/17. D. D. & L., Ltd. Forms/C.2118/14.

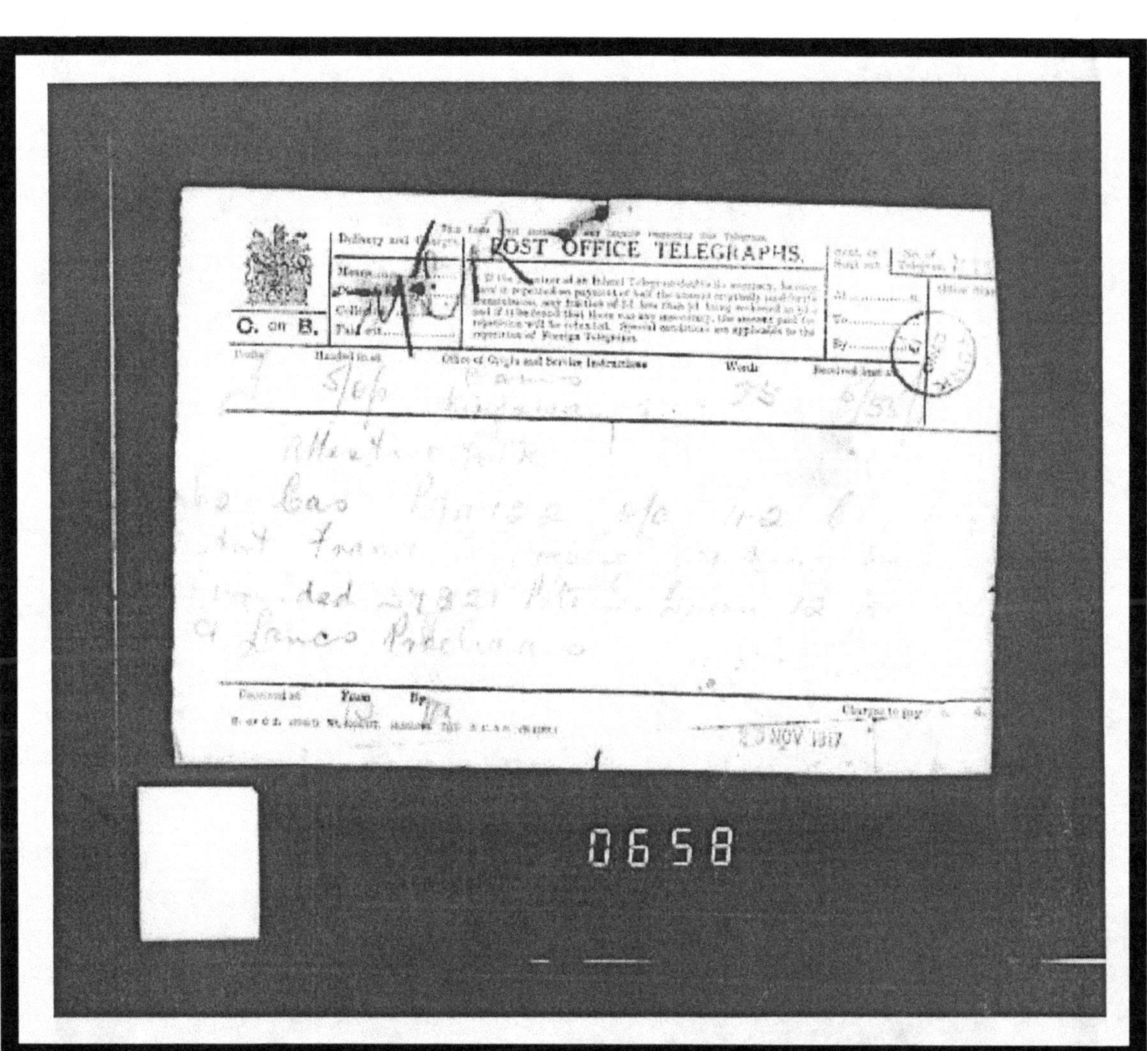

C. or B.

Delivery and Charges

POST OFFICE TELEGRAPHS.

Handed in at

Office of Origin and Service Instructions

Words

Received here at

Received at

From

By

Charges to pay

NOV 1917

0658

Secret Copy No 2

12th York + Lanc Rgt
Operation order No 84

Ref map
MERICOURT (?)
1/20,000 + Trench Map } 5/10/17

1. The 12 Y+L Rgt + attached Coys of 13th + 14th Y+L will be relieved in the front line by the 13th Y+L with one Coy of 14th Y+L attached, tomorrow, 6th Oct, the 12th Y+L proceeding to SPRINGVALE CAMP on completion of relief.
B Coy, 13th Y+L + B Coy 14th Y+L will act under orders from their respective Battn Commanders on completion of relief indicated below.

2. The relief will be carried out as follows:-

A Coy, 13th Y+L relieving B Coy 14th Y+L (Right front line)
C " " " B Coy, 12th Y+L (Centre front line)
B " " " A+C Coys, 12 Y+L (left front line)
HQ " " " HQ

a Coy of 14th Y+L relieving B Coy, 13th Y+L in Support.

Order of Relief

B Coy. 14th Y&L
B " 12th Y&L
A&C " -do-
HQ " -do-

3. The following distances will be maintained on the way out,
100 yds between platoons
50 " " Sections.

4. The leading Coy of relieving Battn will arrive about 10.30am
B Coy, 13th Y&L will not move from their present positions until 10.0am

5. The posts of the left Coy, that cannot be relieved by daylight will be relieved after dark, an Officer of the Coy remaining behind until these posts are relieved
The garrisons of the posts not relieved automatically come under the orders of OC relieving Battn immediately the remainder of the relief of the Battn is completed.

6 The usual advance parties from the 13th Y&L will arrive 2 hours before commencement of relief

to take over Trench Stores etc

7. Trench Store lists will be forwarded to Battn HQ by 6pm on day of relief.

8. Completion of relief will be sent by fullerphone or runner to Battn HQ – Code words GOOD ENOUGH being used.

9 ACKNOWLEDGE.

[signature]
Captain
Adjutant
12th S Bn York & Lanc R

Copies to
No 1 Co
2 Adj.
3-6 Coys 12th Y&L
7 Bgde, 13th "
8 B" 14th "
9 MO
10 TO-QM
11 13th Y&L
12 File
13 } War
14 } Diary

Administrative. Instructions issued with 12th Operation Orders No 84

1. Coys on relief will rendezvous at DAYLIGHT RAILHEAD where trains will be available at 2pm

2 All Lewis Guns, magazines, etc + other stores will be dumped in WINNIPEG RD as near as possible to ration dump. A guard of 1 NCO per Coy + 1 man per LG Section being left in charge until arrival of the Transport. Transport Officer will arrange for removal tomorrow night.

3 25 filled water tins per Coy will be handed over to relieving Coys

4 QM will arrange to hand over all water tins in his possession which are surplus to mobile Reserve to QM 13th Y+L

5 The QM will arrange to take over SPRINGVALE CAMP from 14th Y+L

—

aayt

SECRET.

Copy No.....

13TH.S.BATTALION YORK AND LANCASTER REGT.

Ref. Map :-)
MAROEUIL.) OPERATION ORDER NO 85.

11.10.17.

1. The 13TH.YORK AND LANCASTER REGT will relieve the 11TH EAST LANCASHIRE REGT in Brigade "B" Support Line tomorrow, 12th inst.

2. The relief will be carried out as follows :-

"A" Coy, 13th Y & L will relieve	"W" Coy, 11th.E.L.Rgt in	SUMMER LANE
"B" " " " "	"X" " " "	WINTER LANE
"C" " " " "	"Z" " " "	BROWN LINE
"HQ" " " " "	"HQ" " " "	-do-

3. The Battalion will fall in in Mass at 9.45.a.m. in the above order from Right to Left, for necessary inspections, and will be ready to move off in the above order at 10.a.m. Dress – Marching Order. From the Camp to the BROWN LINE, 100 yds distance will be maintained between platoons.

4. ROUTE. TOMMY ALLEY will be used by all troops.

5. One Officer, 1 N.C.O. and 2 Signallers per Company and H.Qrs will report at Orderly Room at 7.a.m. and will then proceed to H.Qrs 11th.East Lanc Regt to take over Trench Stores, etc., from their respective Companies, on arrival.

6. Trench Store Lists will be handed in to Orderly Room as soon as possible after stores have been taken over.

7. Completion of relief will be notified to Battalion H.Qrs by wire or runner, code word "BRASS" being used.

8. A sketch shewing dispositions will be sent to Battalion H.Qrs by 8.p.m. 12.10.17.

9. ACKNOWLEDGE.

[signature]
Captain & Adjt.,
13th (S) Battn, York and Lancaster Regiment.

Copies to :-
1.....C.O.
2.....2nd in Command.
3.....Adjutant.
4 to 7 Companies.
8.....M.O.
9.....T.O.
10.....Q-M.
11.....R-S-M.
12.....11th.East Lanc Regt.
13.....File.
14)....War Diary.
15)

ADMINISTRATIVE INSTRUCTIONS ISSUED WITH OPERATION ORDER No.85 DATED 11.10.17.

---

1. The Transport Officer will arrange the Transport for all Lewis Guns, panniers, etc., from SPRINGVALE CAMP to TOMMY ALLEY. Two men per Company will proceed with the limbers to act as guard on arrival. Companies will make their own arrangements for collecting the guns and panniers.

2. All water bottles will be filled before moving off for the trenches.

3. Sgt Cook, and Coy Cooks, except one who will be detailed by the Sgt Cook to remain behind, to look after Company cookers, will proceed with their Companies. Quartermaster will arrange for camp kettles to be taken up by the transport.

4. Packs will be taken up to the BROWN LINE, and will be carried on the man. Steel helmets will be worn.

5. Any Officer who wishes, can have his valise taken up to the line. These will be dumped at Guard Room by 8.30.a.m. Blankets rolled in bundles of 10, valises not to be taken, Mess Stores, or other surplus baggage to be dumped opposite the guard room by 8.30.a.m.

6. Transport for baggage detailed in para.5. will be arranged by the Transport Officer.

7. Rations (but not water) will be sent up as usual,

8. Transport Officer will arrange to send up two watercarts nightly; one water man to go up with the Battalion and remain in the line.

9. The 2nd.in Command, Medical Officer, and Quartermaster, accompanied by the Orderly Officer and Area Commandant's representative, will inspect the Camp at 9.30.a.m. The Orderly Officer will obtain from the last named, a certificate of cleanliness for the Camp.

10. The Quartermaster will arrange to hand over SPRINGVALE CAMP to representative of the 13th.S.Battalion York and Lancaster Regiment.

- - - - - - -

SECRET.

Copy No....14...

13TH.S.BATTALION YORK AND LANCASTER REGT.

Ref Maps,
MAROEUIL,
1/20,000
& Tr.Maps.

O P E R A T I O N   O R D E R   NO 86.

17.10.17.

1. The Battalion will relieve the 11TH.EAST LANC REGT in "A" Support tomorrow, 18th October, and will be relieved by the 13TH.YORK & LANC REGT in "B" Support.

2. The relief will be carried out as follows :-

   "A" Company, 13th.Y & L relieving "Z" Company,11th East Lanc Regt, in TRIUMPH TR and WINNIPEG ROAD, coming under orders of O.C.,11th. East Lanc Regt on relief.

   "B" Company, 13th Y & L relieving "X" Company, 11th East Lanc Regt in CANADA TR.(T.28.b.).

   "C" Company, 13th Y & L relieving "W" Company, 11th East Lanc Regt in OTTAWA TR.

   "HQ" Company, 13th Y & L relieving "HQ" Company, 11th East Lanc Regt in RED LINE in B.4.c.

3. Companies will move off in the above order, using TIRED ALLEY and maintaining 100 yds between platoons, and 50 yds between sections, leading platoon moving off at 10.a.m.

4. 2nd.Lt.McNAMARA, the R-S-M and 2 signallers from "HQ", together with 1 Officer, 1 N.C.O. and 1 signaller per Company will parade at the Orderly Room at 8.a.m. and proceed to H.Qrs, 11th East Lanc Regt at B.4.c.6.4 reaching there at 8.30.a.m. to take over accommodation, trench stores, etc.

5. The Asst.Adjutant and 1 N.C.O. per Company will be left behind to hand over accommodation, trench stores, etc to 13th Y & L Regt, rejoining the Battalion in "A" Support on completion.
   1 Officer, 1 N.C.O. and 2 signallers per Company from 13th Y & L Regt will arrive at Battn H.Qrs at 9.a.m. to take over accommodation, stores, etc.

6. Trench Store Lists for both reliefs will be handed in to the Orderly Room by 6.p.m. on day of relief.

7. Sketches, shewing dispositions and location of Anti-Aircraft Lewis Guns to reach Battalion H.Qrs by 6.p.m. on day of relief.

8. Completion of relief will be reported to Battalion H.Qrs by wire or runner - Code Word CHARCOAL.

A.A. Lumbridge

Capt & Adjutant,
13th (S) Battn, York and Lancaster Regiment,

Copies to :-

No.1. C.O.	No.11. R-S-M.
2. 2nd in C.	12. 11th East Lanc Rgt.
3. Adjt.	13. 13th York & Lanc Rgt.
4.to 7. Coys.	14.) War
8. M.O.	15.) Diary.
9. T.O.	16. File.
10. Q.M.	

ADMINISTRATIVE INSTRUCTIONS ISSUED WITH OPERATION ORDER NO 86.

1. Rations and Water will be delivered nightly to the following places :-

RATIONS.		WATER.
"C" Coy.	To Ration Dump S.of WILLERVAL - ARLEUX RD, at B.4.c.5.5.	Tank in OTTAWA filled nightly by water cart.
"A" Coy.	Brought up to WINNIPEG Ration Dump.	35 tins nightly brought up with Rations.
"B" Coy.	To point where limber track crosses CANADA TR in T.28.b.	Tanks filled nightly by water carts at same place.
"HQ"Coy.	Same as for "C" Coy.	Tanks near Battn H.Qrs filled nightly by water carts, also 20 filled tins brought up on transport.

2. All water bottles must be filled before starting from present trenches.

3. All Coys, except "A" Coy, will take their cooks and dixies forward with them, as cooking can be carried out in the trenches to be occupied by them.
"A" Coy's cooks will be sent back to transport lines.

4. Packs will not be taken forward to the RED LINE but greatcoats will be taken rolled in waterproof sheets.

5. BAGGAGE.
   1. All Officers' kits/and other Company stores not required to be taken forward will be dumped near the Canteen by 9.a.m. [Packs inserted above "kits/"]
   2. Officers' valises to be taken forward, Orderly Room stores, etc will be dumped at the same time and place, but separate from stores mentioned in 1.
   3. Transport Officer will arrange for removal after dark.
   4. Each Company will leave a N.C.O. and 3 men in charge of their dump, who will be responsible for the correct distribution of stores, and for loading on to transport.

6. The Quartermaster will arrange to take over 45 petrol tins from the Q.M. of the 11th East Lanc Regt for the use of "A" Company and Headquarters.

[signature]
Capt & Adjutant,
13th (S) Battn, York and Lancaster Regt.

17.10.17.

SECRET. Copy No......10

12TH.S.BATTALION YORK AND LANCASTER REGT.

Ref Map, MAROEUIL, 1/20,000 & Tr Maps.

OPERATION ORDER No.87.

19.10.17.

1. "C" Company, 12th YORK & LANCASTER REGT will relieve a Company of the 6th ROYAL WARWICKS REGT in NEW BRUNSWICK TRENCH at 4.p.m. tomorrow, October 20th, and will hand over their present accommodation and trench stores to O/C "HQ" Coy.

2. Company H.Qrs will be established at ANGLESEA DUGOUT.

3. "C" Company, 12th York and Lanc Regt, after taking over NEW BRUNSWICK will come under the orders of the O.C.,11th East Lanc Regt for tactical purposes in the event of an attack on the Left part of the Brigade Front.

4. On the completion of relief the following will be the Brigade Northern Boundary:-

From present Front Line Boundary to T 27.a.0.0 and via T 26d.5.0 to B 1.a.8.0. to present boundary at B 1.c.1.0.

5. O.C. "C" Coy. will arrange to send an Officer to reconnoitre the new trenches during tomorrow morning.

6. The Signal Sergt will arrange to establish communication between "C" Coy and Battalion H Qs.

7. Rations and Water will be sent up tomorrow night to the junction of SASKETCHAWAN ROAD and HUDSON.

8. Trench Store Lists will be forwarded to Battn HQs on completion of relief.

9. Completion of relief will be notified to Battn.HQs by wire or runner. Code word: COKE.

10. ACKNOWLEDGE.

(Sd). N.L. TUNBRIDGE.
Capt & Adjt.
12.S.Bn,York & Lancaster Regt.

Copies to:
1-4 . All Coys.
5 Adjutant.
6. QM and T.O.
7. R.S.M.
8. 11th East Lancs.R.
9. 6th Royal Warwicks.
10. File.
11 & 12. War Diary.

S E C R E T. Copy No.....13

12TH.S.BATTALION YORK AND LANCASTER REGIMENT.

Ref, Maps.) MAROEUIL:) 1/20,000) & Tr Maps.)

O P E R A T I O N   O R D E R   NO.88.

23.10.17.

1. The Battalion will relieve the 11TH.S.BN.EAST LANC REGT in L.3 Sub-section tomorrow, Oct 24th, and will be relieved in "A" Support by 13TH.S.BN.YORK & LANC REGT.

2. Companies will relieve as follows :-
   "A" Coy, 12th Y & L, relieving "Z" Coy, 11th E.L.R., Nos.1-6 Posts inclusive, in Right front line, relieved by "C" Coy, 13 Y & L.
   "B" Coy, 12th Y & L, relieving "W" Coy, 11th.E.L., Nos 7-15 Posts inclusive, in Centre front line, relieved by "B" Coy, 13th Y & L.
   "C" Coy, 12th Y & L, relieving "X" Coy, 11th.E.L., Nos 16-25 Posts inclusive, in Left front line, relieved by "A" Coy, 13th Y & L.
   "HQ" Coy, 12th.Y & L, relieving "HQ" Coy, 11th E.L., relieved by "HQ" Coy, 13th Y & L.

   "C" Coy, 13th York & Lancs R. will relieve "A" Coy, 12th York & Lancs R. attached 11th East Lancs R. at present in support, coming under orders of O.C. this Battalion on relief.

   "A" Coy, 13th York & Lancs R. will relieve "C" Coy, 12th York & Lancs R. in NEW BRUNSWICK TRENCH, and will come under the orders of the O.C., 12th York & Lancs R. for tactical purposes in the event of an attack on the Left part of the Brigade Front.

3. Companies will take over the existing dispositions of the 11th East Lancs R. in the Front line, remainder of the Company going into support in TRIUMPH or NOVA SCOTIA, as the case may be.

4. The relief will be carried out in the order :- "A", "C", "B", "HQ" Companies, commencing at 10.a.m., 100 yds interval to be maintained between platoons; 50 yds between sectns.

5. O.C."C" Company will arrange to relieve No.24 Post (1 N.C.O.& 6 o.r. L.G.), and No.25 Post (1 N.C.O.& 3 o.r.Riflemen) at 4.a.m. tomorrow, 24th inst. An Officer will be in charge of this party and will report to Coy H.Q. in NOVA SCOTIA on arrival.

6. 2nd.Lt.J.McNamara, the C-S-M and 2 signallers from H.Qrs, together with 1 Officer, 1 N.C.O., & 2 signallers per Coy, will report to 11th East Lancs R. Battalion H.Qrs and Company H.Qrs respectively at 9.a.m. to take over Trench Stores, etc.

7. 1 Officer, 1 N.C.O. and 2 signallers per Coy of 13th York & Lancs R. will report at the respective Coy & Battn H.Qrs at 9.a.m. to take over Trench Stores and accommodation. The R-S-M from H.Qrs and 1 N.C.O.per Coy will be detailed to hand over Trench Stores, accommodation, etc to 13th York & Lancs R.and will if necessary remain behind to do so, rejoining their respective Coys in Front line on completion.

8. Trench Stores Lists, disposition sketches to reach Battn H.Qrs by 6.p.m. on day of relief.

9. Completion of relief to be reported to Battn H.Qrs by Fullerphone or runner - Code Word, BOOTS being used.

10. ACKNOWLEDGE.

(Sd) S CRAWFORD
Capt & A/Adjt.,
12th.S.Battn, York and Lancaster Regiment.

Copies to, No.1. C.O. No.4-7. All Coys. No.10. Q-M.
2. 2nd.in C. 8. M.O. 11. R-S-M.
3. Adjt. 9. T.O. 12 & 13 W.D.
15. 13th Y & L . 16.11th E.L. 17. File.

ADMINISTRATUVE INSTRUCTIONS ISSUED WITH OPERATION ORDER. NO 88.

1. Valises, Dixies and other stores not required by HQs and "B" Coys for the trenches will be dumped by 9-0 a.m. tomorrow, near junction of RED LINE with the WILLERVAL - ARLEUX RD, at a place which will be pointed out by the Regtl-Sgt-Major, a N.C.O. being left in charge by each Company until arrival of the Transport, Any HQs kit or stores to go up the line will be dumped in the same place, ,only separately.
   Transport Officer will arrange removal after dark.

2. All Lewis guns and pans will be carried into the Front Line by Lewis Gun Sections.

3. (a) Rations for HQs will be delivered nightly to Battn HQs in BRANDON and for "A", "B", and "C" Coys, WINNIPEG ROAD.

   (b) Water. The Transport Officer will arrange to send one Water Cart to fill the tanks at WINNIPEG ROAD and one cart to fill the tank in BRANDON TR. nightly.

   (c) The Quartermaster will arrange to take over water tins from Q.M. 11th Bn, East Lancs.R. Twenty-five tins of water will be handed over to each Company by 11th. Bn, East Lancs.R. in the Line.

4. The Sergt-Cook and Coy Cooks will return to the Transport Lines after breakfast tomorrow.

(Sd) S. CRAWFORD. Captain.
A/Adjutant .
13. S. Battn, York & Lancaster Regt .

Addition to Operation Orders
No 89 dated 30/10/17.

1. The 92nd Infantry Brigade is extending its LEFT on October 30th and taking over our Front Line from junction of BRANDY and NOVA SCOTIA up to and including No 7 post. They will also take over SOUTH TRIUMPH and BRANDON TRENCHES.

2. 'C' Coy. 13th York & Lancs will be relieved by 'A' Coy 13th York & Lancs

3. 'C' Coy 13th York & Lancs will hand over accomodation in SOUTH TRIUMPH and any trench stores &c to "B" Coy, 11th EAST YORKS. Receipt to be obtained

All other orders hold good.

ACKNOWLEDGE.

(Sd) S. CRAWFORD Capt
a/adjt
12th York & Lancs Regt

SECRET. Copy No. - - - -

12th. Bn. York & Lancaster Regt.
Operation Order No 89.

Ref. Maps:-
MAROEUIL 1/20,000;
TRENCH MAP. 29. 10. 17.

1. The 12th York & Lancaster Regt. and attached Company of 13th York & Lancaster Regt, will be relieved in the Front Line by the 13th York & Lancaster Regt, with one company of the 14th York & Lancaster Regt. attached, tomorrow 30th. October, the 12th York & Lancaster Regt proceeding to SPRINGVALE CAMP on completion of relief.

"C" Coy. 13th. Y & L. will act under orders from their Battalion Commander on completion of relief indicated below.

2. The relief will be carried out as follows:-

"A" Coy. 13th Y & L. relieving "A" Coy. 12th Y & L. (RIGHT Front Coy)
"C" " " " "B" " " (CENTRE " ")
"B" " " " "C" " " (LEFT " ")
"HQ" " " " "HQ" " "
"one" " 14th Y & L " "C" " 13th Y & L in SUPPORT.

Order of relief:-

"C" Coy: 13th. Y & L Regt.
"B" " 12th Y & L Regt.
"C" " do
"A" " do
"HQ" " do

3. Companies will proceed to SPRINGVALE CAMP by the following route:-

HUDSON - C.P.R - MERSEY - LES TILLEULS Cross Roads - LENS-ARRAS - ROAD.

The following distances will be maintained on the way out as far as LES TILLEULS Cross Roads:-

100 yards between platoons,
50 " " sections.

4. The leading Company of relieving Battalion will arrive about 10.30. a.m.
'C' Coy. 13th Y & L will not move from their present positions until 10. a.m.

5. The 13th Y & L Regt. will relieve Nos 24 and 25 Posts before ~~dawn~~ 4 a.m. tomorrow. The garrisons under an Officer reporting to O.C. 'C' Company, 12th Y & L, ~~at [illegible] a.m.~~ in order to relieve at that time.

6. The usual advance parties from the 13th Y & L will arrive at 9. a.m. to take over Trench Stores, etc.

7. Trench Store lists will be forwarded to Battn H.Qrs by 6 p.m. on day of relief.

Coy Commanders to report relief

8. Completion of relief will be sent by Fullerphone or runner to Battn H.Qrs – Code Words " GOODS DELIVERED" being used.

9. ACKNOWLEDGE.

S. Crawford.
Captain &
A/Adjutant.
12th York & Lancaster Regiment.

Copies to :-

No 1.	C.O.	No 9.	I.O. and L.G.O.
2.	Adjt.	" 10.	13th Y & L.
3/6	Coys. 12th Y & L.	" 11.	File.
7	'C' Coy. 13th Y & L.	" 12 & 13	War Diary.
8.	M.O.		

Administrative Instructions issued with 12th York & Lanc Regt Operation Order No 89, dated 29/10/17.

1. All Lewis Guns, Magazines, etc. and other stores will be dumped in WINNIPEG ROAD, as near as possible to the Ration Dump. A guard of 1 N.C.O. per Coy. and 1 man per Lewis Gun section being left in charge until arrival of Transport.
The Transport Officer will arrange for removal tomorrow night.

2. 25 filled water tins per company will be handed over to relieving companies.

3. The Q-M will arrange to hand over all water tins in his possession which are surplus to Mobile Reserve, to Q-M. 13th York Regt.

4. The Q-M. will arrange to take over SPRINGVALE CAMP from 11th East Lancs Regt.

5. The T.O. will arrange for horses for the C.O., 2nd in Command, M.O. and Adjutant, to be at LES TILLEULS Cross Roads at 2pm.

E. Crawford

Capt & a/Adjt
12th York & Lanc Regt.

SECRET. Copy No. 3

94th INFANTRY BRIGADE ORDER No. 183.

Ref. Map :)
MAROEUIL,)
1/20,000.)

1. 10. 17.

1. A Company of the 12th Bn., York and Lancaster Regt., will raid the enemy's Posts at T.24.d.40.35 and T.24.d.40.55 on the night of 5/6th October, for the purpose of securing identifications and inflicting casualties. The Post at T.24.d.40.35 is possibly hold as a Rifle or Bombing Post ; that at T 24.d.40.55 as a Machine Gun Post.

2. Points of Entry.
Gaps will be cut in the enemy's wire at about T.24.d.4.4 and at T.24.d.40.65, by means of Bangalore torpedoes, which will be fired by electric exploders.

3. Artillery.
The 170th Brigade R.F.A., assisted by guns of the 165th Bde. R.F.A., will co-operate by forming a standing barrage on the following trenches and trench junctions :-

C/165 Bty. (2 18-prs.) enfilading TAMARISK Trench from T.30.b.72.72 to U.25.a.16.86.
C/170 Bty. from U.25.a.16.86 to U.19.c.10. 50.
A/170 Bty. from U.19.c.10.50 to T.24.b.75.00.
B/165 (4 Guns) T.24.b.75.00 to T.24.d.46.91.

4.5" Hows. will engage the following targets :-

Block Trench at T.24.b.27.08.
" " " T.24.b.55.00.
" " " T.24.d.85.20.
" " " T.24.d.55.00.,

and engage the Machine Gun in consolidated Shell Hole at T.30.b.55.64.

The 165 Bde. R.F.A. (less 2 guns) will co-operate on the South.

Rates of fire :-

Zero to Zero plus 5 mins.	-	INTENSE.
Plus 5 to plus 10 min.	-	RAPID.
Plus 10 to plus 15 min.	-	INTENSE.
" 15 to " 20	-	RAPID.
" 20 to " 25	-	NORMAL
" 25 to " 30	-	SLOW.
Plus 30 minutes	....	Cease Fire.

Should the O.C., 13 York & Lanc R. require the Barrage to be continued, he will notify the 170 Brigade H.Q. direct.

The O.C. 170th Brigade R.F.A. is detailing an Officer for Liaison Duties, & this officer will be accomodated in the Coy. dugout at T.24.c.95.50. Arrangements are being made by him to have a direct telephone line to his Brigade H.Q.

4. Machine Guns.
The O.C. 94 M. G. Company will arrange to place barrages on the enemy's Trenches as follows :-

(a) From T.24.b.2.1 to T.24.b.35.45.

(b) From T.24.d.5.1 to T.24.d.8.2.,

and to traverse from U.19.c.15.00 to U.19.c.10.95, thereby assisting the Artillery barrage.

Rate of fire will be decided by M.G. Company Commander. The ammunition required by M G Coy for this operation will be drawn in advance, and will not be used from that held for defence purposes.

5. Trench Mortars.
The 8 Trench Mortars of the 94th T.M.Battery will be utilised as follows :-

4 Mortars placed so as to bring fire to bear on junction of TORTOISE & WINNIPEG Road, T.24.b.25.18.

4 Mortars on enemy M.G. in TULIP at T.24.d.8.2.

Note. Only two Mortars will fire on each Target at a time, the reserve Mortars being ready to fire whilst the others in use are being sponged out, & thus secure continuous fire.

Fire will be maintained at the rate of 10 rounds per Mortar per minute, from Zero to Zero plus 20 mins., and 5 rds. per min. from Zero plus 20 min. until Artillery barrage ceases.

The 92nd Inf. Bde. are being asked to bring Trench Mortar (Stokes), Machine-gun, and Lewis Gun fire to bear on the Northern edge of FRESNOY Park from Zero to Zero plus 30 min.

6. Zero Arrangements.
The following are the Zero arrangements. The approximate Zero Hour is 9.30 p.m. The actual Zero Hour will be fixed by O.C. 170 Bde. R.F.A., on receiving the message in Code from the Front Line that all is ready. He will communicate the Zero Hour he fixes to the 165th Brigade. The Artillery will fire a salvo at the Zero Hour, and Light T.M's, Machine Guns, and Lewis Guns, will take the Zero Hour from the firing of the salvo.

7. Code.

The following Code will be used in connection with this Operation :-

"All Ready" - RATIONS CORRECT.

Zero - BLACKMAIL.

9.0 p.m. - P

10.0 p.m. - Q

11.0 p.m. - R

12 midnight - S

Minutes will be given in clear.

Therefore "Zero, 10.30 p.m." will be sent - "BLACKMAIL Q.30".

8. Watches will be synchronised at 94th Infantry Brigade H.Q. at six p.m. 5th October.

9. A brief report on the Operation will be wired to Brigade H.Q. immediately on its completion. A further written report will be rendered as soon as all details are known.

Captain,
Brigade Major,
94 Infantry Bde.

Copy No. 1 - 11 E. Lan. R.
2)- 12 York & Lanc R.
3)-
4 - 13 York & Lanc R.
5 - 14 York & Lanc R.
6 - 94 M.G.Coy.
7 - 94 T.M.Batt.
8 - 31 Division "G".
9 - 31 Div. Artillery.
10 - 165 Bde. R.F.A.
11 - 170 Bde. R.F.A.
12 - 92 Inf. Bde.
13 - 7 Canadian Inf.Bde.
14 - Staff Captain.
15 & 16 - War Diary.
17 - File.
18)
19) Spare.
20)

CONFIDENTIAL

WAR DIARY

12th.S. Battalion York & Lancaster Regiment.

Period:- November 1st 1917.
to.
November 30th 1917.

Volume XXIIII

Date of despatch.

December 1st 1917.
B.E.F.

Instructions regarding War Diaries and Intelligence Summaries are contained in F. S. Regs., Part II. and the Staff Manual respectively. Title pages will be prepared in manuscript.

WAR DIARY
or
~~INTELLIGENCE SUMMARY.~~
(Erase heading not required.)

Army Form C. 2118.

Place	Date	Hour	Summary of Events and Information	Remarks and references to Appendices
SPRING-VALE CAMP. ROCLINCOURT.	1917 Nov. 1st 2nd 3rd 4th		General training, in which particular attention was paid to the ~~[illegible]~~ fostering of the offensive spirit of platoons and sections, when acting as self contained units in attack. Open air sport was encouraged & inter-company football competition completed. A Battalion Tactical Exercise took place in the vicinity of the camp on the 4th.	[initials]
BROWN LINE.	5th	10 AM.	The Battalion moved into the BROWN LINE to act as 94th Infty Bde "B" Support, relieving the 11th Bn. EAST LANCS REGT. In the evening Working Parties were provided for the Forward Area.	(O.O. 89 att'd) [initials]
	6. 7. 8.		Evening Working Parties provided as on 5th. During the day large parties were engaged on making Barbed Wire Concertinas.	[initials]
	9 10		Do Do Do	[initials]
	11	10.A.M.	The 94th Infty Bde adopted the Defended and Undefended Area scheme of defence, drawn up for the winter campaign. Under this system instead of Battns being 18 consecutive days in the trenches, they will in future — providing hostilities are normal — do duty in the forward area for periods of 6 consecutive days only, each period in the line being followed by a similar period in camp in the Back Area. The troops will benefit considerably by this & sick casualties will be reduced almost to a minimum.	[initials]
			The Battn moved into "A" Support in the RED LINE, relieving the 11th East Lancs. Battn H.Q. were situated in VANCOUVER RD (actually the WILLERVAL – LENS RD) about 1 kilometre from WILLERVAL.	(OO 90 att'd)
			The 15th Bn. WEST YORKS REGT took over the BROWN LINE.	[initials]

A7092 Wt. W128,9/M1293 750,000. 1/17. D. D & L. Ltd. Forms/C2118/14.

Instructions regarding War Diaries and Intelligence Summaries are contained in F. S. Regs., Part II. and the Staff Manual respectively. Title pages will be prepared in manuscript.

WAR DIARY
or
INTELLIGENCE SUMMARY.
(Erase heading not required.)

Army Form C. 2118.

Place	Date	Hour	Summary of Events and Information	Remarks and references to Appendices
RED LINE.	1917 Nov 11		Working Parties provided as usual.	
	" 12		Do	
		11-15pm	Enemy bombarded the Divisional front with gas shell, gas trench mortar shells etc. For an hour the Battn were on the ALERT. There was one casualty — 2/Lt G. H. WOOD being gassed.	
	" 13		Working parties provided & usual routine work carried out.	
	" 14.		Do Do Do The following extracts appeared in Battn Orders for this day:- "York & Lanc. R. 12th Bn. Temp. Major (Actg Lt. Col) T. C. HOOD, 14th Battn, to command Battn, and to be Temp. Lt. Col, vice Lt. Col. J. A. CROSTHWAITE (transferred to 'Regulars attd' 100/Infy/7790 d/18/8/17). 30 Sept. 1917. Temp. Lieut. T. C. NOAKES, General List, to be acting Captain, whilst commanding a Coy, 5th Oct/17. (A.G. List 159. Appointments etc) The under-mentioned is transferred to General List for duty as stated. Temp. Lt. H OXLEY, from York & Lancs. R (attd) for Army Signal Service. 3rd Oct/17. 2/Lt. C.E. BLAD, to be Lieutenant 2.3.17. (Supplement to London Gazette d 2/11/17)"	
	15		Working Parties provided as usual.	
	16		Do	
ECURIE	17	Morning	The Battalion were relieved by the 14th Bn York & Lancaster Regt and proceeded to ROBERTS Camp, ECURIE WOOD.	(0091 attd)
	18		Day spent in general cleaning up and inspections. During the morning the following message was received:- "On 19th inst, the 92nd Infantry Brigade will take over the whole of the 47th	

Army Form C. 2118.

Instructions regarding War Diaries and Intelligence Summaries are contained in F. S. Regs., Part II. and the Staff Manual respectively. Title pages will be prepared in manuscript.

WAR DIARY
or
INTELLIGENCE SUMMARY.
(Erase heading not required.)

Place	Date	Hour	Summary of Events and Information	Remarks and references to Appendices
ECURIE	18th	–	Divisional Front. 11th East Lancs & 12 Y&L will be prepared to move into Support of the 92nd Infantry Brigade on the 20th inst – 94th Infty Bde"	
	19th	–	A quiet day. In the evening the 94th Infantry Brigade Concert party held their opening performance in a former Divisional Cinema Hut at ECURIE. Lt Col. F.T. C. HOOD, is President of the Concert Party Committee, the object of which is to provide variety of entertainment for troops resting after arduous duty in the trenches.	
RED LINE OPPY Sector.	20th	12.15 AM	Battn warned that on 21st it would take over section of the front line in OPPY Sector.	
		7.30 AM	Battn moved off to relieve the 22nd London Regt (47th Div) in the RED LINE in the OPPY SECTOR opposite OPPY WOOD. Weather misty, and drizzling rain.	(0092 att)
FRONT LINE OPPY WOOD	21st	7 AM.	Battalion relieved the 13th Bn EAST YORKS Rgt, 92 I. Bde in the Front Line, the area being defended by three strongly garrisoned Posts backed up by Coy in Support. Hostilities quiet.	(0093 att)
			[Note:- The 31st Div took over the command of the front of the 47th Div on the 19th, the 4th Canadian Infty Bde (2nd Canadian Div) taking over the 94th Infty Bde Front on the 21st inst]	
	22nd	Morning	A general scheme for the improvement of the area drawn up & working parties commenced work. Much is required to be done: Firesteps need re-building, trenches widened & deepened, new shelters erected, berms cleared, sumps dug, trench boards re-laid, & weak spots in the wire strengthened.	

A7092 Wt. W128_9/M1293 750,000. 1/17. D. D & L. Ltd. Forms/C2118/14.

Army Form C. 2118.

WAR DIARY
or
INTELLIGENCE SUMMARY.
(*Erase heading not required.*)

Instructions regarding War Diaries and Intelligence Summaries are contained in F. S. Regs., Part II. and the Staff Manual respectively. Title pages will be prepared in manuscript.

Place	Date	Hour	Summary of Events and Information	Remarks and references to Appendices
OPPY Sector.	22nd.	Afternoon.	Owing to the success of the 3rd Army operations the enemy's positions from MONCHY to the South is weakened & it is not unlikely that the positions of the enemy on our front may thereby be affected. In order to prevent the enemy from withdrawing unmolested arrangements are being made for active patrolling by night & camouflage patrols by day. The object is to keep in constant touch with the enemy & to detect immediately any signs of retirement. Steps are being taken to cut the enemy wire along the whole Divisional front.	(0094 att'd)
do	22/23.	Night	Captain G. C. M. L. PIRKIS O/C "C" Coy wounded by enemy sniper, bullet passing through nose & cheek.	
	23 24 25 26		This period was a very strenuous one. There were continuous heavy working parties and patrol duties were of a more responsible nature than for some time past.	
Railway Cutting	27.	Morning	The Battalion relieved by the 14th Bn. York & Lancaster Regt, moved back to reserve. Battn HQrs & "C" Coy were billetted in the Railway Cutting approx. ½ mile South West of point known as BAILLEUL STATION. "A" & "B" Coys were billetted in the RED LINE in front of BAILLEUL (B 23 sqr: Map FOOTHILL EDN 2.) Working parties provided.	(0095 att'd)
	28.		Working parties provided. Captain N. L. TUNBRIDGE proceeded to 75th Infantry Brigade on appointment as Staff Captain.	

A7092 Wt. W125 9/M1293 750,000. 1/17. D. D & L. Ltd. Forms/C2118/14.

Army Form C. 2118.

Instructions regarding War Diaries and Intelligence Summaries are contained in F. S. Regs., Part II. and the Staff Manual respectively. Title pages will be prepared in manuscript.

WAR DIARY
or
INTELLIGENCE SUMMARY.
(Erase heading not required.)

Place	Date	Hour	Summary of Events and Information	Remarks and references to Appendices
RAILWAY CUTTING RED LINE	29		Lieut J C COWEN rejoined the Battn for duty from England. He was attached to H.Qs as Bombing Lewis Gun Officer.	
			The Battn provided Working Parties.	
"	30		Working Parties as for previous days.	
			The ration strength of the Battn was: 19 Officers, 460 other ranks.	

[signature] Lieut. Colonel Comdg.
12th (S) Bn. York & Lancs. Rgt. (Sheffield.)

A7092 Wt. W128 9/M1293 750,000. 1/17. D. D & L. Ltd. Forms/C2118/14.

SECRET. Copy No.....15

12TH. S. BATTALION, YORK & LANCASTER REGIMENT.

Ref. Map.- MAROEUIL. } OPERATION ORDER. NO 89. 4/11/17.

1. The 12TH. S. BATTN, YORK & LANCASTER REGT, will relieve the 11TH. S. BATTN, EAST LANCS. REGT., in Brigade "B" Support Line tomorrow, 5/11/17.

2. The relief will be carried out as follows:-

"A" Coy. 12 Y & L. will relieve "W" Coy. 11th East Lancs. R. in SUMMER LANE.
"B" " " " " "X" " " " in WINTER LANE.
"C" " " " " "Z" " " " " BROWN LINE.
"HQ" " " " " "HQ" " " " " do.

3. The Battalion will fall in in Mass at 9-45 a.m. in the above order from Right to Left, for necessary inspections, and will be ready to move off in the above order at 10-0 a.m. Dress: Marching Order. From the camp to the BROWN LINE, 100 yds distance will be maintained between platoons.

4. ROUTE: ECURIE Cross Roads, ROCLINCOURT, RIDGE POST Rd and TOMMY ALLEY.

5. Os C. Companies will see that strict march discipline is maintained.

6. One Officer, 1 N.C.O. and 2 Signallers per Company and H.Qrs will report at Orderly Room at 8-0 a.m. and will then proceed to H.Qrs 11th East Lancs. Regt, to take over Trench Stores, etc. from their respective Companies, on arrival.

7. Trench Store Lists will be handed in to Orderly Room as soon as possible after stores have been taken over.

8. Completion of relief will be notified to Battn H.Qrs. by wire or runner, Code word: "COPPER" being used.

9. A sketch showing dispositions will be sent to Battn. H.Qrs by 9-0 p.m.

10. ACKNOWLEDGE.

(Sd) A.N. Cousin Capt
for Captain & A/Adjt.
12. S. Bn, York and Lancaster Regiment.

Copies to:-
1....... C.O.
2.......2 in Command.
3.......Adjutant.
4 to 7...All Coys.
8........M.O.
9........T.O.
10.......Q.M.
11.......R.S.M.
12.......11th Bn, East Lancs. R.
13.......File.
14 & 15. War Diary.

ADMINISTRATIVE INSTRUCTIONS ISSUED WITH OPERATION ORDER. NO 89, dated 4/11/17.

1. The Transport Officer will arrange the Transport for all Lewis Guns, panniers, etc., from SPRINGVALE CAMP to TOMMY ALLEY. Two men per Company will proceed with the limbers to act as guard on arrival. Coys. will make their own arrangements for collecting the guns and panniers.

2. All water bottles will be filled before moving off for the trenches.

3. Sergt-Cook and Company Cooks, except one, who will be detailed by the Sergt-Cook [illegible] to remain behind to look after Coy cookers, will proceed with their Coys. Quartermaster will arrange for camp kettles to be taken up by the transport.

4. Packs will be taken up to the BROWN LINE and will be carried on the men. Steel helmets will be worn.

5. Any Officer who wishes, can have his valise taken up to the Line. These will be dumped at guard room by 8-30 a.m. Blankets rolled in bundles of ten, valises not to be taken, mess stores, or other surplus baggage to be dumped opposite the guard room, by 8-30 am.

6. Transport for baggage detailed in para, 5., will be arranged by the Transport Officer.

7. Transport Officer will arrange to send up two water carts nightly; one water man to go up with the Battalion and remain in the Line.

8. The Second-in-Command, Medical Officer and Quartermaster, accompanied by the Orderly Officer and Area Commandant's representative will inspect the camp at 9-30 a.m. The Orderly Officer will obtain from the last-named a certificate of cleanliness for the camp.

9. The Quartermaster will arrange to hand over SPRINGVALE CAMP to representative of 13th. S. Battn, York & Lancaster Regt.

[illegible signature]
for Captain & A/Adjt.
4/11/17. 12. S. Bn, York & Lancaster Regiment.

SECRET.

Copy No......16.

12TH.S.BATTALION YORK AND LANCASTER REGIMENT.

Ref.Map)
MAROEUIL)
1/20,000)
& Tr.Maps)

OPERATION ORDER No.90.

10.11.17.

1. The Battalion will relieve the 11th EAST LANC.RGT. in "A" Support tomorrow 11th Nov. and will be relieved by the 15th WEST YORKS.RGT in the BROWN LINE.

2. The relief will be carried out as follows:-
"B" Coy 12 Y & L relieving "W" Coy in NEW BRUNSWICK TR, coming under orders of O.C.11th E.LANC R. for tactical purposes in case of an attack on the Brigade Front.
"C" Coy 12 Y & L relieving "Z" Coy 11th.E.L. in HUDSON TR.
"A" " " " "X" " " " CANADA TR.
H.Q " " " "Y"(HQ) " " VANCOUVER RD.

?. "A" Coy 12 Y & L will be relieved by "B" Coy 15 W.YORKS.
"B" " " " " " "C" " "
"C" & H.Q " " " " "D" " "

3. Coys will move off in the order "B", "C", "A" and H.Q using TIRED ALLEY, RED LINE, CANADA TR., MONTREAL, HUDSON, maintaining 100 yds between platoons, and 50 yds between sections, leading platoon moving off at 10.a.m.

4. 2nd.Lieut.McNAMARA, the R.S.M. and two Signallers from H.Q, together with one Officer, one N.C.O and one Signaller per Coy, will proceed to H.Q. of their respective Coys, 11th.E.LANC.R. reaching there at 9.a.m. to take over accommodation, trench stores, etc.
Similar parties from the 15 W.YORKS will report to our respective Coy H.Q, at 9.a.m.

5. Lieut.WESTBY and one N.C.O per Coy will be left behind to hand over accommodation, trench stores, etc., to 15.W.YORKS rejoining the Battalion in "A" Support on completion. A certificate of cleanliness of billets will be obtained.

6. The Adjutant, Medical Officer and Orderly Officer will inspect the Coy areas at 9.a.m. Coy Commanders will see that all trenches and dugouts are clean and tidy by that time.

7. Trench Store lists for both reliefs will be handed to the Orderly Room by 6.p.m. on day of relief.

8. Sketches, shewing dispositions and location of anti-aircraft L.G's to reach Battalion H.Q. by 6.p.m. on day of relief.

9 Completion of relief will be reported to Battalion H.Q. by wire or runner. Code word FUEL.

[signature]
Captain,
A/Adjutant,
12th.S.Battalion York and Lancaster Regt.

Copies to
No.1. C.O.
2 2nd.in.C.
3. Adjt.
4 to 7.Coys.
8. M.O
9. T.O.
10. Q.M.
No.11.R.S.M.
12.11th.E.LANC.R
13.15.W.YORK.R.
14) War
15) Diary
16 File.

ADMINISTRATIVE INSTRUCTIONS ISSUED WITH OPERATION ORDER NO. 90.

1. Rations and water will be delivered nightly to the following places:-

RATIONS.		WATER.
"A" Coy.	To point where limber track crosses CANADA TR. in T.28.b.	25 tins nightly brought up with rations.
"B" Coy.	To junction of NEW BRUNSWICK and SASKATCHEWAN RD.	-do- -do-
HQ & "C" Coy.	To junction of VANCOUVER RD and HUDSON.	One water cart for tanks near ration dump in VANCOUVER RD, and 25 tins nightly brought up with "C" Coy's rations.

2. All water bottles must be filled before starting from present trenches.

3. All Coys will take their cooks and dixies forward with them, as cooking can be carried out in the trenches to be occupied by them.

4. Packs will be taken forward.

5. BAGGAGE.

   1. All Officers' kits and other Company stores not required to be taken forward will be dumped near the canteen by 9.a.m.

   2. Officers' valises to be taken forward, Orderly Room stores, etc, will be dumped at the same time and place, but separate from stores mentioned in 1.

   3. Transport Officer will arrange for removal after dark.

   4. Each Coy will leave a N.C.O. and three men in charge of their dump, who will be responsible for the correct distribution of stores, and for loading on to Transport.

6. The Quartermaster will arrange to take over 80 petrol tins from the Quartermaster of the 11th E.LANC.R.

S. Van Lorel [signature]

Captain,
A/Adjutant.
12th. S. Battn. York and Lancaster Regiment.

SECRET

Copy No. 1.

13TH. S. BATTALION YORK AND LANCASTER REGIMENT.

Ref. Map MAROEUIL, 1/20,000.

OPERATION ORDER No. 91.

16.11.17.

1. The 13th York and Lanc. R. will be relieved in the RED LINE by the 14th York and Lanc. R. tomorrow morning, 17th inst, 13th York and Lanc. R. proceeding to ECURIE WOOD CAMP.

2. The relief will be carried out as follows:-

"A" Coy, 14 Y & L relieving "B" Coy, 13 Y & L in NEW BRUNSWICK.
"B" " " " "C" " " in CANADA and HUDSON.
"C" " " " "A" " " in CANADA.
"D" & Bn HQ " " H.Q " " in VANCOUVER ROAD.

3. Companies will proceed to ECURIE WOOD CAMP by the following route:- HUDSON, MONTREAL, CANADA, RED LINE, TIRED ALLEY, ECURIE CROSS ROADS, and SPRINGVALE ROAD.
All ranks of "A", "B", and "C" Coys must use this route.
Battn HQ details will proceed via HUDSON, C.P.R, and MERSEY.
The following distances will be maintained on the way out:-
100 yds between platoons, and
50 " " sections.
O.C.Coys will see that strict march discipline is maintained and the carrying of sandbags is strictly forbidden.

4. O.C.Coys will detail 1 Officer, 1 N.C.O, and 1 o.r, to report to Battalion H.Q. at 8.a.m. tomorrow; to take over the new Camp at 10.a.m; the other ranks to act as guides and meet their respective Coys at ECURIE CROSS RDS. O.C.H.Q.Coy will detail a similar party and in addition 2 Signallers.
Similar Advance Parties of the 14th Y & L will report to H.Q. of the respective Coys at 10.a.m.

5. No men of the 12th Y & L.R. accommodated in HUDSON or NEW BRUNSWICK will move out on relief until the whole of the 13th Y & L.R. has passed the junction of NEW BRUNSWICK TRENCH and HUDSON C.T.
Two guides from H.Q Coy will meet the 13th Y & L at the junction of HUDSON and VANCOUVER RD, to proceed with them as far as the junction of NEW BRUNSWICK and HUDSON. When the whole of the 13th Y & L have passed this junction, the guides will report this to O's.C "B" and "C" Coys respectively and the relief can then be proceeded with.

6. Trench store lists will be forwarded to Battn H.Q. by 6.p.m. on day of relief.

7. Completion of relief will be sent by Fullerphone or runner to Battalion H.Q. Code word: CANTEEN.

8. ACKNOWLEDGE.

[signature]
Captain,
A/Adjutant,
13th. S. Battalion York and Lancaster Rgt.

Copies to

No.1	C.O.	8.	M.O.	12.	14th Y & L.
2	Adjutant.	9.	Q.M.	13	War Diary.
3 to 6	All Coys.	10.	R.S.M.	14	-do-
7.	T.O.	11.	~~13th Y & L~~	15.	File.

ADMINISTRATIVE INSTRUCTIONS ISSUED WITH OPERATION ORDER. NO.81, dated 16/7/17.

1. All Lewis Guns, magazines, Officers' valises, etc, and other stores will be dumped at the respective Coy Ration Dumps by 9-0 a.m. A Guard of one N.C.O and one man per Company will be left in charge until arrival of Transport.
The Transport Officer will arrange for removal tomorrow night.

2. O.C. Companies will arrange for all water tins to be handed over and a sufficient number of full tins to be handed over for the incoming Battalion to carry on with.

3. The Quartermaster will arrange to hand over all water tins in his possession which are surplus to Mobile Reserve to the Quartermaster, 14th Bn, York & Lancaster Regt.

4. The Transport Officer will arrange for horses for the Commanding Officer and Adjutant to be at THELUS CAVE at 1-30 pm.

[signature]

Captain.
A/Adjutant.
12, S. Bn, York & Lancs. R.

Copies to all recipients of O.O.81.

12

Copy No.......

13TH.S.BATTALION YORK AND LANCASTER REGT.
OPERATION ORDER No.92.

Ref Map.
FRANCE,
Sheet 51,b.N.W.

19.11.17.

1. The 13TH.YORK & LANCASTER REGT, will relieve the 22ND LONDON R. in the REDLINE, in the OPPY-GAVRELLE Sector tomorrow, 20th inst.

2. The relief will be carried out as follows :-
"A" Coy, 13th Y & L, will relieve "A" Coy, 22nd London Regt.
"B" " " " " "B" " "
"C" " " " " "C" " "
"HQ" " " " " H Q & "D" Coy "

3. Companies will fall in for inspections in the Company lines, "A" & "HQ" at 7.15.a.m., "B" & "C" at 7.45.a.m. and be ready to move off at the following times :-
"A" & "HQ" 7.30.a.m. "B" & "C" 8.a.m.
Starting Point. Junction of ECURIE WOOD CAMP and SPRINGVALE ROAD.

4. The Coys will move off in the following order : "A", "HQ" "C" & "B" Coys using routes as follows:
"A" and "HQ" : Train from ROCLINCOURT STATION AT 8am - DAYLIGHT RAILHEAD - OUSE ALLEY.
"C" and "B" : ROCLINCOURT - BAILLEUL Rd - TOWY ALLEY .

5. Guides. 4 per Coy and 2 for HQs Coy will be at the top of OUSE ALLEY at 8-30 a.m. to conduct " A" and "HQ" Coys and 4 guides per Coy will be on the BAILLEUL Rd at H 1 b 8.8 to conduct "B" and "C" Coys to their respective Coy areas .

6. Dress: Field Service Order - Great coats to be rolled up in waterproof sheet . Water bottles to be filled. 100 yds distance will be maintained between platoons as far as TOWY ALLEY and OUSE ALLEY. From these points to RED LINE 50 yds between sections will be maintained. Strict march discipline to be maintained.

7. One Officer and 2 signallers per Coy ,one N.C.O per platoon and one Officer, the R.S.M, 2 signallers and two runners from HQs will report at Orderly Room at 6-0 a.m. to proceed to the respective Coy. H Qs of 22nd LONDON REGT., to take over Trench Stores and fix up accommodation.

8. Trench Store Lists will be handed in to the Orderly Room as soon as possible after stores have been taken over.

9. Completion of relief will be notified to Battn H Qs by wire or runner :Code word: FLAGS.

10. A sketch showing dispositions will be sent to Bn HQs by 8-0 pm

11. ACKNOWLEDGE.

Crawford
Captain.
A/Adjutant.
13.S. Bn, York & Lancs.Regt.

Copies to: 1. C.O.
2, Adjutant.
3-6 All Coys.
7 M.O.
8. T.O.
9. Q.M.
10 R.S. M.
11 & 12 . War Diary.
13. File

ADMINISTRATIVE INSTRUCTIONS ISSUED WITH OPERATION ORDER. NO. 93. dated 19/11/17.

---

1. Sergt Cook and Coy Cooks except one, who will be detailed by the Sergt Cook to remain behind to look after Coy Cookers, will remain with their Coys. Q.M. will arrange for camp kettles to be taken up by the Transport.

2. Blankets rolled in bundles of 10, all packs, Officers' valises, and surplus Mess Stores and baggage will be dumped in front of the Orderly Room by 7-0 a.m. All Field Service caps to be left behind in packs.

   HQ. Officers' kits and all Mess Stores for the Line to be dumped ~~separately~~ near the guard room by 7-0 a.m. Transport Officer will arrange removal.

3. Q.M. will arrange for rations for 21st and onwards to be sent up by train to "A" and "HQ" Coys and by limbers to "B" and "C" Coys.

4. One Water Cart will be sent up with "B" and "C" Coys rations. Water for "A" and "HQ" Coys can be obtained from tanks in the line. One water man will accompany "A" & "HQ" Coy to attend to water supply.

5. The Adjutant, Medical Officer and Q.M. accompanied by the Orderly Officer and Area Commandant representative will inspect the camp at 7-30 a.m. The Orderly Officer will obtain from the last named a certificate of cleanliness of the camp.

. The Transport Officer will arrange for C.Os and Adjutants horses and grooms to be at the camp by 8-30 a.m.

Twelve magazines per Lewis Gun will be carried by the teams and twenty magazines per gun will be dumped near the guard room by 7-0 a.m. Transport Officer will arrange removal of these to the line tomorrow night.

[illegible signature]

Captain.
A/Adjutant.
13.S. Bn York & Lancaster Regt.

Copies to all recipients of O O 93.

Secret

Copy No

1/5th York & Lancaster Regt

OPERATION ORDER No 13

25/4/17

1\. The 1/5th York & Lanc R will relieve the 1/4th [illegible] in the front line in the OPPY Post area tomorrow, 26 inst.

2\. The relief will be carried out as follows:-

A Coy 1/5th will relieve	A Coy 1/5 EYR	in	MARQUOIS POST
B " " " "	B "		WOOD Post
		"	BOYNE Post
C " "	C " "	"	OPPY Post
HQ "	HQ		DUKE ST.

3\. 2nd Lt Dickinson + 1 NCO + 3 OR to be detailed by OC HQ Coy will proceed at [illegible] to the trench at present occupied by D Coy 1/5th EYR to take over trench stores. This trench will not be occupied except by the NCO + 3 OR detailed who will act as guard, till further instructions are issued.

4\. Coys will be relieved in the RED LINE as follows:-

A & B, Coys relieved by 11th Yorks Regt
B & C " " " 13th E Y Regt

5 Coys will move off in the following order – C, B, A and HQ Coy. C & B will move forward at 6.30am and A & HQ at 7am. O.C. Coys will arrange for the trench to be kept clear of all men until B & C Coys have passed.
Rdv. RED LINE and OUSE ALLEY
All Coys to be clear of the junction of OUSE ALLEY & RED LINE by 8am. 50 yds distance will be maintained between platoons

6 Guides 11 (1 per Coy including 1 for Coy HQ) and 3 for HQ Coy will be at the junction of OUSE ALLEY & RED LINE at 7.30am

7 1 officer & 2 signallers per Coy, 1 NCO per platoon & Lewis Gun numbers, 1 NCO & 2 runners from HQ will report at Battn HQ at 6am to proceed to the [illegible] [illegible] Coy HQ of 1st BEYR to take over trench stores & [illegible] accommodation. The Coy officer

to be those who went round the line today.

8. 1 Officer & 1 NCO per Coy with the RQM for HQ Coy will remain behind to hand over to the incoming platoon, afterwards proceeding to join their Coys.

9. OC HQ Coy will detail 2 runners to act as guides to conduct B & C Coys respectively to the junction of OUSE ALLEY and RED LINE & will report to the OC Coys at 6.20am

10. Trench Store Lists will be handed in to the Orderly Room as soon as possible after the store have been taken over.

11. Completion of relief will be notified to Bn HQ by wire or runner. Code word – BREAD

12. Sketch showing dispositions will be sent to Battn HQ by 4 pm

13. ACKNOWLEDGE

[illegible]
Capt
Adjt
12th Bn York & Lanc R

Administrative Instructions
to Operation Order No

1 The Sgt Cook will arrange for breakfast and issue the unexpired portion of the days rations to Coys before moving forward, the Coy Cookers afterwards returning to Transport lines

2 Officers Kits, surplus stores & baggage will be dumped near the HQ ration dump by 6 a.m. OC HQ Coy will detail a guard of 1 NCO & 10 O.R. to remain behind & load up on the returning ration train

3 The QM will arrange for rations to be sent up to all Coys by train. No water is required

Capt
Adjt
26/11/17 12th Bn Glos Rgt

Secret

12th S Bn York & Lancaster Rgt

Ref Map OPPY 3 1/10,000

OPERATION ORDER No 94

1. In the event of the enemy withdrawing from his present position in front of this Battalion, he will be closely pursued by this Battn in conjunction with units on our flanks.

2. The enemy will not be allowed to withdraw unmolested, and if there are any signs that the enemy's resistance is weakening, strong patrols will at once be sent forward to keep touch with the enemy's rearguards.

If the enemy is found to have retired, touch will immediately be regained.

Officers Commanding Coys will arrange that the closest observation is maintained, so that any withdrawal of the enemy can be detected as soon as possible.

Strong patrols will be sent forward under Battn orders, to keep touch with the enemy's rearguards. All ground gained by patrols will be followed up and made good. The line thus reached by the advance troops, will in the first instance be held as an outpost line, the line of resistance being the previous front line. As soon as the outpost line can be adequately supported by artillery, it will be consolidated as a new line of resistance.

3. The advance will be made by bounds, the objective of each bound being securely held, before a further advance is made.

The bounds are shewn on attached map Z as follows:-

1st bound marked in Green
2nd " " Orange.

The bounds will not be made without orders from Battn HQ.

4. The boundaries of the Battn advance, and the dividing line between the two front Coys is also shewn on map "Z".

P.T.O.

4 (Cont) During the bounds, sufficient tools will be carried forward, for carrying out the immediate consolidation of lines gained. Carrying arrangements will be notified later.

5. After these lines have been occupied, ammunition and wiring material will be carried forward in sufficient quantity to meet requirements; under Battn arrangements.

6. The area vacated by this Battalion in moving forward will be occupied by the Battalion in "A" Support, other Battns being moved up correspondingly into Reserve etc.

7. The advance will be made in three lines, two Coys in the first two lines, one Coy in the 3rd line.

The following formations will be adopted where the ground & hostile resistance make them possible:

(a) 1st line One platoon from each front line Coy, in line of section columns at about 100 yds interval, protected by scouts working in pairs at 150-200 yds in advance.

(b) 2nd line (Supports). Remaining platoon of front line Coys, with sections in Artillery formation. 2nd line to be 300 yds distance from 1st line. This 2nd line will also be responsible for mopping up and thoroughly clearing the whole area between Coy boundaries.

(c) 3rd line (Bn Reserve). Support Coy from MARQUIS Post with platoons in Artillery formation, 500 yds distance from 2nd line.

Note. The above intervals are approximate only and the Right Coy which has to pass through OPPY WOOD and VILLAGE may not find it possible to maintain the formation exactly, but it is particularly important that touch is maintained between all lines, and that support is quickly available at any point where resistance is met with.

PTO

8. The advance beyond the first bound will not be made without orders from Battn HQ, and when ordered, a similar procedure will be adopted to that detailed in para 7.

9. <u>Dispositions after Bounds have been Completed</u>

The general line will be as shewn on map Z. The following "Strong points", shewn on map by blue circles will be established:-

1. <u>By the Right Coy</u>

(a) C15a45.45

(b) C9c7.3.

2 <u>By the Left Coy</u>

(a) C9c75.80.

The Left Coy on reaching objective and making good will send out one platoon to take & occupy IZEL-HOF Farm. When taken, to be garrisoned by 1 Off, 1 corr., 2 LGs.

The remaining dispositions taken up by Coys will be such as to procure the fullest possible value from a defensive point of view

A sketch shewing these dispositions will be rendered to Battn HQ immediately after such dispositions have been taken up.

10. <u>Machine Guns & Trench Mortars</u>

2 MGs and 2 TMs will probably be detailed for duty with this Battalion & come under the order of the Battalion Commander.

11. When the first bound is ordered, Battn HQ will move forward to the left front Coy HQ.

12. All lines must keep close touch with units operating on their flanks. This is of the greatest importance. Disposition sketches will shew the position of nearest posts of neighbouring units.

24/11/17

Secret. Copy No. —

12th S. Bn York & Lancaster Regt.

Operation Order No 95.

Ref Map
FOOTHILL 1/20,000.

26/11/17.

1. The 12th Y&L Regt will be relieved in the C2 Front Line tomorrow 27th inst.
On relief Battn HQ & "C" Coy will proceed to RAILWAY Cutting, and "B" & "A" Coys, to the RED LINE taking over from the 14th York & Lancaster Regt.

2. "A" Coy, 12th Y&L, will relieve "C" Coy, 14th Y&L, on the Right, in Red Line
"B" " will relieve "A" Coy, 14th Y&L on the Left in RED LINE
"C" " will relieve "B" Coy, 14th Y&L in the Cutting.
"HQ" " will relieve "HQ", 14th Y&L in the Cutting.

3. 50 yds intervals will be maintained between Sections.

4. Guides. Guides as follows will be at the Junction of OUSE ALLEY & RED LINE at

page 2

at 4.15 am to guide relief. "A", "B" & "C" Coys, 1 guide per platoon (2 platoons per Coy) and 1 for Coy HQrs. "HQ" Coy, 3 guides

5. Advance Party. 1 Officer, 1 N.C.O and 2 signallers per Coy and the R.S.M, 1 N.C.O and 2 signallers & a runner from HQrs, will report at Orderly Room at 6.30 am to proceed to take over trench stores & accomodation for their respective Coys from the 14th Y & L Regt.

6. Coy Commanders will hand over all maps, papers etc which were taken over, to the incoming battalion.

7 Trench Store Lists will be handed in to Orderly Room as soon as possible after relief.

8. Completion of relief will be notified to BHQ by ~~code~~ wire or runner, the following codes being used –
"A" Coy "Order No 95 complied with"
"B" " "Pte Jackson"
"C" Plenty of Water

9. Sketch, shewing dispositions, will be sent to Batt HQrs by 9 pm. 10. Acknowledge.

Copies to 1 CO. 2/5. Coys. 6. TO + QM.
7 14th Y & L. 8 File.
9/10 War Diary.

(Sd) S. CRAWFORD Capt a/Adjt
12th Y & L Regt

Administrative Instructions
issued with 12th York & Lancaster Regt
O.O. No 95

1. The QM will arrange for the Sgt Cook & Coy Cooks (except 1 who will be detailed to remain behind to look after Coy Cookers) to join their respective Coys tomorrow. Camp kettles will be sent up by ~~Transport~~ Train.

2. The QM will arrange for HQ Officers valises and any Coy Officers valises required, to be sent up. Coy Officers requiring their valises will notify their CQMS's tonight. Coy Officers will cut down their requirements to a minimum

3. OC "A" Coy will arrange for the 8 camp kettles at present in their cookhouse to be dumped near ration dump by 8. am tomorrow. The 2 cooks to remain in charge & return them by the ration train to the RED LINE.

4. Rations will be sent up by train as usual. No water is required.

5. OC "C" Coy will arrange for the LG panniers etc to be dumped near the ration dump and taken back by tram to the Cutting.
One NCO + 2 men to remain i/c as guard and loading & unloading party.

Copies issued as per Operation Orders.

(Sd) S. Crawford Capt
a/adjt
12th S Bn York & Lanc Rgt

26/11/17

CONFIDENTIAL

WAR DIARY

12th S Battalion York & Lancaster Rgt.

Period:- December 1st 1917.
to
December 31st 1917.

Volume XXIV

Date of despatch
January 2nd 1918
B.E.F.

WO 22

Instructions regarding War Diaries and Intelligence Summaries are contained in F. S. Regs., Part II. and the Staff Manual respectively. Title pages will be prepared in manuscript.

WAR DIARY
or
INTELLIGENCE SUMMARY.
(*Erase heading not required.*)

Army Form C. 2118.

Place	Date	Hour	Summary of Events and Information	Remarks and references to Appendices
RED LINE & RAILWAY CUTTING	1/12/17	–	Working Parties provided. Capt A.N. COUSIN assumed the duties of Adjutant, vice Capt. N. L. TUNBRIDGE & a/Capt S. CRAWFORD took over the command of "C" Coy, the vacancy created by the evacuation of a/Capt PIRKIS, wounded.	D.H.
	2/12/17	–	Working Parties provided & preparations made for taking over the Front Line tomorrow.	
OPPY WOOD FRONT LINE	3/12/17	8 AM	Battalion relieved the 1st Bn. York & Lancaster Rgt in the Front Line. Quiet relief. Warning received of an impending move of the Division.	D.H.
	3/12/17 4/12/17	Midnight	At midnight the sentries on duty at the two Bombing Posts on the ARLEUX-OPPY ROAD, suddenly observed a party of about 6 Germans approaching the post, and apparently quite close to the road. Rifle fire was opened on them and they disappeared. Very shortly afterwards a party of 50 of the enemy were seen following up in the direction of the previous 6, and approaching the same posts. They appeared to move in what the sentries describe as "artillery formation"; later reported as small groups at a few yards interval. As soon as the larger party was seen Lewis Gun & rapid fire was immediately opened on them, the posts all being very alert on account of the firing on the smaller party just previously. Rifle grenade fire was also opened on them. The party then withdrew in a direction half-right from the posts, and almost immediately were lost sight of.	
	4/12/17	Dawn	At daybreak this morning, new work was found to have been dug about half-way between the Bombing Posts on ARLEUX RD & CANDLE TRENCH. It	D.H.

Instructions regarding War Diaries and Intelligence Summaries are contained in F. S. Regs., Part II. and the Staff Manual respectively. Title pages will be prepared in manuscript.

WAR DIARY
or
INTELLIGENCE SUMMARY.
(Erase heading not required.)

Army Form C. 2118.

Place	Date	Hour	Summary of Events and Information	Remarks and references to Appendices
			appears to consist of a trench about 30 yds long and judging by the amount of earth thrown up, is fairly deep & wide. The centre of the work would be approximately at B12 d 87.60 (OPPY 2 Map)	
			The garrison of the post consider they inflicted casualties on the enemy and ~~that~~ some of them got within 50 yds of the Bombing Post.	
			A camouflage patrol sent out before dawn to investigate the new work reported that it was a communication to a post. No enemy dead was found.	
			The general opinion of the incident is that the enemy were attempting a silent enterprise against one or more of our posts, but on the other hand the party might have been out in connection with the new work referred to. Things generally quiet.	L.H.
	5/12/17		Quiet day. During night of 5/6 enemy gas was reported on both flanks.	
	6/12/17		Enemy displayed more activity than usual with heavy artillery, causing a few casualties.	
	7/12/17	6-50 am	Capt A.N. COUSIN, whilst walking "over the top" from one post to another, in pursuance of his duties, was shot in the throat by a sniper and died. Lieut J.C. COWEN assumed the duties of Adjutant. Activity normal. Administrative work was abnormal owing to move.	L.H.
MONT ST ELOY.	8/12/17	–	Battn were relieved in the line by the 1/4 Bn London Regt (56th Divn) & moved back to LANCASTER CAMP, MONT ST ELOY (F8 c 90.40). Transport moved to lines in ECOIVRES. Utmost secrecy is being maintained & ultimate destination of Battn unknown.	

A7092 Wt. W128_9/M1293 750,000. 1/17. D. D & L. Ltd. Forms/C2118/14.

Instructions regarding War Diaries and Intelligence Summaries are contained in F. S. Regs., Part II. and the Staff Manual respectively. Title pages will be prepared in manuscript.

WAR DIARY
or
INTELLIGENCE SUMMARY.
(Erase heading not required.)

Army Form C. 2118.

Place	Date	Hour	Summary of Events and Information	Remarks and references to Appendices
MONT ST ELOY	8/12/17		There was a draft of 7 Officers & 33 men awaiting the Battn. The Officers were:– Lieut. H. V. L. ROBINS (1/5. East Lancs) 2/Lt. A TURNER. " H. R. BOWEN " E. F. WYRILL " J. G. BEAUMONT " P. C. MORTON. " R. KENYON. The subalterns were from the following Regts: East Lancs, Duke of Wellington (WR). The men came from 2/Westminster Dragoons, 3rd Hussars. R.Z.A. [NOTES:– During the tour of duty in the line much patrolling was done as hitherto, but more attention was devoted to lateral patrols, involving special time-tables & codes. Each Coy in the Front line detailed two qualified men to go out each day into NO MAN'S LAND for about 6 hours. These Camouflage patrols were very successful & much useful information was obtained. Some of the enemy were sniped. A special enterprise patrol consisting of 1 Officer & 30 men including a Lewis gun went out nightly to:– (i) Obtain prisoners. (ii) Inflict casualties on the enemy. (iii) Locate posts, observe any enemy movement and record anything of interest. No prisoner was captured however.	DH

A7092 Wt. W128.9/M1293 750,000. 1/17. D. D & L. Ltd. Forms/C2118/14.

Army Form C. 2118.

Instructions regarding War Diaries and Intelligence Summaries are contained in F. S. Regs., Part II. and the Staff Manual respectively. Title pages will be prepared in manuscript.

WAR DIARY
or
INTELLIGENCE SUMMARY.
(Erase heading not required.)

Place	Date	Hour	Summary of Events and Information	Remarks and references to Appendices
MONT ST ELOY	9/12/17 10/12/17 11/12/17 12/12/17 13/12/17 14/12/17 15/12/17 16/12/17		This period was devoted to special training in the absence of further orders to move. The daily programme consisted of Platoon & Coy Tactical exercises, Setting Up drill, Musketry, Range firing etc. Specialists were trained including a special party for patrol work. There was a great revival in sport & in the afternoons there were football matches with other Battns & smaller units, by both Officers & men. 2/Lts J. WINN & H.W.B. HANSFORD joined Bn. 11/12/17. On the 15th Major D. C. ALLEN took over command of the Battn Lt-Col F. J. Courtenay Hood proceeding on leave to U.K. Sunday the 16th, was a day of rest.	D.H.
	17/12/17		Battalion Tactical exercise as per General Idea attached.	D.H.
	18/12/17 19/12/17 20/12/17		Training as above.	D.H.
	21/12/17		Route March, by Companies. The undermentioned Officers joined the Battalion 2nd Lieut. H. GIBSON 2nd Lieut. A.J. PURKESS " C.R. WRAY " W.H. RYLANCE	D.H.
A.22.c, 6.4. (Near ROCLINCOURT)	22/12/17		Battalion moved to SPRINGVALE CAMP Headquarters at A.22.c.6.4 (Sheet 51 B)	D.H.
	23/12/17		Owing to the Battalion being under orders to move to the line on the 25th (Xmas Day), the 23rd was observed as Xmas.	D.H.

A7092 Wt. W128 9/M1293 750,000. 1/17. D. D & L. Ltd. Forms/C2118/14.

Instructions regarding War Diaries and Intelligence Summaries are contained in F. S. Regs., Part II. and the Staff Manual respectively. Title pages will be prepared in manuscript.

WAR DIARY
or
INTELLIGENCE SUMMARY.
(Erase heading not required.)

Army Form C. 2118.

Place	Date	Hour	Summary of Events and Information	Remarks and references to Appendices
A22c64 (Sheet 51B)	24/12/17		One Company on Working Party making Barbed Wire Concertinas. Other Companies paraded under Company arrangements.	S.H.
ACHEVILLE (HUDSON POST)	25/12/17		Battalion relieved the 14th YORK & LANCASTER REGT in HUDSON POST. (Front Line). Quiet relief.	
	26/12/17 27/12/17 28/12/17 29/12/17 30/12/17 ~~31/12/17~~		During the tour of duty (25th to 30th), lateral patrolling to the Battalions on our flanks was carried out nightly as for the previous tour of duty, also patrols, composed of specially trained N.C.Os and men, went out nightly into No-mans-land to obtain information & if possible identifications. Some useful information was obtained but no identifications were secured. Daylight camouflage patrols were out each day & were very successful in gaining particulars of the enemy and enemy work etc. Owing to the ground being under snow the whole of the period all patrols both by day & night, wore white suits.	S.H.
NEUVILLE ST VAAST.	31/12/17		The Battalion was relieved in the line on the 31st inst. by the 13th YORK & LANCASTER REGT, & moved to CUBITT CAMP, NEUVILLE ST VAAST. Battalion H/qrs at A9a24.	S.H.

Douglas Allen Major,
12th (S) Bn. York & Lancs. Regt.

(A7092). Wt. W12839/M1293. 750,000. 1/17. D. D. & L., Ltd. Forms/C.2118/14.

ADMINISTRATIVE INSTRUCTIONS TO ACCOMPANY OPERATION ORDER NO.96.

1. Cooking. The Sergeant Cook will arrange the following:-
   (a) Breakfast to be eaten before Coys move off.
   (b) Unexpended portion of days ration to be issued to Coys before they move forward.
   (c) Two cooks to move forward with the Battalion to attend to Battalion Soup Kitchen.
   (d) Remainder of Coy Cooks to return to Transport Lines after Coys have moved forward.

2. Surplus Stores. Officers' Kits and surplus stores and baggage will be dumped at places shown below by the times indicated:-

"A" & "B" Coys near RATION DUMP at "B" Coy H.Q. by 6.30.a.m.
"C" & H.Q " " Battalion H.Q in the CUTTING by 6.30.a.m.

"A" Coy will detail one N.C.O and one man and "B" Coy one man to act as baggage guard and loading party for loading baggage on returning ration train. They will then rejoin their Coys.

"C" Coy will detail one N.C.O and one man and H.Q. Coy one man to act similarly with the Dump in the CUTTING.

3. RATIONS. The Q.M. will arrange for rations to be sent up to all Companies by train as far as Ration Dump where ration parties will assemble.

4. Ration Parties, and Water carrying. "B" Coy and H.Q Coy will carry for themselves, "C" Coy will carry for "A" Coy and themselves.

RELIEF TABLE. December 3rd.

Coy 13 Y & L	From.	To.	Relievg Coy 14 Y&L	Route.	Time of Starting from H.Q.
"B"	RED LINE	WOOD Post & BOYNE Post.	"C"	OUSE TR. to junction with South DUKE ST.	To follow "A" Coy.
"A"	Do.	OPPY Post.	"A"	Do.	7-35 a.m.
"C"	CUTTING.	MARQUIS Post.	"B"	CUTTING - OUSE TR. to junctn with S.DUKE ST.	7-45 a.m.
"HQ"	Do.	DUKE STREET.	"HQ"	Do.	To follow "C" Coy.

50 yds distanse will be maintained between sections.

R. [signature] Captain & A/Adjt
13.S.Bn.York & Lancs.Regiment.

SECRET. Copy No. 16.

12th. S. BATTALION YORK & LANCASTER REGIMENT.

Ref. Map FOOTHILL 1/20,000

OPERATION ORDER. NO 86.

2.12.17.

1. The 12th. S. Bn. York & Lanc. R. will relieve the 14th. S. Bn. York & Lanc. R in the C.2. Sector of the Front Line to-morrow, 3rd. Dec 1917.

2. The relief will be carried out in accordance with attached relief table.

3. Advance party. 2nd. Lieut. DICKINSON will be in charge of the Advance Party detailed as follows, which will assemble at 7.a.m. at the junction of OUSE TRENCH and the RED LINE, and will proceed to take over trench stores at Battn and Coy H.Q. and arrange accommodation:-

(a) A, B & C Coys only, 1 Officer, and two Signallers per Coy, and 1 N.C.O per platoon.

(b). H.Q. Coy. 1 N.C.O, 2 Signallers and 2 runners.

4. Coys will be relieved in the RED LINE & CUTTING as follows:-

"A" Coy 12 Y & L by "C" Coy 13th Y & L.
"B" " " "B" " "
"C" " " "A" " "
H.Q " " H.Q. " "

1 Officer and 1 N.C.O. per Coy will remain behind to hand over to relieving Coys of 13th Y & L and will then proceed to rejoin their respective Coys.

5. Guides. 1 guide per platoon will be provided by 14th Y & L at the junction of OUSE & SOUTH DUKE STREET at 8.30.a.m.

6. Trench Store Lists:- Will be handed in to Battalion Orderly Room by Coys as soon as possible after relief is complete.

7. Relief Complete will be notified to Battalion Orderly Room by wire or runner. Code words as follows:-

"A" Coy Sgt. JONES. "C" Coy. Sgt. FRANK.
"B" " Cpl. HARRIS. H.Q. " Cpl. THOMAS.

8. Sketch Map shewing dispositions of each Coy to reach Battalion Orderly Room by 6.p.m.

9. ACKNOWLEDGE.

A.H. Cousin Captain,
A/Adjutant,
12th. S. Battalion York and Lancaster Regt.

Copies to. No.1 C.O.
2. 2nd. in. C.
3. Adjutant.
4-7 Coys.
8 M.O.
9. T.O.
10. Q.M.
11. R.S.M.
12. 13th. Y & L
13. 14th Y & L
14. War
15 Diary.
16 File.

SECRET. Copy No. .... [illegible]

[illegible]

[illegible] 27.

[illegible]

[illegible] 7.[illegible].17.

1. The [illegible] Work and [illegible] [illegible]

2. [illegible] detailed.

3. [illegible] [illegible] the [illegible]

"A" Coy will provide 3. "C" Coy will provide 2 (1 platoon)
"B" " " " 3. "D" " " " 2.

[illegible] runner from "B" [illegible]

4. [illegible]

5. [illegible]

"A" " [illegible] "C" " [illegible]
"B" " [illegible] "D" " [illegible]

6. [illegible]

7. [illegible]

8. [illegible]

(Sd.) [illegible]

[illegible]

[illegible] :-

[illegible]

[illegible]

[illegible]

1. [illegible]

2. [illegible] Officers kits and Surplus Stores will be sent to the Light Railway Ration Dump by 8 p.m. [illegible] day. Each Company Commander is responsible that his own stores are there at the time stated.

3. O.C. Coys will ensure that all the posts etc are handed over in a clean and sanitary condition, and a certificate will be obtained to that effect.

R E L I E F T A B L E.

[illegible]	Relieved by Coy. of 4th London Regt.	Move from	Route.
"A"	"A"	OPP Y POST	Via OUSE ALLEY to DAYLIGHT RAILHEAD.
"B"	"D"	WOOD & BOYNE POST S.	-do- -do-
"C"	"C"	MARQ UIS POST.	-do- -do-
"HQ"	"HQ"	S. DUKE STREET.	-do- -do-

"B" Coy. 4th London Regt. will move into M.G. TRENCH.

Interval of 50 yards between sections will be maintained when moving out.

SECRET. Copy No.....13

12TH.S.BATTALION YORK AND LANCASTER REGIMENT.

OPERATION ORDER No.98.

21.12.17.

1. The 12TH YORK & LANCASTER REGT will move to SPRINGVALE CAMP tomorrow.

2. ORDER OF MARCH. "HQ", "A", "B", "C". The Band will move with "B" Company. Coys will maintain 100 yds interval. The first company will pass the starting point, H.Q.Mess, at 10.0.a.m. Cookers and Water Carts will move behind rear Coy.

3. DRESS. Full Marching Order. Steel helmets on pack. Officers will be dressed as the men, unless mounted, when haversacks will be worn on the back.

4. STORES. All Officers' Kits and Mess Stores will be dumped outside H.Q.Mess by 9.15.a.m.
   Lewis Guns and Medical Stores will be dumped outside Q.M.Stores by 9.15.a.m.
   1 N.C.O./(L.G.) will be left with each Coys Lewis Guns.

5. ROUTE. Camp - ANZIN - ECURIE - SPRINGVALE CAMP. First Company must not reach destination before 12.30.p.m.

6. ADVANCE PARTY. 2nd.Lt.Dickinson and 1 Officer per Coy with C.Q.M.S's will parade outside Orderly Room at 8.30.a.m. They will take over Springvale Camp.

7. REAR PARTY. 2nd.Lt.Simpson and 6 men per Coy will be left behind to clean the Camp. They will move independently when the work is completed.

8. All billets must be evacuated by 9.30.a.m., in a thoroughly clean condition.

9. ACKNOWLEDGE.

C Cowlin
Lieutenant & Adjutant,
12th York & Lancaster Regt.

Copies to :-

No.1. Cmdg Officer.
2. Adjutant.
3 - 6. O.C.Coys.
7. Medical Officer.
8. Transport Officer.
9. Quartermaster.
10. Regtl-Sgt-Major.
11. War Diary.
12. -do-
13. File.

S E C R E T. Copy No. 12.

13TH. S. BATTN YORK & LANCASTER REGT.

O P E R A T I O N O R D E R No. 99.

Ref Maps:-
MAROEUIL &
Trench Maps.

24.12.17.

1. The 13TH. YORK & LANCASTER REGT will relieve the 14TH. YORK & LANCASTER REGT in HUDSON POST, tomorrow, 25.12.17.

2. The Battalion will fall in at 8.15.a.m. and march by platoons at 100 yds interval to the Starting Point - the end of THELUS Duck-boards, which will be passed by the first platoon at 9.30.a.m.

3. ROUTE. THELUS DUCK-BOARDS - MERSEY - C.P.R. - & HUDSON.

4. RELIEF. Companies will relieve Companies of the 14th Y & L as under :-

"C" Coy, 13th Y & L	will relieve	"C" Coy, 14th Y & L	on Right.	
"A" "	" "	"B" " "	" Left.	
"B" "	" "	"A" " "	in Support in BRANDON TRENCH.	

5. DISPOSITIONS. Will be as taken over by the Company Officers today.

6. MARCH. Order of march, "HQ", "C", "A", "B".

7. ADVANCE PARTY. 2nd. Lt. Harrison, 2nd. Lt. Judd & ~~1 N.C.O.~~ per 1 Officer & 1 N.C.O per Company will go forward to take over Trench Stores, etc.

8. GUM BOOTS. Will be brought up with the rations tomorrow night. Company Commanders are responsible for the number they take over. These will be returned in full 24 hours after we leave the line.

9. SKETCHES of dispositions taken up will be rendered to Orderly Room two hours after relief is completed. Trench store lists will accompany them.

10. Relief complete will be reported by wire as under :-

"A" Coy.	BLACK.	"B" Coy.	BROWN.
"C" "	RED.	"HQ" "	GREEN.

11. REAR PARTY of Orderly Officer and 12 men from "B" Coy will remain behind. They will be responsible that the Camp is handed over in a thoroughly clean condition and obtain certificates to that effect from the incoming Unit. They will then rejoin the Battalion in the Line.

12. All huts will be evacuated by 7.45.a.m. when they will be inspected by the M.O. and reported on.

13. STORES. All surplus Kits will be dumped outside Orderly Room by 8.a.m. All Stores, Kits, etc., to be taken up the Line will be placed in the Guard Room at the same time.
Dixies will be taken up the line with rations, as cooking will be done there. The Cpl-Cook will detail 1 cook to remain behind to look after the cookers.

14. LEWIS GUNS will be sent up to THELUS CAVES on limbers at 8.a.m. Companies will detail 1 N.C.O. and 1 man to accompany each limber.

15. Acknowledge.

[signature]
Lieutenant & Adjutant,
13th York & Lancaster Regiment.

Copies to:-
1. C.O. 7. M.O. 10. R.S.M.
2. Adjt. 8. T.O. 11/12 War Diary.
3/6 Coys. 9. Q.M. 13. File.

SECRET   Copy No. 9

13th. S. Battn York and Lancaster Regt.

Ref Map
[illegible],
1/20,000   Operation Order No. 101.   30.12.17.

1. The Battalion will be relieved in the line tomorrow, 31st inst, by the 12th York & Lancaster Regt and on relief will proceed to [illegible] Camp, NEUVILLE ST VAAST, at about 12.30 p.m.

2. An advance party of the 13th Y & L will report to Battn H.Qrs 1½ hours before the time notified for relief to take over dispositions, trench stores, etc. [illegible] material will be included in trench stores. [illegible] possible.

3. Companies will be relieved in order :-

"[illegible]", "[illegible]", "[illegible]", "[illegible]".

4. Relief will be [illegible] :-

"[illegible]" Coy. [illegible]   "C" Coy [illegible]
"[illegible]" [illegible]   "[illegible]" [illegible].

No Company to leave until incoming unit is all in position. Any odd parties of men which O.C. Coy may wish to send out must leave before 7 a.m.

5. On relief Coys will move out independently by [illegible] – [illegible] – [illegible] – [illegible] – NEUVILLE [illegible], keeping usual distances.

6. Packs and blankets will be sent out by [illegible] train tonight. Gum boots, in full, will be sent out at the same time.

7. Lewis Guns, [illegible] and [illegible] will be [illegible] in the [illegible] in the [illegible] at the [illegible] of [illegible] TR. [illegible] detailed by O.C. "[illegible]" Coy, and 1 man per Coy will be left on guard.

8. An advance party of the Q-M, 2nd Lt. J. McNamara, [illegible], and [illegible] will take over [illegible] Camp from the 12th Y & L at 8.30 a.m. tomorrow, and have all in readiness for the Battalion's arrival.

9. (1) The Q-M will hand over to the Q-M, 12th Y & L Regt all water tins and Hot Food Containers.
(2) Only breakfast rations will be brought up on the night of Dec 30th except for the Lewis Gun Guard.
(3) A full water supply will be brought up tonight.
(4) The Transport Officer will arrange for the transport of Lewis Guns and [illegible] from [illegible] TR tomorrow night.

10. All trenches, dug-outs and shelters must be left in a clean and sanitary condition and a certificate to this effect obtained from the incoming Unit. This to be rendered to Orderly Room as soon as possible [illegible].

(Sd.) J. C. CORRY, Lieut & Adjt.,
13th York and Lancaster Regiment.

Copies to :- No. 1 to 4 O.C. Coys, 5 [illegible] and [illegible], 6 12th Y & L,
7 [illegible], 8 File, 9 [illegible] 10 War Diary.

12TH. S. BATTALION YORK & LANCASTER REGIMENT.

Ref. Map. Training Area "A" (issued by Brigade).

T A C T I C A L   E X E R C I S E.

General Idea.

The Battalion is holding t he present Sector in the Line, with

"B" Coy in Support in MARQUIS POST.
"A" " " OPPY POST .
"C" " " WOOD POST and BOYNE POST.
H.Q " " SOUTH DUKE STREET.

Special Idea .

1. OPPY POST is attacked and oc cupied by the enemy (By day).

2. The unoccupied portion of trench between WOOD and OPPY POSTS is attacked and occupied by the enemy. (By night).

Counter attack will be carried out as l id down in the Battalion Defence Scheme.

CONFIDENTIAL

WAR DIARY.

12. S. Bn, YORK + LANCASTER
Rgt.

Period. January 1, 1918
to
January 31, 1918

VOL. XXV

Date of Despatch.
Feby 1/18.

Instructions regarding War Diaries and Intelligence Summaries are contained in F. S. Regs., Part II. and the Staff Manual respectively. Title pages will be prepared in manuscript.

WAR DIARY
or
~~INTELLIGENCE SUMMARY.~~
(Erase heading not required.)

Army Form C. 2118.

Vol 23

Place	Date	Hour	Summary of Events and Information	Remarks and references to Appendices
CUBITT CAMP. NEUVILLE ST VAAST. A 9. a 24	1/1/18	-	A day of rest. Major D. C. ALLEN proceeded to TANK Corps and Major J. V. KERSHAW. D. S. O., 11th East Lancashire Rgt assumed Temporary Command of the Battn. Lieut- Col- F. J. COURTENAY- HOOD. the Commanding Officer of the Battn. was awarded the D. S. O, the announcement appearing in the Supplement to the "London Gazette" of 1/1/18.	
"	2/1/18, 3/1/18, 4/1/18, 5/1/18		This period devoted to "refresher" training.	
	6/1/18.	8 AM	Battn moved into Brigade Close Support at VANCOUVER ROAD, relieving the 14th S. Bn. York & Lancaster Rgt; 'A' Coy being attached to Front Line Bn. 11. East Lancs. Major D. C. ALLEN struck off the strength of the Battn on transfer to Tank Corps being approved.	O.O. 101
VANCOUVER ROAD	7/1/18, 8/1/18, 9/1/18, 10/1/18, 11/1/18		The Battn provided working parties for forward area. Nothing of moment to record.	
			2/Lt. J. McNAMARA was transferred to R. F. C. 8/1/18.	

(A7092). Wt W12839/M1293 75,0.0. 1/17. D. D. & L., Ltd. Forms/C.2118/14.

Army Form C. 2118.

Instructions regarding War Diaries and Intelligence Summaries are contained in F. S. Regs., Part II. and the Staff Manual respectively. Title pages will be prepared in manuscript.

WAR DIARY
or
~~INTELLIGENCE SUMMARY.~~
(Erase heading not required.)

Place	Date	Hour	Summary of Events and Information	Remarks and references to Appendices
SPRING-VALE CAMP.	12/1/18.	-	Battn. relieved by the 13th Bn. York & Lancs. R. moving back to Reserve at SPRINGVALE CAMP, ROCLINCOURT.	OO 102
ROCLINCOURT	13/1/18 14/1/18 15/1/18 16/1/18 17/1/18		Owing to the severe winter conditions the Battn. training was greatly restricted. Lieut-Col. F. J. C. HOOD. D.S.O. rejoined the Battn from leave 17/1/18 & resumed command of the Unit.	
	18/1/18		Battn relieved the 14th Bn York & Lancs. Regt in HUDSON Post (Front Line). The relief was a night relief, the bad state of the trenches making it necessary for overland tracks to be used.	OO 103
Front Line.	19/1/18	1-30pm to 4-30pm	A Daylight patrol consisting of 235720 L/Cpl Poole J. & 235212 Pte CLARKE W. A. performed very creditably, seriously interfering with a German working party & shooting 3 of the enemy. The G. O. C. 9th Infy Bde expressed his appreciation of their work.	
	20/1/18 21/1/18		Very active patrolling was done both by day & night & valuable information on the increasing activities of the enemy was obtained. Hostile patrols were engaged.	
	22/1/18	2.45 AM. to 5 AM	A patrol of 1 Offr (2/Lt. G.V. BURGESS) & 16 OR observed parties of the enemy approaching our lines, near ALBERTA ROAD. The enemy – some 60 strong – finally took up a position in front of our wire & 100 yds in front of our line. As the position of the patrol was not a suitable	

(A7092). Wt. W12839/M1293. 75,0.0. 1/17. D. D. & L., Ltd. Forms/C.2118/14.

Army Form C. 2118.

Instructions regarding War Diaries and Intelligence Summaries are contained in F. S. Regs., Part II. and the Staff Manual respectively. Title pages will be prepared in manuscript.

WAR DIARY
or
~~INTELLIGENCE SUMMARY.~~
(Erase heading not required.)

Place	Date	Hour	Summary of Events and Information	Remarks and references to Appendices
Front Line			one for engaging the enemy it withdrew. Our posts who were already "Stood to", opened Lewis Gun fire & the enemy dispersed.	[initials]
	23/1/18	6-30 to 9-30 AM	A Daylight Patrol went out with a view to finding out further information of the enemy's intention. The patrol brought in 2 Granatenwerfers (one with Base Plate).	[initials]
			Stick Grenades, & Egg Bombs were found laid about in confusion in our wire & along our front. Shell holes contained many bombs. The Granatenwerfers were found 50 yds off our wire & one was fixed in position. A Demolition Charge of about 8 lbs in weight was also found. It seemed obvious that the enemy had been frustrated in an attempted raid.	[initials]
	24/1/18	2 AM to 6 AM	Further patrols again reported increased liveliness on the part of the enemy. ~~[struck out]~~ Three parties, about 30 strong in all, were fired upon about 4-40 AM & they replied without effect. Later, a Daylight Patrol reported fresh blood stains in the area where the enemy had been, but no identifications were secured.	[initials]
CUBITT CAMP.		Afternoon.	The Battn. relieved by the 13th S. Bn. York & Lancaster Rgt, moved to CUBITT CAMP, NEUVILLE ST VAAST. "B" moved to RED LINE being attached to 14th Bn. York & Lancs. Rgt.	O.O. 104. [initials]

(A7092). Wt. W12839/M1293. 75,0.0. 1/17. D. D. & L., Ltd. Forms/C.2118/14.

Instructions regarding War Diaries and Intelligence Summaries are contained in F. S. Regs., Part II. and the Staff Manual respectively. Title pages will be prepared in manuscript.

WAR DIARY
or
~~INTELLIGENCE SUMMARY.~~
(Erase heading not required.)

Army Form C. 2118.

Place	Date	Hour	Summary of Events and Information	Remarks and references to Appendices
CUBITT CAMP.	25/1/18.	—	General cleaning up.	
NEUVILLE St VAAST.	26/1/18		Working parties provided for Communication trenches in Forward Area.	
	27/1/18			
	28/1/18			
	29/1/18			
RED LINE	30/1/18	8.0 AM.	The Battn. relieved the 14th Battn York Lancaster Rgt in Brigade Close Support in RED LINE. "C" Coy were attached to the 11 East Lancs. Rgt in the Front Line for Carrying purposes.	O.O. 105
	31/1/18	—	Nothing important to record.	
			NOTES :- The Battn Ration strength this day was 25 Officers 431 Other Ranks. The Battn Effective strength was 39 Officers 667 Other Ranks. Of those detached 4 Officers and 85 O.R. were on leave to the UK; 1 Officer & 41 O.R. were employed on work for 211 Field Coy. REs; 4 Officers & 27 O.R. were attending various Courses of instruction.	
			It is noteworthy that during the past 3 months 251 Officers & men have been granted leave to the UK after service overseas, in the case of the men, varying from 18 to 12 months.	
			In Novr/17. 48	
			Decr/17. 58.	
			Jany/18. 145	
			Total 251	

[signature] Lieut. Colonel Comdg.
12th (S) Bn. York & Lancs. Rgt. (Sheffield.)

A7092 Wt. W128 9/M1293 750,000. 1/17. D. D & L. Ltd. Forms/C2118/14.

12th. S. Battalion York and Lancaster Regiment. Copy No...15

OPERATION ORDER No.101.

Ref. Map.)
MAROEUIL)
1/20,000.)

5.1.18.

1. The 13th. S. Battn York and Lancaster Regt will relieve the 14th S. Battn York and Lancaster Regiment in close Support, VANCOUVER ROAD, tomorrow, Jan. 6th.

2. "A" Coy will be detached from the Battalion, and will be attached to the front line Battalion, 11th. East Lanc. Rgt, and will come under the orders of the Officer Commanding that unit for tactical purposes. This Coy will move off from the Camp at 8.0. .m. and march by platoons at 100 yds interval to the starting point - THELUS Duckboards, and will arrive there at 9.15.a.m.
The remainder of the Battalion will fall in at 8.20.a.m. The first Coy will move off at 8.30.a.m. to arrive at the starting point at 9.30.a.m. The usual intervals will be maintained.

3. ROUTE THELUS Duckboards, MERSEY, C.P.R., HUDSON.
Equipment. Trench order with greatcoat and waterproof sheet rolled on back. Jerkins will be worn. All waterbottles to be filled.

4. Relief. Coys will relieve Coys of the 14th Y & L as under:-

"B" Coy	13 Y & L	will relieve	"C" Coy	14 Y & L	in CANADA.
"C"	"	"	"A" "	"	in NEW BRUNSWICK.
H.Q	"	"	H.Q "	"	in VANCOUVER RD.
"A"	"	"	Coy of	13 Y & L	in BRANDON TRENCH.

5. Dispositions will be as taken over by Coy Officers to day.

6. March. Order of march:- H.Q. "B", "C".

7. ADVANCE PARTY. 2nd. Lt. Harrison, 2nd. Lt. Judd, one Officer and One N.C.O per Coy will go forward to take over Trench Stores etc., This party will move off at 7.30.a.m.

8. Limbers to carry L.G's up to Thelus Caves will report at this Camp at 7.30.a.m. All other necessary Transport will be here at the same time. Coys will detail 1 N.C.O and 1 man to accompany each L.G. limber.

9. All blankets will be dumped outside the guard room by 7.0.a.m. Officers' Kits, Mess Stores, and kits to be taken up the line will be dumped outside "A" Coy Orderly Room at 7.15.a.m. Stores for the line to be kept separate. Dixies will be taken up the line with rations, as cooking will be done there. The Sgt Cook will detail 1 cook to remain behind to look after the cookers.

10. Sketches of dispositions taken over will be rendered to Orderly Room two hours after relief is complete by all Companies. Trench Store lists will accompany them.

11. Relief complete will be reported by wire as under.
"A" Company ALBERT. "C" Company CODIN'
"B" " BERTRAM. H.Q " DONALD.

The Rear party consisting of the Orderly Officer, 1 Cpl and 6 men from "C" Coy will remain behind. They will be responsible that the Camp is handed over in a thoroughly clean condition, and obtain certifica... to that effect from the incoming unit. The Cpl and the 6 men will then rejoin their Coy in NEW BRUNSWICK. The certificate for cleanliness of Camp should be sent in to Orderly Room.

12. All huts will be evacuated by 7.30.a.m. when they will be inspected by the M.O. and reported on.
13. Sick parade. 7.0.a.m.
14. ACKNOWLEDGE.

J C C[illegible] Lieutenant,
Adjutant.
13th. S. Bn. York and Lancaster Regiment.

Copies to.

No.1. C.O.	7.Q.M.	10. R.S.M.	13. File.
2. Adjutant.	8.T.O.	11. 14 Y & L	14) War
3-6 Companies.	9.M.O.	12. 11 E.L.R.	15) Diary.

SECRET

[illegible] Bn York & Lanc R. [illegible]

OPERATION ORDER No 102

11/1/18

1. The Battalion will be relieved tomorrow by [illegible] York & Lanc. R, & on relief will move to SPRINGVALE.

2. Relief The Coy of the 1/4th Y&L will be relieved by Coy of [illegible] by [illegible] 30am, and will join rear of column of 1/4 Y&L proceeding to front line.

   A Coy 12 Y&L will be relieved by A Coy 13 Y&L
   B " " C "
   C " " B "
   HQ " " D

   A Coy will move out independently of the Battalion.

3. Order of March B C HQ.

4. Route HUDSON, CPR, MERSEY, THELUS duckboards, SPRINGVALE.

5. Advance Party 2/Lt Simpson & 4 CQMS's will take over Springvale Camp at 9.30am tomorrow & have all in readiness for the Battalion's arrival.

6. Cooks [illegible] will go out tonight.

7. Rations for breakfast only will be brought up. Beyond this, rations for [illegible] (dinner etc) will be brought up.

8. Lewis guns & other stores will be dumped in shed opposite [illegible] HUDSON on VANCOUVER RD. A guard of [illegible] men will be detailed by C Coy to remain & load the above stores. [illegible] to collect the above [illegible] tomorrow night.

9. Relief complete will be reported by runner as under. A Coy [illegible]

   D Coy BOOK C CHALK
   B [illegible] BANK HQ HOUSE

10. Trench Stores All RE material [illegible] Trench Stores [illegible] Dump [illegible] separately. [illegible] at Camp.

11. All dugouts & trenches etc will be handed over in a thoroughly clean condition, and certificates obtained to this effect.

12. Acknowledge.

Copies to
No 1 A Coy No 6 [illegible]
2 C 7 [illegible]
3 RB [illegible]
4 [illegible] 9 } War
5 [illegible] 10 } Diary

J Clowm [illegible]
[illegible] York & Lanc Rgt

SECRET. Copy No. 14

12TH.S.BN.YORK & LANCASTER REGIMENT.

OPERATION ORDER No.103.

Ref Map.
MAROEUIL,
1/20,000.

17.1.18.

1. The Battalion will relieve the 14TH YORK & LANCASTER REGT in the Front Line tomorrow, 18.1.18.
2. The Battalion will fall in at 3.30. p.m. and march by platoons at the usual intervals.
3. ROUTE. Duck-boards - MERSEY TR. to VIMY-FARBUS RD, thence overland by Track as per details submitted by Coy Officers today. No smoking will be allowed when parties are crossing overland.
4. RELIEF. Companies will be relieved as under :-

"A" Coy will relieve "C" Coy, 14th Y & L in Front Line.
"B" " " " "B" " " " " "
"C" " " " "A" " " " " "
"HQ" " " " "HQ" " " " WINNIPEG ROAD.

One Company of ~~13th Y & L~~ will be attached in BRANDON.

5. RELIEF COMPLETE will be wired through as under :-

"A" Coy. RED. "C" Coy. GREEN.
"B" " YELLOW. "HQ" " BLUE.

6. EQUIPMENT. Trench Order - Greatcoats rolled in waterproof sheets. All water-bottles filled.
7. DISPOSITIONS - As taken over by Coy Officers today. Sketches of these to be rendered to Orderly Room 2 hours after relief is completed. Trench Store Lists will accompany them.
8. MARCH. Order of march. "HQ", "C", "B", "A".
9. GUM-BOOTS. Will be brought up with rations at night. Coy Commanders are responsible for the number taken over. They must be returned in full 24 hours after we leave the line.
10. ADVANCE PARTY. One Officer & One N.C.O. per Coy will go forward to take over Trench Stores, etc. The R-S-M. will represent "HQ" Coy. They should leave at 2.30.p.m.
11. STORES. All Officers Valises will be dumped in hut opposite Canteen by 11.30.a.m. All Stores, Kits, etc., to be taken up to the Line will be dumped at 2.p.m. in the same place. Box periscopes will be sent up. Dixies will be taken up the line with rations. The Cooks - except 1 left behind to look after Cookers - will accompany them. Blankets and men's packs to be dumped in hut opposite Canteen by 10.a.m
12. LEWIS GUNS. Will be sent by limber to the end of THELUS Duck-boards at 3.p.m. 1 N.C.O. & 1 man per Coy will accompany them.
13. REAR PARTY. The Q-M. and 2nd. Lt. Drury and 3 men per Coy will remain behind. They will be responsible that the Camp is handed over in a thoroughly clean condition and obtain certificates to that effect from the incoming Unit. A list of all Stores handed over will be kept and a receipt obtained. The party (except the Q-M.) will then rejoin the Unit in the Line.
14. BILLETS. All Billets will be evacuated by 2.45.p.m. when they will be inspected by the 2nd in Command, Medical Officer, Quartermaster and Orderly Officer.
15. ACKNOWLEDGE.

J C Cowan
Captain & Adjutant,
12th S.Bn York and Lancaster Regiment.

Copies to :-

No.1. Commanding Officer.
2. 2nd in Command.
3. Adjutant.
4/7. Companies.
8. 14th York and Lancaster Regt.
9. Transport.
10. Quartermaster.
11. Regtl-Sergt-Major.
12. Medical Officer.
13. File.
14/15. War Diary.

SECRET — Copy No 10

REF MAP MAROEUIL 1/20,000

12th [illegible] Bn York & Lancaster Regt.

Operation Order No 104

23 [illegible]

1. The 12th Bn [illegible] Lancaster Regt will be relieved by the [illegible] Bn [illegible] Lancashire Regt tomorrow 24.1.18. When relieved the Bn will proceed to CUBITT CAMP.

2. Reliefs. Coys will be relieved in the following order.
A [illegible] LEFT
B [illegible] CENTRE
C [illegible] RIGHT
HQ [illegible] HQ [illegible] WINNIPEG RD
[illegible] OTTAWA [illegible] for attachment to 14th [illegible] for rations purposes. [illegible] advance party of [illegible] & signallers to take over trench stores [illegible] by 7-30 a.m.
W [illegible] 11th East Lancs Regt will be relieved by [illegible] 14th [illegible] Regt [illegible] will proceed to SPRINGVALE CAMP [illegible] will be [illegible] at CUBITT CAMP.

3. Relief Complete will be wired to HQ [illegible]
A ORANGE C BLUE W [illegible] VIOLET
B GREEN D INDIGO [illegible]

4. Route HUDSON – C P R – MERSEY – DUCKBOARD [illegible] TILLEUL – NEUVILLE ST VAAST – CUBITT CAMP

5. All trenches dugouts etc will be handed over in a thoroughly clean condition & certificate obtained.

6. Stores
(a) All [illegible] will be dumped in No 1 SHAFT WINNIPEG RD. All [illegible] & Periscopes will be dumped in the same place.
(b) C & HQ Coys will each detail 4 men and A Coy 3 men & 1 Lce Cpl as a [illegible] party to take charge of above stores and to load them on the ration train at night.

Stores (cont:)

c). The T.O. will arrange to collect all above stores from the Railhead in 5 Limbers.

7. Rations Breakfast & haversack rations will be sent up. Full days rations for the rear party of 12 men and for 'B' Coy will be sent up in addition

8. Cooks will take all dixies and the other cooking utensils out of the line by the returning ration train on the night of 23.1.18.

9. Parties Any small parties which O.C. Coys may wish to send out in advance must leave their H.Qrs by 7. am.

10. Advance Party of 2nd Lt. H.W.B. Hansford & 4 C.Q.M.S. will take over CUBITT CAMP at 9-30. am. on 24.1.18. They will see that all is in readiness for the Battalions arrival. The Band will be in readiness to play the Coys. into Camp at about 3 p.m.

11. Acknowledge

[signature]

Captain & Adjutant
12th York & Lancaster Regt.

Copies to:-

No.1 O.C. 'A' 12th York Regt.
2. 'B' "
3. 'C' "
4. 'H.Q'
5. 'W' 11th E. Lancs Regt
6. 13th York Regt.
7. 14 " "
8. Q.M. and T.O.
9. File
10. } War Diary
11

Ref Map, MAROEUIL, 1/20,000.

12TH.S.BN.YORK & LANCASTER REGT.

Copy No. 15

OPERATION ORDER NO.105.

29.1.18.

1. The 12th YORK & LANCASTER REGT will relieve the 14th YORK & LANCASTER REGT in Close Support, VANCOUVER RD, tomorrow, 30.1.18.
2. Relief will be carried out as under:-

"A" Coy, 12th	will relieve	"B" Coy, 14th	in	NEW BRUNSWICK.
"C" " "	"	"A" "	"	BRANDON.
"HQ" " "	"	"HQ" "	"	VANCOUVER RD.
"B" " "	"	remain	in	OTTAWA TR.
"C" " 14th	"	"	"	CANADA.

"C" Coy, 12th Y & L will come under O. C. 11th E.L.Rgt for tactical purposes.

3. ROUTE. THELUS DUCKBOARDS - MERSEY - C.P.R. - HUDSON.

   Equipment. Trench Order, with greatcoat and waterproof sheet rolled on back. Jerkins to be worn. All water-bottles to be filled.
4. PARADE. "C" Coy will parade at 8.a.m. and move off at 8.15.a.m. joining rear of 11th E.L.Regt column at Thelus Duckboards at 9.15.a.m. "HQ" and "A" Coys will parade at 8.15 .a.m. and first platoon of "HQ" will move off at 8.30.a.m. 100 yds distance between platoons to THELUS, thence by sections at 50 yds.
5. RELIEF COMPLETE will be wired as under :-

   "A" Coy, ROSE. "C" Coy, PANSY. "HQ" Coy, LILY.

   Sketches of dispositions taken over will be sent to Orderly Room as early as possible. Trench Store Lists will accompany them.
6. ADVANCE PARTY 2nd.Lt.Dickinson, 1 Officer per Coy & 1 N.C.O. per platoon will leave CUBITT CAMP at 7.a.m. and move forward to take over dispositions, trench stores, etc.
7. ACKNOWLEDGE.

[illegible] Capt & A/Adjt.,
12th. York & Lancaster Regt.

Copies to :-

No.1.	C.O.	No.8.	T.O.	No.12.	14th Y & L Rgt.
2.	2nd in C.	9.	M.O.	13.	File.
3/6.	Coys.	10.	R-S-M.	14/15.	War Diary.
7.	Q-M.	11.	11th E.L.Rgt.		

ADMINISTRATIVE INSTRUCTIONS.

1. **REVEILLE.** 6.a.m.
2. **SICK PARADE.** 6.15.a.m.
3. **BREAKFAST.** 6.45.a.m.
4. All blankets, packs, Officers' vali ses, mess stores and stores for the Line will be dumped on the duck boards near "A" Coy Orderly Room by 7.30.a.m. Stores for the L ine will be kept separate.
5. **LEWIS GUNS** . Limbers to take Lewis Guns up to the end of Thelus Duckboards will report outside Orde rly Room at 7.a.m. They must leave here by 7.15.a.m. C oys will detail 1 Lewis Gun N.C.O. & 2 men to take charge of and unload the guns.
6. All men must be clear of huts by 7. 30.a.m. The huts and camp will then be inspected by the 2nd in Com mand, Medical Officer and Orderly Officer.
7. **REAR PARTY.** Orderly Officer and 4 men from each of "A" & "HQ" Coys will remain behind to hand over the Camp. They will obtain receipts for all stores handed over and a ce rtificate as to cleanliness. They will then rejoin the Battalion in the Line.
8. **RATIONS** for "C" Coy will go up to B RANDON by train, for the remainder by limbers to VANCOUVER RD . The Q.M. will send up two watercarts nightly and as many tins of water a s possible.

29.1.18.

Captain &
A/Adjutant,
12th.S.Bn York an d Lancaster Regiment.

Secret

12 (S) Batt.
York & Lancaster
Regiment.

LAST
VOLUME.

Feb 1 to Feb 26
1918.

Feb 28/18.

Vol 24

Army Form C. 2118.

Instructions regarding War Diaries and Intelligence Summaries are contained in F. S. Regs., Part II. and the Staff Manual respectively. Title pages will be prepared in manuscript.

WAR DIARY
or
INTELLIGENCE SUMMARY.
(Erase heading not required.)

Place	Date	Hour	Summary of Events and Information	Remarks and references to Appendices
VANCOUVER ROAD.	1/7/18		Battn provided Working Parties.	J. C. C
Brigade Support.	2/7/18		HQs informed that this Battn had been selected for disbandment, under War Office instructions that Divisions should be cut down to 9 Infantry Battns.	J. C. C
	3/7/18		Arrangements for disbandment commenced.	
	4/7/18		do do continued.	J. C. C
	5/7/18		do do do . Battn relieved by 13 Bn York & Lancaster Rgt, moved to CUBITT CAMP, NEUVILLE ST VAAST.	
CUBITT CAMP.	6/7/18		Arrangements for disbandment completed.	J. C. C
	7/7/18			
	8/7/18			
	9/7/18			
	10/7/18		13 Officers, 280 other ranks transferred to 7th Bn York Lancaster Rgt. T/Capt S. CRAWFORD in charge, the party proceeding by bus to new Battn at 2-0pm. Remainder of Battn moved to LANCASTER CAMP. MONT ST ELOI.	

A5834 Wt. W4973 M687 750,000 8/16 D. D. & L. Ltd. Forms/C.2118/13.

Instructions regarding War Diaries and Intelligence Summaries are contained in F. S. Regs., Part II. and the Staff Manual respectively. Title pages will be prepared in manuscript.

WAR DIARY
or
~~INTELLIGENCE SUMMARY.~~
(Erase heading not required.)

Army Form C. 2118.

Place	Date	Hour	Summary of Events and Information	Remarks and references to Appendices
LANCASTER CAMP	11/2/18	–	Nothing of importance to record except that the Battn moved to YORK CAMP ECOIVRES.	J.C.C.
YORK CAMP.	12/2/18	4-30 pm.	15 Officers 300 other ranks transferred to 13th Bn. York Lancs. Rgt.	J.C.C.
		12 noon.	Battn transport of 1 Off. 34 O.R. & all equipment transferred to Guards Division being attached to 3rd Bn. Grenadier Guards.	
YORK CAMP.	13/2/18.		Nothing to record.	
"	14/2/18.		The Battn Band 1 N.C.O & 18 men transferred to 2/4 Battn York & Lancs. Rgt, 62 Division.	J.C.C.
	15/2/18.		Battn Staff: 3 Officers, & surplus personnel 27 O.R. proceeded to 13 Corps Musketry & Reinforcement Camp to await orders from G.H.Q as to disposal.	J.C.C.

Notes:– The Battn was disposed of as under:–

Effective Strength: 38 Officers 660 Other Rks.

To	9 York & Lancs	13 Officers	280 O.R.
To	13 York & Lancs	15 Officers	300 "
To	Guards Division	1 "	34 "
To	2/4 York & Lancs	–	19 "
To	Pool (13 Corps M & R C)	9x	27
		38	660

x Includes 6 detached.

A5834 Wt. W4973/M687 750,000 8/16 D. D. & L. Ltd. Forms/C.2118/13.

Instructions regarding War Diaries and Intelligence Summaries are contained in F. S. Regs., Part II. and the Staff Manual respectively. Title pages will be prepared in manuscript.

WAR DIARY
or
~~INTELLIGENCE SUMMARY.~~
(Erase heading not required.)

Army Form C. 2118.

Place	Date	Hour	Summary of Events and Information	Remarks and references to Appendices
PERNES.	16/7/18		Capt & Adjutant J. C. COWEN & Hon. Lieut. & Q.M. C POLDEN. M.C., together with the surplus 27. O.R, were transferred to the 4th Entrenching Battn.	J. C. C
PERNES & YORK CAMP.	17/7/18 to 28/7/18		Affairs of the Battn gradually cleared up. The Commanding Officer applied for 6 months Home Service in England & on this being granted left for England on the 2d of March.	J. C. C

F. Courtenay Hood
Lieut-Colonel
Commanding
12 S. Bn York & Lancs Regt.

A5834 Wt. W4973 M687 750,000 8/16 D. D. & L. L[illegible] C.2118/13.

SECRET. 12TH.S.BATTALION YORK AN D LANCASTER REGIMENT.

O P E R A T I O N O R D E R No.110

10.2.18.

1. Tomorrow 11.2.18. the Battalion will move to YORK CAMP, ECOIVRES.
2. The Battalion will parade in ful l marching order on the South side of the huts, facing Eas t, at 10.45.a.m.
3. ROUTE. CART Rd South of the Cam p - AUBIGNY RD - YORK CAMP.
4. Advance party. 2nd.Lieut JUDD, P ioneers, 1 Signaller, and 1 Sgt per Coy will leave here at 9.0.a.m. to take ove r YORK CAMP.

ADMINISTRATI VE.

1. Reveille. 6.0.a.m.
   Breakfast. 7.0.a.m.
   Dinne r. 12.30.p.m.

2. All blankets will be neatly rolled in bundles of ten and placed on the duckboards South of the huts by 8.0.a.m.
   All stores to be moved will be dump ed in the same place at the same time. Officers' valises and Mess Stores will be dumped at the side of the road near HQ Me ss at 9-0 a.m.
3. One Motor Lorry will report here after drawing rations and will take all Stores to YORK CAMP.

4. After breakfast the Field Cooker s belonging to "A" and "HQ" Coys will return to the Transport Lin es to be put in readiness for handing over. Private Williams , of "A" Coy, will accompany them to see that this is carried out. He will rejoin the Battn. as soon as this work is complete d. Coys. will make arrangements for future cooking to be done in the dixies.
5. The Camp will be cleaned up by 1 0- 15 a.m., and will be inspected by the Second-in-Command and Med ical Officer.

[signature]
Capt & Adjt.
NAPKIN.

Copies to: 1 Adjt.
2 "A" Coy.
3 "HQ" "
4 Q.M. and T.O.
5 R.S.M.
6. M.O.
7 and 8 War Diary.

Army Form C. 2118.

Instructions regarding War Diaries and Intelligence Summaries are contained in F. S. Regs., Part II. and the Staff Manual respectively. Title pages will be prepared in manuscript.

WAR DIARY
or
INTELLIGENCE SUMMARY.

(*Erase heading not required.*)

Place	Date	Hour	Summary of Events and Information	Remarks and references to Appendices

A5834 Wt. W4973/M687 750,000 8/16 D. D. & L. Ltd. Forms/C.2118/13.

SPECIAL ORDER OF THE DAY

BY

BRIGADIER-GENERAL G.T.C. CARTER-CAMPBELL, D.S.O.,
COMMANDING 94TH INFANTRY BRIGADE.

29. 1. 18.

I have to say to my Comrades of the 94th Infantry Brigade a regretful farewell.

We have served together now for well over two years, two years to me full of pride and esteem of those I have had the honor to command. Your discipline, your valour, your endurance, have ever given me confidence in any operation that we have had to undertake.

I trust that the ties of comradeship that have bound us together in War may not be relaxed in Peace, and that one and all of you will regard me as your Friend.

Good-bye, and God bless you.

G Carter Campbell

Brigadier-General,
Commanding 94th Infantry Brigade.

Bde. Hdqrs.,
29.1.18. Please say as early as possible how many copies of the above you desire

10 copies

Secret 12 Bn. York & Lancs R. Copy No 1

OPERATION ORDER No 108

Ref. Map MAROEUIL 4/2/18

I. Tomorrow, (Feby 5) the 12. S. Bn. York & Lancaster Regt will be relieved by the 13th. S. Bn. York & Lancaster Regt and will proceed to CUBITT CAMP.

2 "A" Coy 12 Y & L will remain in the Line. They will relieve "C" Coy, 14th Y & L by 9-30 AM & will leave a Rear party in NEW BRUNSWICK to hand over dispositions Trench Stores. etc.

Other Coys will be relieved as under:-

"A" in NEW BRUNSWICK by "A" Coy 13 Y & L.
"B" in OTTAWA by "C" Coy. 13 Y & L.
*"C" " BRANDON " "B" " 13 Y & L.
*(On relief they will move independently).
"HQ" in VANCOUVER by "HQ" 13 Y & L.

The inter relief between "A" Coy. 12 Y & L & "C" Coy 14 Y & L will be carried out as shewn above. "C" Coy 14 Y & L will form rear of their own Bn as it passes down HUDSON

3.– Relief complete will be wired to this office as under:–

"C" Coy. 14th. LILY! "A" 12th. VIOLET!
"B" " 12th. HEATHER "HQ" " ROSE.

4. Route:– HUDSON — C.P.R — MERSEY — LES TILLEULS — CUBITT.

5. Trench Store Lists including R.E. material will be handed in to Orderly Room on arrival at CUBITT CAMP.

Lists of "C" Coy will be handed in to 11th E. Lancs. Rgt. Handing over Lists of "A" Coy, 12 Y&L. & "C" Coy 14 Y&L will be handed in to Orderly Room, 12 Y&L, as soon as relief is completed.

6 All trenches, dugouts & shelters will be left in a thoroughly clean condition and certificates to that effect obtained from incoming unit.

The Second-in-Command will inspect the lines at 10·0 AM.

7 All parties when on the march will be under the command of an Officer or N.C.O. who will see that correct march discipline is maintained.

3

Copies to:-

No 1. ~~Adjutant~~
2 O/c "A" Coy.
3 O/c "B" "
4 " "C" "
5 " "HQ" "
6 QM.
7 T.O.
8 13 Y & L.
9 M.O.
10 File
11 } War Diary.
12 }

[signature] Capt & Adjt
12 S. Bn York & Lanc R.

4/7/18

4

Administrative Instructions

I. Cooks will leave the Line tonight (4/3/18) & will take with them all cooking utensils.

2. Rations for breakfast only will be brought up tonight. Full rations for "A" Coy & the 12 O.R. remaining will also be sent. Rations for the 12 men will be given to the R.S.M. for safe keeping.

3. Lewis Guns, Stores, Kits, etc., of "B", "C" & "H.Q." Coy, will be dumped in the small shed on the W. side of VANCOUVER opposite the end of HUDSON. "B", "C" & "H.Q." Coy will each detail 4 men to look after & load up the above on the limbers which the Transport Officer will send. "A" Coy will retain all guns, stores etc.

4. Advance Party: 2/Lt H G IBSON & 4 C.Q.M.S. will proceed to CUBITT CAMP. to take over stores, hutments etc. They will be there by 7-30 AM. They will have everything in readiness for the Bn's arrival. Dinners at 3pm. The Band will play each party into camp.

[signature]

AW

RE-POSTINGS.

Details of Move tomorrow.

1. 13 Officers + 280 men of this unit are transferred to the 7th York & Lancaster Regt and will proceed there tomorrow.
2. A/CAPT. S. CRAWFORD will be in charge of the party and will see that all rolls & documents are handed over to O.C. 7th Y/L
3. A/Capt Crawford will call at Orderly Room for Rolls etc at 10 a.m. tomorrow.
4. Officers valises & other stores which will accompany the party will be dumped at the junction of CAMP Rd. with MAIN Rd. by 12·30 p.m.
5. The whole party will fall in for inspection by the C.O at 10·30 a.m.
6. The whole party will embus at 2 p.m. and proceed direct to their destination Parade at 1·30 p.m. and move on to the CAMP ROAD, the head of the column being on its junction with the MAIN Rd.
7. Breakfast will be served at 7 a.m. Dinner will be served at 12 noon. After dinner the cookers for "B" & "C" Coys will return to the Transport Lines.

[signature]
Capt & Adjt
12th Bn York & Lancaster R.

9/2/18

SECRET. OPERATION ORDERS. No. 109.

Ref Map MAREUIL.

1. The Battalion (less "A" Coy & party for 7th Y&L) will proceed to LANCASTER CAMP tomorrow.
2. They will parade at 11·15 a.m. and will move off at 11·30 a.m. by platoons at 200 yds interval.
3. ROUTE LA TARGETTE – MONT ST ELOI – LANCASTER CAMP.
4. EQUIPMENT Full marching order.
5. BLANKETS will be neatly rolled in bundles of 10 & placed on the Duck Boards near "A" Coy Orderly Room by 8 a.m. Officers' Valises, MESS STORES etc will be dumped at the same place by 9. a.m.
6. REVEILLE 6. a.m.
BREAKFAST. 7 a.m.
DINNER at 1·30 (on arrival at destination).
7. Cookers of "A" & "HQ" Coys will move off as soon as breakfast is finished. Rations will be sent direct to LANCASTER CAMP for HQ Coy. Those for "B" & "C" Coys to CUBITT.
8. The MO & Orderly Officer will inspect the camp at 10 a.m. All men will be outside their billets at that time.
9. The Band will move with the front party

9/2/18

www.ingramcontent.com/pod-product-compliance
Lightning Source LLC
Chambersburg PA
CBHW080854010526
44117CB00014B/2249
* 9 7 8 1 4 7 4 5 1 5 8 0 1 *